SECURING THE BLESSINGS OF LIBERTY:
THE CONSTITUTIONAL SYSTEM

ARTHUR N. HOLCOMBE
Eaton Professor of the Science of Government, Emeritus
Harvard University

with an introduction by
SENATOR HUBERT H. HUMPHREY

SCOTT, FORESMAN AMERICAN GOVERNMENT SERIES
Joseph C. Palamountain, Jr., Editor

SCOTT, FORESMAN AND COMPANY
Chicago • Atlanta • Dallas • Palo Alto • Fair Lawn, N.J.

L. C. # 64-23298

Printed in the United States of America

PREFACE

The American system of government strikes a balance between unity and diversity. There is a unity to our system, but it is a unity which tolerates — indeed, requires for its vigor and viability — a broad diversity of institutions, processes, and participants. By organizing the analysis of the sprawling complexity of the American system into smaller, coherent, but interlocking units, the Scott, Foresman American Government Series attempts to reflect this pluralistic balance.

This approach, we believe, has several important advantages over the usual one-volume presentation of analytical and descriptive material. By giving the reader more manageable units, and by introducing him to the underlying and unifying strands of those units, it puts him in a better position to comprehend both the whole and its components. It should enable him to avoid the not-uncommon circumstance of viewing the American system as a morass of interminable and unconnected facts and descriptions.

This approach certainly permits us to tap the expertise and experience of distinguished scholars in the fields of their special competence. Each writes about his specialties, and none is forced to deal with subjects remote from his ken or heart for the sake of "completeness." The unity of the series rests on the interlocking of the various volumes and, in the general emphasis on policy and policy-making, on the method of analysis as opposed to simple description. It does not rest on a unity of approach. The authors vary in their values, their accents, and the questions they ask. To have attempted to impose unity in these matters would have been to water down the series, for the diversity of approach reflects the diversity of the system, its participants, and its commentators. But the final value of this series and its ultimate balance between unity and diversity rest, of course, in the use to which it is put by the reader.

I am most pleased and grateful that this series is opened by a scholar as distinguished as Arthur N. Holcombe. His long and productive career has been marked by the almost constant discovery of new answers to old questions and of new truths in old answers. In this book he has both illumined with new light the historical bases of our political system and used that historical experience to shed new light on our contemporary problems. I am sure the reader will share my sense of gratitude.

Joseph C. Palamountain, Jr., *Editor*

INTRODUCTION

It gives me deep satisfaction to contribute an introduction to this book. Dr. Holcombe has made a most important contribution to the political education and faith which the final paragraph of this book holds to be essential. I agree whole-heartedly with it:

> In the long run the American system of political education is the foundation of the American constitutional system. The American political way of life rests upon the faith that a real sovereignty of the people may coexist with an actual reign of law. Since 1776 the American people have learned that by taking thought they can make such progress toward their political goal as to justify that traditional and rational faith.

Understanding is of two kinds: academic, or learning from the study of books and theory; and experiential, or learning from direct participation in the practical work of politics. Understanding by experience is crucial, but all of us will be much more aware of the meaning of our constitutional system after studying this road map of its history which Dr. Holcombe has prepared. This book provides an admirably clear and accurate outline. Better yet, it has been done with what William James called a sense of the "thickness" of ideas. A rich sense of the socio-historic context of thought comes through at all times. Therefore we grasp the essential point, that our constitutional system is a living organism. As a human being grows, changes, adapts, yet retains a continuity of identity with all of the occasions of his life, so our constitutional system has grown while remaining the same. In this present moment of history, profound changes are taking place with great rapidity. All political and social institutions are being tested severely. This book gives us a basis for reassurance about the constitutional anchor of our liberties. It presents as well a challenge to the future.

The sovereignty of the people and the rule of law—these are the two basic propositions of the American constitutional system, and they are the theme of this book. These propositions were stated clearly in the Declaration of Independence, which is the theoretical cornerstone of our political system. "All men are created equal" and have certain inalienable rights. To secure them, the people are justified in assuming a separate and equal station among the powers of earth by "the laws of Nature and of Nature's God."

It is not easy to reconcile these two propositions in theory. Indeed, when the "sovereignty of the people" and the "rule of law" are viewed abstractly or with the strictness of logic, they appear to present a certain contradiction or paradox. To the extent that the law has an objective, impersonal quality about it, governing equally the actions of Presidents and ordinary citizens, the law has a majesty we revere. The integrity of "the law" gives stability to government and is the bastion against the caprice of individuals who would wield power arbitrarily. All of us value this, and "strict constructionists" of the letter of the law from the earliest days of our founding as a nation to the present remind us that we must be careful to preserve a government of laws, not of men.

On the other hand, the ongoing life of men and societies presents new conditions continually. The positive law—the law of human contrivance—sometimes begs for change in order to preserve an old sense of justice in a new circumstance. If the law cannot be changed in time, the law itself may come to represent a tyranny. Few of us have difficulty understanding that. But if the people—even by a majority—can change the law at will, what is the law except what men of the moment say it is? The objectivity of the law seems to be breached. The law appears to be made subordinate to some momentary coalition of power among men. Can a majority do anything it pleases? For example, can a majority revoke the guarantees of freedom of worship, freedom of speech, or other liberties in the Bill of Rights? No, a majority cannot—not without destroying our constitutional system. The people can adapt the law; they cannot abrogate it.

Dr. Holcombe makes it clear that it is the genius of the American constitutional system to reconcile these two propositions. The Founding Fathers did not attempt a purely theoretical resolution. Such always emphasizes the law at the expense of popular sovereignty, or vice versa. Rather, the political architects of our constitutional system devised a political structure that would permit both principles, the rule of law and the sovereignty of the people, to *work* together and reinforce one another independently. Thus out of *a* revolution, the groundwork was laid for a *continuing* revolution, in which both freedom and stability would be maintained.

Dr. Holcombe also makes it clear that if the men of 1776 and 1787 were revolutionaries, they were not iconoclasts. Although they faced forward with a sense of destiny in a New World, they kept continuity with the moral values and the distilled political wisdom of western civilization. Dr. Holcombe emphasizes that success at the Constitutional Convention in Philadelphia was due to this moral sense, the spirit of responsibility, and the equal homage of these men to both order and change. The author stresses that this spirit is the key to what has made our system work from then until now and is the key to its future adequacy. I could not agree more.

The Founding Fathers believed that the people may make and remake the positive law by which the everyday affairs of the political community are conducted. But they also believed that these decisions must be judged by a higher law—the "natural law." This concept the Founding Fathers inherited from its long existence in the thought of western civilization. The Greeks of pagan antiquity had conceived of a natural law defined by a universal "reason" to which every individual had access and which he could reflect through his own powers of reason and logic. Both Jews and Christians came to be deeply influenced by this idea. By the time of St. Thomas Aquinas in the thirteenth century, Christianity had welded the idea of natural law into its theological structure. In the system of Aquinas, men could by a natural reason discern a divine moral order. Where finite men differed in insight, it was the task of the Church to complete the insight. There are practical limitations to the power of reason, both in individuals alone and when they reason together. No individual or group can claim to have the "absolute" truth. Yet, by presuming to adjudicate all differences, the Church involved itself deeply in the temporal affairs of men, including affairs of State. The Church did recognize, in theory, the distinction between the political and spiritual orders, and it granted an independent integrity to the former. In practice, the Church was tempted to assume responsibility for both. As a result, Christianity suffered considerable internal convulsion and came into sharp conflict with secular powers.

In England the concept of a "natural law" underwent a modulation during its long development from the "judicious Hooker" to the practical Locke. As inherited by the Founding Fathers of our constitutional system, it was disengaged from ecclesiastical control, but the ethos of the Judeo-Christian tradition—its spirit, its values, its sense of divine authorship—was maintained.

Dr. Holcombe makes it clear that if American Englishmen were sensitive to the possible tyrannies of the Church, they were equally determined to keep absolute power from the State. The *people* were sovereign. By contracting continually with one another, they could form and re-form the State. By reasoning together in search of the higher law, they might not find it absolutely, but, as Abraham Lincoln was to say later, they could approximate it continually.

At no time have Americans been much inclined to philosophy, let alone to theology. They have been practical people or, as the jargon goes, "pragmatic." Yet they have also been a morally committed people. They have taken the Judeo-Christian values for granted and have desired to get on with the task of making them work.

Dr. Holcombe underscores the fact that the framers of our Constitution did not try to solve all of the practical issues of their own day—let alone settle the future—and write the solution into the Constitution. They were not absolutely definitive on the exact limits of property rights, the specific boundaries of Church and State, the detailed rights of States, or the full prerogatives of citizenship. They were embarrassed by the institution of slavery and simply did not know what to do with the problem other than to live with it and somehow work it out.

Rather, the constitutional architects set themselves the task of framing a structure of government within which men could live with freedom and stability while finding practical answers to their problems and preserving a viable political community. They arrived at the now famous tripartite division of government—executive, legislative, and judicial—in which each autonomous branch is a check and a balance on the other two.

As Dr. Holcombe illuminates with brilliance, this was not done easily, and could not have been done at all had not the delegates to the Constitutional Convention possessed a common commitment to reason together. It was a remarkably able group assembled at Philadelphia. There were different opinions, all strongly held and cogently reasoned. There were differing sectional and economic interests. Comparatively speaking, there were just as many differences to harmonize then as there are now. The content of the differences varies from age to age, but the form is the same. We may expect that honest and intelligent men always will differ, as each views the world from a different and partial perspective.

The tripartite framework fashioned in 1787 has worked well. The Executive was not given as much power as the Virginia delegation wanted, but the office was given independence. In the intervening years the inherent powers of the Executive have transformed the office into something closer to what the Virginians had in mind. In recent years some observers have feared that the legislative branch has declined in effectiveness, although I believe that the record of the 88th Congress would have reassured the Founding Fathers who were partisan to that branch. Others fear that the States have suffered from the growth of Federal government, but Dr. Holcombe finds, and I agree, that the States today are a healthy part of our Federal system. The creative powers of the Supreme Court in giving interpretation to the basic constitutional document were perhaps not envisioned fully, yet the creation of an independent judiciary has turned out to be a stroke of genius. Each of these branches checks and balances the others, and all are sensitive to public opinion. Lawmakers and Presidents may be replaced in periodic elections. The Supreme Court has a constant struggle of conscience. The Court may not always follow but it always listens to the expressed spirit of the times. In the recent school prayer decision, *Abington* v. *Schempp,* Justice Brennan, in a concurring opinion, recalled the words of the early Chief Justice, John Marshall: ". . . we must never forget that it is a *constitution* that we are expounding." The Court does not just balance the other two branches. It conducts a continual dialogue on adapting the spirit of the law to changing times.

The times and conditions have changed enormously in 177 years. Dr. Holcombe traces the interrelationships of our three major branches of government as they have evolved to meet the successive cultural, social, and economic revolutions. The constitutional system as developed in America has had both the flexibility and durability to meet and master every challenge.

Although there is not a line in the Constitution about political parties, Dr. Holcombe rightly considers our two-party pattern to be a part of our constitutional system. In the beginning parties were feared. George Washington warned of the divisiveness they would create. Our two-party system did not emerge until the 1820's, but it did take shape as non-legislated, practical wisdom.

Periodically, some persons fear the death of the two-party system. I do not, and Dr. Holcombe reassures me. A given party may die, like the Whigs, when it cannot any longer command a national base or when it can no longer reflect all of the diverse elements in the American pluralism and evolve from those elements a consensus with which to contest an opposing party which has to do the same thing. But if either major party should go out of business because of this failure, a new and more vigorous leadership would bring another party into being. Rather than fear the death of the two-party system, I would fear a sharp polarization of the parties in which both departed too far from the mainstream of American politics. Yet this dangerous development would require that both parties become erratic and irresponsible at the same time. I do not believe this will happen.

Our constitutional system will survive only if there is a recommitment in every generation of the people to its moral basis and to responsible participation in it. Americans must do this in every generation, to preserve their own liberties and to keep up the momentum of their continuing revolution. This is necessary also if we are to give democratic leadership to all of the new revolutions arising in the many new countries around the world. The new countries do not always understand us. Leaders there look for the meaning of our "ideology" as an alternative to the Communist "ideology." We do not have an ideology in the Communist sense of a doctrinaire, absolutist position. But we have principle, integrity, and stability. Our Founding Fathers had a larger idea than to stop with a revolt from one tyranny. They wished to be free of future ones and to create an instrument to keep their revolution going. They desired a way to continue working together with both the rule of law and sovereignty of the people as guiding principles. We will teach best by example. This is the best answer to Communist propaganda.

We know we are living in times of exploding knowledge and accelerated social change. But if events are taking place faster, we do not really look forward to changes essentially greater than the ones we have come through. Our constitutional system has proved to be supple yet firm. Now it has maturity. Dr. Holcombe has given us great reason to believe that it will continue to be adequate as long as the people are committed to work within it.

Students will find this book invaluable. So, I trust, will a much wider general audience.

Senator Hubert H. Humphrey

TABLE OF CONTENTS

PREFACE iii

INTRODUCTION iv

CHAPTER ONE ★ THE DECLARATION OF INDEPENDENCE 1
The Philosophy of the American Revolution
The Interests Behind the Revolution
The Major Parties of 1776

CHAPTER TWO ★ THE REVOLUTIONARY PRINCIPLES OF GOVERNMENT 19
The Purpose of Government
The Governmental Process
The Governmental Performance

CHAPTER THREE ★ TOWARD A MORE PERFECT UNION 39
A New Model of Political Planning
The Fundamental Principles of Free Government in the Federal Convention of 1787
The Revolutionary Principles of 1776 in the Federal Convention of 1787

CHAPTER FOUR ★ THE CONSTITUTIONAL PRINCIPLES OF 1787 . . 63
Federalism
Checks and Balances
Pluralism

CHAPTER FIVE ★ THE DEVELOPMENT OF THE CONSTITUTIONAL SYSTEM 87
The Unplanned Party System
The New Nationalism and the Free-Enterprise System
The Welfare State

CHAPTER SIX ★ A LIVING CONSTITUTION 115
The Nature of the American Community
Changing Views of the Principles of 1776
Changing Views of the Principles of 1787

CHAPTER SEVEN ★ FRONTIERS 145
Political Consequences of the New Technology
Political Consequences of the Organization of Peace
The Spirit of the Constitutional System

FOOTNOTES 168

BIBLIOGRAPHICAL ESSAY 174

APPENDICES 179
Declaration of Independence ★ Articles of Confederation
Constitution of the United States

INDEX 195

CHAPTER ONE

The Declaration of Independence

The foundation of the American constitutional system is the Declaration of Independence, and its cornerstone is the inherent right of the self-determination of peoples.[1] The most cogent evidence in support of these two propositions is the opening sentence of the Declaration itself. In this sentence the representatives of the thirteen United Colonies declared that the people for whom they spoke were entitled to assume a separate and equal station among the powers of the earth by "the Laws of Nature and of Nature's God."

THE PHILOSOPHY OF THE AMERICAN REVOLUTION

These two kinds of laws were as closely associated in the thinking of the people of the United States as in the text of the Declaration of Independence. These people thought of themselves as a Christian people. Their culture was built on their heritage from medieval Christendom. Their ideas of law were derived from the great medieval thinkers, who had supplied the most acceptable explanation and justification of the medieval way of life. The outstanding expounder of these ideas was St. Thomas Aquinas, whose *Summa Theologica* was an epochal work which helped win for the thirteenth century its reputation as the greatest century of the Middle Ages.

Aquinas thought of the world as a manifestation of the will of God, the Creator of all things. The concept of creation and the purpose to give it substance and form produced the eternal law of the universe which existed in the mind of the Creator and was the original source of all other kinds of law. These other kinds of law fell into three classes—divine law, natural law, and human or man-made law. The first consisted of that part of the eternal law which had been revealed to man in the Holy Scriptures and possessed throughout Christendom a higher sanctity than either natural or human law. Natural law comprehended that part of the eternal law, not revealed in the Bible, which was discoverable by human reason; its source was the nature of things and natural processes and relationships of all kinds. Any need for guidance in human affairs, not satisfied by divine or natural laws and too urgent to be endured without a struggle, could be met by laws of human contrivance, designed for man's convenience pending better knowledge of the eternal law.

Under the conditions of life in the Middle Ages this system of laws was highly favorable to the influence of the clergy in political affairs. Churchmen by the nature of their profession possessed a practical monopoly of the important business of interpreting the sacred writings. Moreover, in a period of all but universal illiteracy, when even kings might be unable to write their own names, the systematic and purposeful study of natural phenomena was practically restricted to churchmen. Furthermore, if there was need for human lawmaking in states where ordinarily only warriors could be kings, churchmen could most conveniently fill the role of statesmen. Under the circumstances it is not surprising that such a legal system should have been readily accepted and strongly supported by the medieval Church.

The enhanced authority of the Church made for greater stability in the political order of the later Middle Ages. In the earlier Dark Ages, when the authority of the clergy was considerably less, the warriors had held sway almost unchecked by law of any kind. The papal coronation of Charlemagne as Holy Roman Emperor emphasized the felt need for some kind of a higher law than barbarian customs, the arbitrary will of tribal leaders, or the uncertain authority of *de facto* kings. The development of the feudal system in the high Middle Ages blended the power of warriors and ecclesiastics in a mixture more favorable, when in good working order, to political stability and economic and social progress. Though the system was difficult to keep in order, medieval ecclesiastics managed to maintain a more than tolerable reign of law in both church and state. Though the Supreme Pontiff often had his troubles with the temporal rulers and sometimes even with his spiritual associates, respect for law became widespread and deep. The medieval legal system left little room for claims to a right of revolution by ordinary subjects, but it did help protect the common people against lawless violence by the feudal lords.

The medieval political order was threatened with subversion by the consequences of its own success. Respect for law facilitated the extension of markets for the products of medieval artisans and craftsmen. The extension of markets encouraged the growth of cities and improved opportunities for the profitable employment of capital in business enterprise. The rise of urban industry and commerce produced a growing class of men who were neither warriors nor ecclesiastics and who were hampered in their operations by the medieval legislation against usury. These precursors of modern businessmen gained power behind the protection of their city walls and grew restless under the medieval ban on the pursuit of profits by the employment of capital.

The restlessness of these early businessmen was stimulated by technological changes in the medieval way of life. The revolution in the art of war, brought about by the invention of gunpowder, subverted the feudal system. The revolution in the system of education, brought about by the invention of printing, subverted the monopoly of the clergy. The revolution in the mode of thinking, brought about by the discovery that Rome was not the center of the world and that the earth was not the center of the solar system, to say nothing of the rest of the universe, profoundly altered the relations between church and state. Roger Bacon, legendary inventor of gunpowder, Johannes Gutenberg, authentic pioneer in the development of printing, Columbus and Magellan, Galileo and Copernicus and the other early scientists made inevitable a thorough reconsideration of the nature and sources of law and of the sanctity of the religious and political institutions supported by the law.

The early religious and political reformers did not think of themselves as revolutionists. Erasmus in the Holy Roman Empire and Sir Thomas More in Tudor England hoped by their criticisms to strengthen rather than to weaken the established religious and political order. When the Lutherans protested against their treatment by the agents of the Emperor Charles V at the Diet of Speier, they still hoped to make a reformation rather than a revolution. When the leading Calvinists took refuge in Geneva and made that prosperous city an outstanding model of their new way of life, they still regarded the doctrines set forth in Calvin's *Institutes of the Christian Religion* as a logical development of the orthodoxy of the Middle Ages. The medieval system of laws was not to be cast aside but merely adapted to the changing requirements of the new times.

Nevertheless there was a revolution, and neither the Christian Church nor the Holy Roman Empire nor the Tudor monarchy and other states of western Christendom would ever be the same again. In the British North American colonies, popular thinking about "the Laws of Nature and of Nature's God" was affected in different ways in different places. The Puritan colonies derived their unquestionable respect for law from the Calvinists.[2] Oliver Cromwell, victorious commander in the British civil war of the mid-seventeenth century and Lord High Protector of the Puritan Commonwealth, was their greatest political hero, and John Milton, one of Cromwell's secretaries of state, was their favorite defender of the faith. But in those colonies where the Church of England was established by law the Puritan Cromwell was the outstanding villain of recent English history, and William Shakespeare, a dutiful subject of Queen Elizabeth I and King James I, rather than the Puritan Milton, provided the most respected model of polite literature.

The chief problem of political thinkers in the Anglican colonies, as in the home country, was to explain and justify the changes in the monarchy brought about by the Tudor reforms and the Revolution of 1688. There had been widespread interest in religious reform in England even before Martin Luther nailed his ninety-five theses to the door of the castle church at Wittenberg, but it was King Henry VIII's resolute search for a male heir to the throne that precipitated the struggle for supremacy in matters of religion between the papacy and the monarchy. The traditional interpretation of the fundamental law, divine and natural, did not support Henry's version of the proper relationship between church and state. In order to tip the balance against the Pope's claim to higher authority, it was necessary to strengthen the case for the supremacy of the Crown by introducing a new view of the law of nature. This was accomplished during the reign of King Henry's Protestant daughter, Queen Elizabeth I. The adroit statesmanship of the great Queen, sustained by the skill of ministers who were no longer medieval ecclesiastics but laymen learned in the common law and familiar with the ways of the new class of merchant-adventurers and of the rising world of capitalistic business enterprise, was equal to a provisionally acceptable solution of the problem.

The most important feature of the new view of natural law was its fresh emphasis on the old doctrine of the social compact. This doctrine was at least as old as Plato's *Republic*, in which one of Socrates' pupils advanced a version of the doctrine that did not meet with the master's approval. The essence of the doctrine in all its various forms was reliance on the power of reason in the search for a sanction to the authority of emperors, kings, and other established heads of state. A people should obey the ruling churchmen and statesmen, when it was reasonable to do so. A social compact afforded acceptable evidence of a mutual obligation to govern well and to submit to good government. It was not necessary that there be an actual compact, binding the people of a state and their rulers to perform their appropriate duties and to respect each other's basic rights, duly signed, sealed, and delivered. It was enough that under the special conditions existing at a particular time and place the maintenance of a specific political and religious order was a reasonable mode of action by rational men.

The most impressive statement of the case for emphasizing reason rather than revelation, in arguing in favor of Queen Elizabeth's claim to the English throne and to superior authority over the English Church as well as over the Tudor kingdom, was Richard Hooker's *The Laws of Ecclesiastical Polity*. The "judicious" Hooker, as John Locke later described him, was primarily concerned with the Queen's claim to be the head of the Church, but he succeeded in setting forth the reasons for supporting the Elizabethan form of union between church and state cogently enough to command the assent, either active or at least passive, not only of the royal household, members of Parliament, great landlords holding land confiscated from the clergy after the dissolution of the monasteries, merchant-adventurers and other capitalistic businessmen, and all other special beneficiaries of the Tudor revolution, but also of the English Protestants generally and most of the whole body of English people. Under the circumstances of the time the social compact enjoyed one great advantage over the Bible, which was regarded as a source of fundamental law; its meaning could be ascertained and declared by properly trained civil servants and other educated laymen as well as or better than by ecclesiastics. Acceptance of its authority tended to exalt the influence of all orders of magistrates and civil officers and of the rising new classes of citizens from whose ranks these officials were likely to be drawn. The new view of natural law greatly strengthened the position of that part of the eternal law, not revealed in the Bible, which was discoverable by human reason, and of the political authorities who had been brought into power by the Tudor revolution.

The problem of justifying the "Great and Glorious" Revolution of 1688, as later English historians liked to call it, made greater demands upon the law of nature and the doctrine of the social compact. This revolution, though one of the least sanguinary of modern times, cost a legitimate monarch his throne and put an end to lingering fears that the results of the Protestant Reformation in England might be undone by a tyrannical king, unresponsive to the wishes of the bulk of his subjects. Time was, when most subjects would have recognized the right of their sovereign to determine his subjects' religion as well as his own. But the Reformation, with its insistent emphasis on the right of the people to read the Bible for themselves in their own language and to find its meaning in the light of their own consciences, encouraged the idea that sovereignty was not absolute but limited by the nature of the state and the purposes of its people. The new version of the social compact, best stated by John Locke, author of the most successful defense of the English revolutionists, supplied an acceptable account of the natural limits on the functions of Protestant kingdoms and on the powers of royal sovereigns therein.[3]

Locke's version of the social compact divided it into two parts. The first part was designed to show how reasonable it is for men to pass from a state of nature into a civil society or political state where all are to be governed by their common concern for the general welfare. It sought to explain also, where the only law is that dictated by each man's concern for himself, why some, but not all, of their natural rights should be exchanged for civil or political rights. The second part set forth the terms of a rational arrangement between the political state and its sovereign concerning the extent of his authority over his subjects and described the conditions under which the subjects would be justified in deposing their sovereign and choosing another in his place. These conditions proved to be substantially the same as the cases in which King James II was accused of abusing his powers and Prince William of Orange, who was chosen by the Parliament in his place, was required to accept them before ascending the English throne. The English Bill of Rights of 1689 and the later Act of Settlement incorporated as much of the substance of the Lockean version of the social compact as seemed necessary and proper to the prudent Whig statesmen, who organized the revolution and nominated the new sovereign.

A summary account of the social compact political philosophy, as illustrated by the English Revolution of 1688, and a persuasive description of the natural and civil rights of Englishmen were contained in the favorite textbook of American lawyers on the eve of the American Revolution, Sir William Blackstone's *Commentaries on the Laws of England*.[4] This account met with the full approbation of the revolutionary leaders in the colonies where the Anglican Church was established by law. The interests of their ancestors had been well served by the Revolution of 1688 and their sympathies lay with the English Whigs. In the Puritan colonies also, the Whig revolution had been favorably received, though it had not wholly repaired the damage done to the colonials under the tyranny of the last of the Stuart kings. Massachusetts lost the original Company Charter under which the Puritan church-state had functioned like an independent commonwealth in all but name, and the new Province Charter granted by the government under King William reserved greater power to the Crown, including the appointment of royal governors in place of those previously chosen in the colony by its freemen. The Plymouth Colony, which had governed itself under the self-made Mayflower Compact—the outstanding historical example of an actual social compact—lost its independent existence altogether, becoming a mere subdivision of Massachusetts.

In the Puritan colonies the influence of a different religious tradition and in most of them the legal establishment of Calvinistic Congregational churches created a need for a more systematic and comprehensive political philosophy than that afforded by the form of the social compact theory used to justify the revolutions which had given the English people the great Queen Elizabeth and the good King William. Of course loyal English subjects could always recognize the divine right of Protestant kings to rule over them, if they wished to accept the Anglican version of the medieval philosophy of law; but men like the New England Puritans, accustomed to reading the Bible in acceptable translations and thinking for themselves under the guidance of their own consciences—but not without help from their appointed ministers—could not be content with the conventional form of the doctrine of the divine right of kings. They could read and enjoy the arguments of Hooker and Locke and still crave more filling food for thought. This craving found its most satisfying nourishment in the theological politics of Calvinism.

John Calvin held a place in the affections of the Puritan Protestants in France, Great Britain, and the Netherlands like that of Luther among the Germans and Scandinavians. Born in the north of France, he was bred in one of the regions most deeply marked by the influences which were breaking up medieval Christendom. His followers set greater store by conscience than by authority in matters of religion and emphasized righteousness over penance, faith over ritual. In dealing with more worldly affairs they rejected the medieval doctrine of usury and produced an intellectual climate more favorable to the rise of modern capitalism and to the shifting of political power from feudal magnates and manorial landlords to corporate magistrates and urban businessmen. The most systematic and comprehensive formulation of the arguments for these changes in the traditional mode of thinking and way of life was Calvin's contribution to the literature of modern Protestantism.

Among English Puritans the need to vindicate the rule of Oliver Cromwell against the Cavaliers' charge of usurpation provided the most searching test of the Calvinistic political philosophy. The task of justifying the Cromwellian Protectorate fell to John Milton, Cromwell's Latin Secretary, who responded with two of the most impressive Puritan tracts for the times, his *Tenure of Kings and Magistrates*, designed for the defense of the regicides after the execution of King Charles I, and his *Ready and Easy Way to Establish a Free Commonwealth*, planned to help stabilize the new Puritan political order. Milton drew upon his vast erudition to put together a medley of Biblical tradition, Calvinistic theology, and social compact rationalism which did little for his literary fame and less for the Puritan Commonwealth. But the Miltonian tracts left a permanent record of Puritan political thinking which showed how the inhabitants of the Puritan colonies in British North America might be expected to justify themselves in the event of their assuming a separate and equal station among the powers of the earth alongside the descendants of the Cavaliers.

Milton, like Calvin, accepted the traditional Christian doctrine of the Two Kingdoms, derived from the Scriptural injunction to render unto Caesar what is Caesar's and unto God what is God's. But he could not be content with Calvin's dogma that tyrannical kings should be judged and, if necessary, deposed only by civil magistrates duly entrusted with the care of their communities without the intervention of common people. Milton agreed with Calvin that the prime function of those entrusted with authority in a temporal kingdom should be to protect the true religion. But he could no longer believe that the particular reforms recommended by Calvin would suffice to make the medieval spiritual kingdom acceptable under the changed conditions of the western world. He was convinced of the need for a radical revolution rather than mere reform.

Specifically, Milton was convinced that all good people should come to the help of the magistrates, or even act for them, if they refused to do their duty when it became in order to put down a tyrant. "It is lawful," Milton wrote, "for any who have the power to call to account a tyrant, or wicked king, and after due conviction to depose him and put him to death, if the ordinary magistrate hath neglected or denied to do it." Milton retained what he believed to be a Christian's respect for law, but he intended that the law should command the approval of all good people and be administered with the consent of the governed. Popular consent was implied in Locke's justification of the English Revolution of 1688, but the people were obviously expected to follow right leadership. The Puritan tradition sanctioned the emergence of new leadership, suitable to the occasion, when good people were called upon by their consciences to deal with a tyrant.

But Milton went further in his liberalization of Calvinistic political philosophy than was really necessary for the purpose of justifying the Puritan Commonwealth under the Lord High Protector Oliver Cromwell. Good men, he argued, might depose magistrates as well as kings, and might do this at their discretion, even if the discarded rulers were not actual tyrants, "merely by the liberty and right of free-born men, to be governed as seems to them best." Milton accepted Aristotle's definition of tyranny, that is, the abuse of power in the special interest of the ruler instead of its use primarily for the benefit of the ruled. When he spoke of the right of freeborn men, he meant not particularly men fortunate enough to be born in a democratic monarchy or republic but all men everywhere by virtue of their birth in a state of nature, that is, in a state of mind hospitable to a purpose to be governed only by reason. His version of the social compact was broad enough to justify a more radical revolution than even that of Cromwell.

The multiplication of dissenting sects under the impact of the Protestant emphasis on freedom of conscience caused further complications in the interpretation and application of "the Laws of Nature and of Nature's God." Calvinists, like Anglicans and Catholics, were taught that there should be a union of church and state for their mutual advantage, and that it was only the true religion which rightly constituted states were bound to protect. Error did not have the same rights as truth, according to their mode of thinking, and toleration of misguided subjects in a Christian body politic was regarded as not only impolitic but also sinful. Where Calvinistic rulers had the power, like Anglican or Catholic rulers, they tolerated no more dissent among their subjects than was deemed prudent, and they consistently protected the particular form of Christianity which they believed to be true. Where they lacked the practical capacity to exercise such power with satisfactory results, the problem of intolerance was bound to plague them.

In the British North American colonies on the eve of the American Revolution there were numerous dissenting sects which ordinarily were constrained by circumstances to submit to the laws that others made or interpreted. Presbyterians, Baptists, and Quakers in the seventeenth century and Methodists in the eighteenth century had been foremost in insisting on the right of dissenters to practice their own religions, whatever might be the established religious order in a particular colony. It was difficult to satisfy these various dissenters without introducing a spirit of toleration into colonial politics which would eventually lead to the separation of church and state. Both Locke and Milton had advocated the practice of at least a limited toleration in England—Milton more boldly than Locke—and their writings contributed to the development in the colonies of greater freedom in the practice of religion than had existed generally in western Europe. Locke's carefully reasoned version of the social compact was more logical and persuasive than Milton's relatively casual treatment of the science of government, but by the middle of the eighteenth century the spirit of Milton's approach to the political problems which chiefly concerned the colonists was more suited than Locke's to the changing circumstances of the times, at least in the Puritan and Quaker colonies.

The problem of justifying the eventual American Revolution had to be solved under radically different circumstances from those which existed in England at the time of either the attempted Puritan Revolution under Cromwell or the successful Anglican Revolution of 1688. It was likely that the approach to a solution of the problem would also be at least somewhat different in different colonies. Jefferson and his associates on the drafting committee which wrote the opening sentence of the Declaration of Independence had to bear these differences in mind. The language they used disclosed their greater interest in natural rather than in divine rights. It portended a greater interest also in the rights of common people than in the prerogatives and pretensions of princes and magistrates of whatever religious persuasion.

It was the Founding Fathers' faith in the reality of the higher law that enabled them to speak so confidently of the self-evident truths which they accepted as axioms of the free society they intended to compose. All men were obviously not equal in their physical or mental attributes, or even in their legal status under the laws made by man himself, in any existing political society, but it was possible to speak of their equal relationship to that higher power which Jefferson called "Nature's God." What God had given God could take away, but divine gifts were not to be taken away by one's fellow men without due cause and due care. Thus divine as well as natural rights to life, liberty, and the pursuit of happiness could be said to be inalienable in the sense that they ought not to be taken away without putting in their place equivalent civil and political rights. Jefferson, when writing the Declaration, did not stop to define these inalienable rights, because presumably the people for whom he was writing already possessed a sufficiently exact notion of their nature to accept the political principles associated with them. In attempting to describe the constitutional system which was the fruit of the American Revolution, however, it is necessary to examine more closely the nature of the basic political ideas which animated that Revolution.

THE INTERESTS BEHIND THE REVOLUTION

The members of the select committee which drafted the Declaration of Independence were chosen with special care by the Continental Congress. They were of course men of outstanding revolutionary prestige and special competence for the business assigned to them, the preparation of the official statement of the case for political separation from Great Britain. But they were also symbols of the major forces in American politics which would have to be brought together into an effective working system, if the colonial peoples were to gain that equal station among the powers of the earth to which they aspired.

Benjamin Franklin, the oldest member of the committee, was a veteran of both colonial and imperial politics. In Pennsylvania he had taken a leading part in the perennial struggle between the privileged Proprietors of the Province and its vigorous and spirited inhabitants for influence over the conditions of its development. He had been one of the recognized colonial leaders summoned by the British Lords of Trade to the Albany Conference of 1754 to prepare a general plan for regulating relations with the Indians. He had been the most prominent and effective colonial agent in London, first of the Province of Pennsylvania and later of other colonies as well, during the troubled years of intra-imperial negotiation following the Stamp Act of 1765. Now he was the most famous and one of the most resourceful members of the Continental Congress, where he pushed ahead with the task of political organization on a continental basis begun at Albany more than a score of years before.

Franklin spoke not only for the enterprising and prosperous merchants and tradesmen of Philadelphia but also for the far more numerous settlers—poor, doubtless, but self-respecting and self-reliant—in the back country and on the frontier. Born in Boston of humble parentage, he had in his youth gone west to seek his fortune in the manner afterwards traditional for ambitious and energetic young Americans. The West for him was Pennsylvania, and from his printing office in Philadelphia he made himself the most popular spokesman for all the various kinds of people who, like himself, had left their native lands in search of the greater opportunities that they believed were awaiting them in the Quaker-founded colony which was then the freest and most cosmopolitan country in the world. But Franklin was no mere provincial politician. No man in the Congress could speak more convincingly for all the plain people of the colonies who were seeking a larger measure of control over what was called in the Declaration their lives, their fortunes, and their sacred honor. He was indeed the first great representative of the American West in continental politics. He came as near being a truly national leader as was possible for the accepted champion of one of America's major historical sections.

Roger Sherman, the next oldest member of the committee, was the foremost spokesman for the Connecticut delegation in the Continental Congress. Born in Massachusetts near Boston, Sherman, like Franklin before him, went west to seek his fortune. Like many early colonial Puritans, his westward migration carried him no farther west than Connecticut, where he became first a self-taught surveyor and then a lawyer and eventually gained an honored place in colonial politics as lawmaker and judge. At the Continental Congress he became the foremost spokesman not only for all Connecticut Yankees but also for Puritan farmers and tradesmen generally. He was the only revolutionary statesman who signed all four of the great revolutionary state papers—the Articles of Association of 1774, the Declaration of Independence, the Articles of Confederation, and the Constitution of the United States.

The Puritan farmers and tradesmen, for whom Roger Sherman was an outstanding champion, constituted the hard core of a second major section in continental politics, the Rural North. It included most of New England and New York, lying back from tidewater, forming a homogeneous region where hay and timber were the leading crops and mixed farming predominated over the characteristic corn and wheat growing of the Middle West. In later years this would be the well-developed Northeastern dairy belt, but in the eighteenth century it was largely a land of subsistence farming, where the established way of life made for a high degree of economic and social equality. Together with the New England town meeting, the prevailing form of local government, these conditions constituted a solid foundation for a comparatively democratic political system.

John Adams, third in order of age among the draftsmen of the Declaration of Independence, had just passed forty in 1776. Born on a modest farm within the limits of the present metropolitan Boston, he elected to make his career in his home town. Instead of going west like Franklin and Sherman, he went to Harvard College and became eventually one of the most learned as well as one of the most belligerent of the revolutionary leaders. He offered the motion naming George Washington to be Commander-in-Chief of the Continental Army and led the fight on the floor of the Congress for the adoption of the Declaration of Independence. Like Sherman, he could speak effectively for Puritan farmers and tradesmen throughout the Rural North.

Adams could also speak for another one of the major sections in continental politics, the Maritime North. This sectional interest began simply enough when the earliest settlers took to the coastal waters and high seas in order to supplement their meager food supplies with fish. The spectacular growth of the productive cod-fisheries led to the development of a sturdy shipbuilding industry and that in turn to profitable lumbering and the production of naval stores. A burgeoning foreign commerce, though restricted by British navigation acts to the confines of the Empire, helped the growth of busy seaports up and down the coast and gave to this section of the continent a strong and distinct character of its own. Years later, when Emerson in his "Boston Hymn" declared that "fishers and choppers and ploughmen shall constitute a state," he was describing with no more than a reasonable poetic license the basic composition of the colonial Maritime North.

Thomas Jefferson was in his early thirties when he wrote the first rough draft of the Declaration of Independence. Born on one of the great Virginia plantations, which gave character to the first and in 1776 the most populous and wealthy of the colonies, he completed his formal education at William and Mary College and could look forward to the life of cultivated leisure and public service which at that time was the natural heritage of a superior gentleman in the Old Dominion. Jefferson was not the foremost representative of Virginia in the Continental Congress. Older delegates were more typical representatives of the big tobacco planters, who formed the hard core of the colonial economy in that part of the continent which may best be described as the Upper South, and enjoyed greater prestige in the Congress. But Jefferson was known to wield a mighty pen and was a natural selection for his particular assignment.

In the colonial period the Upper South extended to the Mississippi River. Virginia included the present states of West Virginia and Kentucky together with apparently valid, though not uncontested, claims to most of what history has called the Old Northwest. North Carolina included the present state of Tennessee, and only Maryland was confined to the eastern seaboard. Tobacco was the leading money crop of the continent, and the region in which its cultivation was still the dominant occupation naturally took the lead in colonial politics. The first families of Virginia, the Randolphs and Lees and the others, furnished effective leadership for the Continental Congress from the beginning and gave a higher tone to its proceedings than might have been expected by the courtiers and politicians in the mother country whose short-sighted policies were bringing on the troubles with the colonies.

The Lower South had no representative on the committee charged with drafting the Declaration of Independence. This omission proved to be a mistake, since the one important change in the draft, made on the floor of the Congress, was the elimination of the paragraph which Jefferson regarded as the climax in his list of grievances against the British Crown. This was the paragraph in which he denounced most bitterly the royal opposition to measures of the Upper South for limiting the importation of Negro slaves. The interest of the Lower South in the African slave trade was already radically different from that of Virginia and Maryland. There was a shortage of cheap labor for the rice and indigo plantations of South Carolina and Georgia, whereas the tobacco planters of the Upper South possessed a plentiful supply. This circumstance magnified the natural differences between the two regions. It condemned the Lower South to a position of marked inferiority in the continental economy until the invention of the cotton gin and the great expansion of cotton growing brought about a veritable revolution in the relations between the sections.

The fifth and youngest member of the drafting committee was a scion of one of the great aristocratic families of colonial New York. Robert R. Livingston was born on a manorial estate situated up the Hudson but spent much of his time in New York City. He was a graduate of King's (now Columbia) College and a lifelong protagonist of capitalistic enterprise. His partnership with Robert Fulton in the development of the steamboat was merely the culmination of an active business career. His presence on the committee symbolized the role of the rising capitalistic interests in the continental economy. His preoccupation with local affairs in New York City caused him to leave the Congress before he had time to sign the Declaration, to the drafting of which his contribution was a modest one, but two of his uncles were active Congressmen, and one of them, Philip Livingston, was a signer. In general the big New York and Philadelphia merchants who attended the Continental Congresses gave perhaps disproportionate representation to the special interests of the Maritime North.

In 1776 the urban population of the colonies, despite the prominence of big urban merchants among the leaders of the Revolution, was very small. Fourteen years later, when the first census was taken, 96 percent of the American people lived in small villages or in the open country. Only two cities, New York and Philadelphia, were populous enough to be entitled to a representative of their own in the Congress. The only other considerable urban centers were Boston, Baltimore, and Charleston. A substantial part of the maritime interests was scattered along the coast in smaller places. Eight of the thirteen original states boasted of no town with as many as eight thousand inhabitants. The Maritime North owed its importance in the national economy to the activity of its leading merchants and the need for its shipping and salt fish rather than to the size of its population.

The ability of the Lower South to force the elimination of Jefferson's antislavery plank from the text of the Declaration does not mean, however, that the South as a whole was the dominant partner in the Union. The slavery issue was not a paramount issue in continental politics. Slavery existed in all sections of the country and, while widely disliked in the northern and middle sections and to a lesser extent in the Upper South, was regarded as a local issue. The principle of politics upon which the revolutionary leaders operated was not that of majority rule, but rather that of consensus. They wished to proceed by general consent, at least by unanimous agreement among the thirteen colonies, and sectional differences were tacitly kept out of continental politics as much as possible. The political leadership of the Continental Congress was divided between Virginia and the Maritime North, and the big planters and merchants were careful to maintain a united front. There were plenty of potential sources of contention between them, but sectionalism was not permitted to take the form of open conflict between North and South.

Conflict between East and West was more active in 1776 but was largely confined to the local politics of the separate colonies. In the Upper South the big planters and in the Maritime North the big merchants had to struggle to maintain their ascendancy over the growing numbers of small farmers in the back country and pioneers on the frontier. Propinquity to navigable rivers was a circumstance of major importance in an age when roads were few and bad and when money crops were brought to market by water-borne carriers. In colonial politics all settlers who lived at a distance from tidewater were naturally arrayed against their more prosperous fellow colonials. The circumstances of their lives created a demand for more democratic ways than were favored on the great plantations and in the maritime centers. The local political divisions in all the colonies suggested the traditional division between court party (Tories) and country party (Whigs) in British politics. But in American continental politics at the time of the Revolution, the small farmers and pioneers generally accepted the leadership of the big planters and merchants.

The five members of the drafting committee formed a fair sample of the effective leadership in the American Revolution. A majority of them were college graduates and the minority were self-educated men of extraordinary all-round competence. A majority of them also were rich men, judged by the standard of their time, and the minority were at least successful professional men. Only one could be described in modern terms as a capitalist, and none of them represented anything even remotely comparable to a Marxist proletariat. Two of them could be described in eighteenth-century terms as wellborn, and the other three belonged to what would then have been recognized as the middling rank. All were members of what Adams and Jefferson agreed in later life to call the natural aristocracy. Though each doubtless was responsive in some measure to what the language of modern politics terms a special interest, the group as a whole was well equipped to represent the general interests of the American people.

THE MAJOR PARTIES OF 1776

Whigs and Tories flourished in the colonies long before there was serious talk of separation from the mother country. The names, as applied to political parties, originated in England in 1679, when the Parliament and the country were divided by the great controversy over the attempted exclusion of the Duke of York, on account of his religion, from the line of succession to the throne. The earliest Tories were Irish bandits and the earliest Whigs were Scottish malcontents, suggesting to the original contenders over the Exclusion Bill suitable bad names for their political opponents. But if the names did not originally lend dignity to the two great parties in subsequent British politics, the respective partisans eventually succeeded in giving dignity to the names. The Exclusion Bill failed, and the Duke of York, though a Catholic, presently became King James II. He also became a tyrant in the eyes of most of his Protestant subjects, and the Whig party rode to an enduring ascendancy through the ensuing struggle for what its members claimed as their ancient rights and liberties.

In the colonies the factions advocating greater influence in colonial politics for the colonists naturally called themselves Whigs, and the defenders of the authority and pretensions of the royal and proprietary governors were forced to accept the name of Tories. In England by 1776 it was hard to distinguish the two great parties from one another except for personal differences among the parliamentary politicians, since the traditional issues between them had lost most of their practical importance. But the dissensions in the colonies were real and after 1765 were of rapidly growing importance. The fortunes of the colonial parties became involved in the struggle of King George III for greater personal influence in British politics, and the rising party of the King's Friends in Parliament became involved in the colonial struggle for a more satisfactory place in the British Empire. By 1776 the point was reached in the struggle where the colonial Whigs could no longer rest their case logically on their claim to possession of equal rights with British subjects at home, and the King's Friends could not rest their case conveniently on the plea that the King and Parliament together possessed sovereign power to rule the Empire. The time had come for an appeal to the inherent right of peoples to self-determination.

This appeal took the then familiar form of an appeal to the higher law represented by "the Laws of Nature and of Nature's God." If King George had broken his compact to govern his subjects in North America well, they could feel free to enter into a new compact with one another to establish an independent government of their own. Jefferson did no more than cast his argument in support of independence in the form most acceptable to British subjects who cherished the memory of the temporarily successful Puritan Revolution of 1649 or the permanently successful Anglican Revolution of 1688. It is particularly significant that the Continental Congress did not mention Parliament in its enumeration of the colonial grievances against the British government. These grievances were not in themselves the grounds upon which a right to make a revolution was asserted. The grievances were merely the evidence of an evil intent on the part of King George to establish "an absolute tyranny" over the North American colonies. It was that evil intent which justified the breaking of the social compact that bound the King of England and the people of the United Colonies together in a lawful body politic.

Whigs and Tories alike were dedicated to submission to law, but the social compact theory of the state could supply a theoretical justification for radically different revolutions. The English Revolution of 1688 caused no more than a termination of the relations between King James and the Parliament, that is, a revision of the second stage of the social compact. But the American Revolution dissolved the social compact in its first stage, the creation of the body politic itself. The American Tories would not consent to a dissolution of the political bands, to use the language of the Declaration, which connected them with the people of Great Britain, but the American Whigs were bent on assuming for themselves as an independent "people" a separate and equal station among the powers of the earth.

According to the doctrine of the social compact, either kind of revolution was "legal" under the appropriate circumstances. An evil intent to govern in a tyrannical manner could justify a limited revolution such as that of 1688. An evil intent to establish "an absolute tyranny" could justify a more radical revolution such as that of 1776. How much more evil was the intent of George III than that of James II or Charles I? On this decisive point American Whigs and Tories parted company. Their differences were temperamental as well as political and economic and social. But on one essential truth they were agreed: all men should be subject to a government of law, and the higher "Laws of Nature and of Nature's God" should reign supreme over man-made laws as well as over man himself.

Whigs and Tories were not agreed, however, on the theoretical location of sovereign power. Sovereign power in an independent national state, believers in the divine right of kings since Tudor times could assert, might be located in the king alone, as English Tories used to maintain, or in the "King-in-Parliament," as English Whigs contended. Later, in the nineteenth century, Englishmen would say that sovereignty was located in the Parliament or even, in the twentieth century, in the House of Commons. But to say that sovereignty was permanently located in the people themselves seemed to eighteenth-century Englishmen to be indulging in an excessively unrealistic legal fiction. It might be true at the moment of entering into a social compact, Whiggish political theorists could concede; thereafter, however, there could be no such thing as genuine popular sovereignty. After all, what was the social compact but a manner of speaking about the rational basis of a well-ordered state.

American Whigs insisted nevertheless that the sovereignty of the people was a rational concept at all times. If the people could make a social compact, they could unmake it and make a new one in its place. The right of revolution, to their way of thinking, was a natural right, to be exercised at any time at the discretion of the people themselves. It was not one of those rights to be exchanged by virtue of the social compact for civil or political rights of any kind. The real question among men governed by reason and the law was a different one. When was a particular population, or part thereof, a "people"? To that question the answer seemed obvious. A population becomes a "people" by thinking of themselves as a people. It is the state of mind that molds the basic material of a well-ordered political state.

Thus the American Whigs explained the first of the two fundamental political principles of 1776. The principle of popular sovereignty was of course a legal fiction. Women and children as well as men are people, and obviously they do not all participate actively in the government of the state. But there was also a sense of the term in which popular sovereignty appeared to be a political fact. In this sense, the term meant that the authority of the constitutional rulers was supported in the long run by opinion, the opinion of all those members of the state who thought about the matter, and only immediately by physical force or the threat of official violence. Even in the most despotic state the authority of the ruler depends in the last analysis on opinion, in this case the opinion of his palace guard at least, since they possess the physical force to destroy him, should they be so minded. But in a truly popular state the power of public opinion must be the ultimate sanction for the authority of the government.

The second fundamental political principle of 1776 was that of an actual reign of law. This principle is more difficult to explain. How can the government actually be a reign of law when in fact it is men who hold the offices and seem to be making and enforcing the laws? The essential characteristic of a political state is the organization of power, and all organized power seems to be placed in the hands of power-conscious men. To the end that there may be a government of laws and not of men, power must be defined and classified and distributed among them so that no man or single body of men can abuse that portion of it in his or their possession. In short, the practical problem is to control the use of power in order that it may not be abused. In other words, the reign of law is contingent upon the acceptance and application of right principles of government; that is, it depends upon the existence of a suitable constitutional system.

CHAPTER TWO

The Revolutionary Principles of Government

The second paragraph of the Declaration of Independence contains the essentials of the American Whigs' program of political reconstruction. This program consisted of three propositions. The first related to the purpose of government; the second, to the governmental process; and the third, to the governmental performance.

THE PURPOSE OF GOVERNMENT

The purpose of government, as the Declaration describes it, seems clear and definite. Governments are instituted among men to secure their rights, namely, those inalienable rights with which they are endowed by their Creator. The Declaration proceeds to enumerate three of these rights—the rights to life, liberty, and the pursuit of happiness. Thus an element of uncertainty creeps into the Declaration. Does the enumeration of these rights exclude others not specifically included? Or are the enumerated rights to be construed so broadly that no right of importance need be lost? Or are life, liberty, and happiness so important that governments may treat other human interests as of inferior concern or leave them to other agencies?

For instance, the Declaration says nothing in this connection about the protection of property. Is the protection of property, or more specifically of private property, a primary purpose of government, as conservative politicians have always been quick to assert? In the federal Constitutional Convention of 1787, when the purpose of government was again under discussion, several delegates contended that the protection of property was the primary purpose of government. Others replied that the protection of human rights should always come first, as if there were an irrepressible conflict between the two kinds of rights. Perhaps it is less important what politicians say than what they do, and the best evidence concerning the respective rights of property owners and of other men may be found in the laws which they make rather than in their speeches. Doubtless it is possible to construe a right to liberty, or to pursue happiness,[1] broadly enough to include the acquisition and enjoyment of property, but surely the good citizen will not go as far as Humpty Dumpty in his oft-quoted conversation with Alice of Wonderland fame, who said that when he used words he made them mean just what he wished them to mean, neither more nor less.

In 1776 conservative politicians in most of the colonies would have contended that the protection of religion, or more particularly the protection of the true religion, is a primary purpose of government. This purpose also may be implied in the rights which were specifically expressed in the Declaration. But the further conversation between Humpty Dumpty and Alice comes to mind. The question is, responded Alice, how can you make the same words mean such different things? The question is, Humpty Dumpty replied with an air of finality, who is the master here, that's all! The proper relations between church and state were indeed a matter of deep concern to both American Whigs and Tories, but the matter was not to be disposed of by general observations in the Declaration of Independence. It remained to be fought over in the governments of the states, where doubtless the triumph of the Whigs in the Continental Congress gave them some advantage over their opponents.

The right to life may be defined in the language of the social compact school of political theorists as the right to live a natural life, limited and restricted by civil laws as far as may be necessary and proper in the public interest and no further. In the eighteenth century there was much discussion concerning the true nature of a natural life. Some said that a natural life meant, in general, doing as one pleased. If there were no civil laws to guide the natural man, the nature of a natural life would depend primarily on the nature of man himself. If men were naturally good, as Jean Jacques Rousseau believed,[2] life in a state of nature would be good, at least as long as there was no scarcity of the things men wanted to supply their needs or support their pleasures. If, however, men were naturally selfish creatures, inconsiderate of others except insofar as they might be made to serve their own interests, as Thomas Hobbes, writing in the seventeenth century, had contended,[3] a state of nature would be a state of war of all against all, in which life would be more miserable than any reasonable man would be willing to endure.

The arguments of the various social compact theorists merit further examination. If men were naturally good, the civil state would also be good, according to Rousseau, since the general will, which in a rightly constituted state would be directed toward the common good, could prevail over the separate wills of disorganized individuals who might prefer life in a state of anarchy. If men were naturally bad, any kind of civil government, according to Hobbes, even that directed by a tyrannical dictator, would be preferred by reasonable men to life in a state where every man did as he pleased regardless of the feelings of others. Thus these two eminent political theorists reached by different routes some identical conclusions, both agreeing that reasonable men should support the law and order furnished by the established rulers of civil states, in which the sovereign power would be absolute, provided there was general compliance with the terms of their respective versions of the social compact. But neither Hobbes nor Rousseau possessed a noteworthy following in the British North American colonies on the eve of the Revolution.

The favorite philosopher of the American Whigs was John Locke. He believed that man was naturally good, but that life in a state of nature would naturally become difficult on account of the eventual scarcity of desirable things. Hence a reasonable man would naturally wish to gain greater security and the other advantages of a well-ordered state of civil society by consenting to suitable man-made laws. If civil laws were actually made for the common good, there could be no doubt in the mind of a reasonable man concerning the superiority of the civil state over the natural state. If the man-made arrangements for the maintenance of law and order were not satisfactory, then, under Locke's version of the social compact, men would still possess their natural right to change the arrangements, if necessary by resort to physical force and revolutionary violence. The kind of civil state that Locke's philosophy was designed to justify was one in which the sovereign power would be limited by the purposes of its people, and the exercise of this limited sovereignty would be further restricted by the obligation to respect duly established processes in the making and enforcement of law. Thus Locke's version of the social compact led reasonable men to willing acceptance of the two fundamental political principles which were most highly esteemed by the American Whigs, that of the sovereignty of the people and that of the reign of law.

There was some confusion in the political thinking of the eighteenth-century Whigs, both British and American, on account of the prevailing uncertainty concerning the historical existence of the natural state. Some of them readily accepted the romantic vision of the favorite poet of the eighteenth century in the English-speaking world, Alexander Pope. The author of the classical masterpiece *Essay on Man* might have been mistaken for a true follower of Locke when he wrote the celebrated lines:

> Nor think in Nature's state they blindly trod;
> The state of Nature was the reign of God:

Self-love and Social at her birth began,
Union the bond of all things, and of man.

But in the eighteenth century Englishmen knew little of the modern science of anthropology and were apt to confuse the rational man's concept of how reasonable men would behave, if left to their natural devices, with the actual behavior of the most primitive societies with which they were then acquainted. This exposed the Whigs to the criticism that there was no historical basis for their favorite political philosophy, and that, if their concept of natural rights possessed any practical validity, it must apply not to the past or present condition of men but to some distant future in which an ideal state of society might perhaps be realized. On the other hand, the authors of the Declaration of Independence were practical politicians who knew what they wanted and how to make their political theories serve their revolutionary purposes.

The essence of the revolutionary claim to a natural right to life was the revolutionary purpose to make more secure a civil right not to be deprived of one's life without due process of law. The right to life did not include any particular formula for determining how far the civil government should go in making life richer and happier. In general, revolutionary theories concerning the functions of government were dealt with under the heads of liberty and the pursuit of happiness. But the Whig political philosophy was capacious enough to contain a set of policies designed to make life safer against injurious physical violence and, to a more limited extent, against contagious disease. There were no uniformed colonial or municipal police officers, but there were local constables and sheriff's posses to hunt down murderers, and gaolers and hangmen to punish them after conviction by juries of their peers. There were special officers in the more important seaports to quarantine merchant ships with crews or passengers suffering from dangerous diseases. There were militiamen to deal with hostile Indians on the frontiers. But in all the colonies the individual subject was encouraged to regard his home as his castle and to rely upon himself for the protection of his life.

An important practical consequence of the Whig interpretation of the right to life was extraordinary emphasis on the concept of due process of law. Colonial judges were not always learned in English common law. In the Puritan colonies they could supplement the deficiencies of their legal education by their knowledge of ancient Hebraic law as recorded in the Bible. But most British subjects in the colonies were familiar with the English system of trial by jury. The right to appeal to the judgment of their peers, when charged with heinous crime, was the most highly valued of the securities against violation of the first of their natural rights. A resolute purpose to strengthen and improve the legal processes constituting the traditional basis of colonial law and order was therefore a foremost characteristic of the American Revolution.

The American Whigs' concept of "liberty" has stimulated more discussion than their concept of "life." The best-known definition of the term and the most acceptable to members of the Continental Congress in 1776 was that of Sir William Blackstone. "Political liberty is no other than natural liberty," Blackstone wrote in his widely read *Commentaries on the Laws of England*, "so far restrained by human laws, and no further, as is necessary and expedient for the general advantage of the public." This may be regarded as the standard interpretation of the term as used in the Declaration of Independence. But general political terms acquire practical significance through their application to controversial situations.

The situation that caused the American Whigs the greatest difficulty in applying their theory of liberty was the institution of Negro slavery. Slavery existed in all the colonies, and Negroes were numerous in many of them. Except in the Lower South, dislike of the institution was widespread, and the revolutionary fervor of 1776 precipitated vigorous efforts to bring it to an end. It was easy for the committee which drafted the Declaration of Independence to agree on a scathing denunciation of King George for blocking efforts in various colonies to put an end at least to the importation of slaves from Africa. But the Continental Congress, moved by a desire for unanimous support of the Declaration, prudently struck out this limited antislavery provision. Thereafter the Congress treated the abolition of slavery as a local issue and refused to be drawn into any general discussion of the meaning of liberty. Efforts to give practical significance to the term were reserved to the newly liberated states of the Union.

Another situation which put the American Whigs' conception of liberty to the test of reason under the circumstances of the time was that resulting from the traditional relationships between church and state. The existence of different established churches in the Anglican and Puritan colonies, as well as the multiplication of dissenting sects, ensured the adoption of a generous measure of toleration as a national policy. But it did not necessarily lead to an immediate separation of church and state within the states. Appeal to the authority of Blackstone could not bring a generally acceptable explanation of religious liberty, because Blackstone was an English Tory, primarily concerned with explaining and justifying the position of the established church in England. He allowed no more than a narrow liberty for the freedom of conscience and the practice of religion by dissenting Protestants, Roman Catholics, and Jews. This problem would have to be attacked in each state in the light of the circumstances and traditions of that particular state. Years would pass before a uniform policy could be worked out, whatever political theorists or politicians might say about the revolutionary principles of 1776.

A third situation which put the Whig concept of liberty to the test of allowable practice was that resulting from the attempts by colonial governors to discourage popular criticism of the conduct of government by the agents of the Crown. Blackstone taught that freedom of the press meant no more than the absence of a royal censorship of books and newspapers prior to publication. Local juries were to determine merely the fact of publication, whereas the royal judges would decide whether an offending report or editorial threatened an injurious disturbance of the king's peace, or of his agent's peace of mind, and called for punishment. This narrow view of freedom of the press could not be satisfactory in an age of growing popular interest in public affairs and increasing disposition to criticize royal governors and even the king himself. Here again was a field of government in which the people of the several states would have to work out by trial and error an acceptable adjustment between popular aspirations for a new freedom and official anxiety lest there be a lack of effective power to govern.

Adam Smith's *Wealth of Nations* and Jeremy Bentham's *Fragment on Government* appeared in 1776, bringing visions of a new freedom in the relations between government and business as well as in those between colonies and mother countries. Both books, particularly the first, were read and admired by discerning friends of liberty in the United States, but the idea of economic freedom made slower headway than that of political freedom. The long-established mercantilist approach to the problem of the economic functions of government, involving extensive regulation of private industry and commerce by governmental authority, was less popular in the colonies than in the mother country, principally because of colonial opposition to the imperial policy of excluding colonial merchants from direct trade outside the Empire. Nevertheless, in dealing with matters within the domestic jurisdiction of the colonies, the colonial governments were generally devoted to mercantilist principles. They favored North American producers of all kinds by the usual expedients—bounties, subsidies, grants-in-aid, special manufacturing and marketing privileges, and the rest—whenever encouragement of domestic manufacturers and tradesmen seemed likely to promote more rapid development of colonial industry. Governmental intervention in the operations of industry and commerce for the purpose of strengthening or enriching the state was regarded not as an objectionable infringement of natural liberty but as a necessary and proper activity in the public interest. The mercantilist system was accepted in principle as thoroughly consistent with the Whig concept of political liberty. Economic freedom, as advocated by Smith and Bentham, was no part of the liberty claimed by the authors of the Declaration of Independence.

The perennial conflict between liberty and authority was not solved by the pleasing generalities in the Declaration of Independence. The social compact political philosophy indeed was not well designed to serve that general purpose. It was well suited to the requirements of particular controversies between unpopular rulers and their subjects. The list of grievances against the Crown, cited in the Declaration of Independence, supplies impressive illustrations of the particular liberties which the colonists feared were in jeopardy. Their leaders wisely abstained from theoretical discussions of other liberties, which did not concern them, or of the nature of liberty in general.

This conclusion is confirmed by the contemporary treatment of the third of the inalienable rights specified in the Declaration of Independence, the pursuit of happiness. It is significant that Jefferson did not specify a right to the enjoyment of happiness. He was concerned only with a right to its pursuit. The Whig Congressmen, for whom Jefferson was drafting the Declaration, might have expected him at this point to say something about the rights of owners of property. Controversies over property have had as much to do with most revolutions as those over liberty, at least those over liberty as an abstract proposition. Controversies over particular liberties get involved with those over properties of one sort or another—printing presses, books, meeting places, and other things. But Jefferson seemed not to want to talk much about land, shipping, farm produce, and the other kinds of property over which the controversies of 1776 raged. He had become by force of circumstances a revolutionist and properly wished to put his case for so drastic a remedy as revolution on the firmest possible grounds.

Now happiness, or even its pursuit, is an elusive objective. There is the happiness of the individual, which should be something more intense than mere contentment, and something more refined than sensual pleasure, if it is to be an important concern of statesmen. There is also the happiness of the body politic, which requires the adjustment of the desires of the individual to the wants and needs of the whole community to which the individual belongs. The most satisfactory pursuit of happiness, from the individual's viewpoint, would seem to require unrestricted opportunity to do as he pleases. The greatest happiness of the whole community, or at least of the greatest number of its members, would seem to require ample opportunity for the community to protect its members from injury by selfish pleasure-seekers and, if possible, to promote the general welfare by public-spirited measures transcending the petty aims of unsociable individuals.

The pursuit of happiness inevitably leads statesmen to a concern with processes rather than with properties. If all the implications of the term *liberty* are fully understood, there is nothing a property owner might like to do with his possessions that could not be covered by an appeal to his liberties, duly considered in the light of all the circumstances of a particular case. Shall he be free to keep his money in order to pay his debts and provide for his private wants, if the people of his state need some of it for public purposes? Shall he be free to keep land which is needed for a public park, if he would prefer to use it as a private hunting ground? Shall he be free to operate his factory and work his employees for long hours to the hazard of their health and the ultimate injury of the society of which they are a part? The answer depends presumably on the circumstances of the case, and the important matter is that the choice between the liberty of the individual and the liberty of the whole body of people, which constitutes a state, be reached by a process that allows an adequate hearing to all interested parties and insures the use of the best judgment at the command of the government. Thus the pursuit of happiness comes to depend on due process of law.

In the eighteenth century the pursuit of happiness, even more than the enjoyment of life and liberty, was influenced by conflicting ideas concerning the natural state of man. Theological doctrines of original sin conflicted with poetic visions of primitive bliss. John Dryden, a favorite poet in the latter part of the seventeenth century, was a contemporary of John Locke and equally interested in natural man. In one of his most popular poems he made his hero say:

> I am free as Nature first made man,
> Ere the base laws of servitude began,
> When wild in woods the noble savage ran.

Lawyers might prefer the language and thought of Locke and Blackstone, but their clients could not be blamed for liking the style and imagery of Dryden and Pope. Still the question remained, how happy actually was the noble savage, running wild in his native woods? More important, how should a good American Whig go about the pursuit of happiness under the far more complex conditions of his contemporary world?

THE GOVERNMENTAL PROCESS

The second of the revolutionary principles of government followed closely after the first. The governments, which according to the Declaration were instituted among men in order to secure their rights, would derive "their just powers," in Jefferson's impressive phraseology, "from the consent of the governed." It should be noted that Jefferson was not speaking of all governments, but only of governments rightly instituted, and that he did not say that even such governments would derive all their powers from the consent of the governed, but only their just powers. Jefferson was not dealing with abstractions here, but with the actual processes of government which should be established for the benefit of the American people. He was looking forward to the revision of colonial institutions under the impact of the new revolutionary principles as well as to the formation of a new continental government to replace that of the British Empire in the service of the American people.

In 1776, whatever might be the popular view concerning the nature and pursuit of happiness, Blackstone was obviously more useful than the poets in dealing with due process of law. Having treated as best he could what he considered the primary rights of Englishmen—the rights to life, liberty, and property—he turned his attention to what he called their subordinate rights. These, in his opinion, served to protect the primary rights and were five in number. Blackstone listed them as (1) "the constitution, powers, and privileges of Parliament," (2) "the limitation of the royal prerogative by certain and notorious bounds," (3) "the right to apply to courts of justice for redress of injuries," (4) "the right to petition for redress of grievances," and

(5) "the right of bearing arms." These five subordinate rights—the right of self-defense, the right of petition, the right to one's day in court, the right to impose limits on the discretionary power of kings, and the right to representative government, as we may conveniently describe them—may well have seemed to most American Whigs to be of greater practical utility than the philosophical abstractions in the Declaration of Independence. Be that as it may, Blackstone's subordinate rights furnish clues to the further discovery of the meaning of the Declaration to the American people at the time of the Revolution.

There could be no question about preserving the right to bear arms. The American Whigs were making vigorous use of that right, as the Declaration was being written, and expected to continue to do so. In an age when wars were fought with muskets and when powder and shot could be manufactured with the facilities available in almost any colonial town or village, the right to bear arms was a valuable possession of free men. In an age of atom bombs and intercontinental ballistic missiles, the less said the better about the value of this particular right. It is so greatly subordinate to the primary rights as to play no significant part in the calculations of practical statesmen, responsible for the maintenance of law and order and the promotion of the general welfare. But in 1776 the wildest visionaries among the revolutionists did not dream of atom bombs and intercontinental missiles. The assertion of a right to bear arms was a foremost concern of the authors of the declarations of rights and was inserted in the front of the new constitutions adopted in most of the original states.

The importance attached to this right by the American Whigs is well attested by the elaborate form in which it was stated in the Virginia Declaration of Rights, carefully drafted by George Mason, the wealthy planter and outstanding Whig leader, and adopted by the provincial legislature a few weeks before the Declaration of Independence. This influential document declared that "a well-regulated militia, composed of the body of the people, trained to arms, is the proper, natural, and safe defense of a free state; that standing armies, in time of peace, should be avoided, as dangerous to liberty; and that, in all cases, the military should be under strict subordination to, and governed by, the civil power." This detailed statement was a substantial improvement over Blackstone's version of the right to bear arms and thoroughly in keeping with the spirit of a people already fighting for their primary rights. In later years it was sometimes criticized as being merely a piece of good advice which might or might not be respected in the actual conduct of government. But those who believed the advice to be sound and essential to good government were well satisfied to have it cast in a form which the sovereign people would not easily let their rulers forget.

Blackstone's right to petition for redress of grievances was not mentioned in the Virginia Declaration of Rights. George Mason and his fellow Virginia Whigs evidently believed that they possessed more valuable means of protection against the abuse of power by public officers of their own choosing, acting under a written constitution of their own making. They would tolerate no king, to whom by tradition petitions were humbly submitted. They would not petition their representatives in the state legislature but would issue instructions to them. In short, a sovereign people, they seemed to think, would have no need of a right of petition.

Much greater importance was attached to Blackstone's right to apply to courts of justice for the redress of injuries. The Virginia Declaration of Rights contained numerous provisions designed to make a person's right to his day in court of substantial benefit to him. Trial by jury, both in civil and in criminal cases, was carefully protected; excessive bail and fines were frowned upon; and cruel and unusual punishments were forbidden. The area of good advice respecting the incidental processes of trial and conviction was widely extended. This manifest trust in the practical utility of such advice clearly indicated a strong disposition to rely on juries for the protection of the rights of the people.

The Virginia Declaration of Rights had little to say about Blackstone's various devices for imposing limits on the discretionary power of kings. This was not a major problem to men who had gotten rid of kings and had no intention of replacing them with new tyrants of their own contrivance. The second paragraph of the Virginia Declaration clearly expressed the conviction of George Mason and the Virginia Whigs "that all power is vested in, and consequently derived from, the people; that magistrates are their trustees and servants, and at all times amenable to them." There followed an explicit endorsement of the right of revolution and an explicit repudiation of the notion that public offices of any kind should be hereditary. But there was no explicit endorsement of the proposition that the chief executive officer of the state should be elected directly by the people.

In fact, the election of the Virginia governor was left to the state legislature. The Virginia Whigs were content that the responsibility of the governor to the people should be maintained by frequent elections, and the legislature was expressly authorized to provide for the further limitation of the governor's influence by making him ineligible for re-election at the end of his term. The legislature subsequently further restricted the governor's authority by depriving him of the power to veto acts of the legislature and by vesting the power of appointment to inferior offices in the legislature or in local assemblies. Whatever the Virginia Whigs may have thought about King George personally, long experience with oppressive, or at least unpopular, colonial governors had left them with little taste for vigorous executive leadership. Their strong disposition to put their trust mainly in legislative representatives was plainly manifest.

Evidently, in practice much would depend upon the system of legislative elections. On this point the Virginia Declaration of Rights was more emphatic than precise. It declared that such elections should be "free" and that all men, "having sufficient evidence of permanent common interest with, and attachment to, the community," should have the right to vote and should not be taxed or deprived of their property for public use without their own consent or that of their representatives. Finally, they should not be bound by any law "to which they have not, in like manner, assented, for the public good." This was indeed good advice, but much was left unsaid concerning the kind of evidence of attachment to the community that would be consistent with an effective sovereignty of the people.

Under the Virginia Constitution, adopted by the legislature under the authority of the Declaration of Rights, the right to vote was restricted to property owners, and somewhat higher property qualifications were required for election to the legislature. Jefferson, who complained later that the property qualification for voting excluded from the electoral franchise a majority of those Virginians who were liable to pay taxes or to serve in the militia, declared that the test for voting was too high. He wanted an early reform of the state constitution in order that the will of the sovereign people might be more clearly expressed in the public elections. However, more than a half century was to pass before there would be an opportunity to give this aristocratic frame of government a more democratic cast. Meanwhile, for practical purposes, sovereign power remained vested in the state legislature.

The Virginia solution of the problem of protecting the people against the abuse of power by the possessors of the remnants of the royal prerogative was acceptable in a majority of the original states. Manhood suffrage was not established in any of them, and substantial property qualifications for legislators were maintained in most. The states in which the frontier populations were large and influential possessed the nearest approaches to manhood suffrage and to democratic legislative bodies. In 1776 Pennsylvania, Vermont (which, though not admitted to the Union until 1791, adopted an independent state constitution in 1777), and Georgia were the outstanding frontier states. In Pennsylvania any taxpayer, even one who paid no more than a poll tax, could vote, and in the other two states the practice was still more democratic. But in the states in which the big planters and merchants had been most influential in colonial politics, more aristocratic practices prevailed. Not yet was every man to be a king.

The first and most important of Blackstone's subordinate rights of Englishmen, the "constitution, powers, and privileges of Parliament," led him to the conclusion that in Great Britain the theory of the separation of powers was supported in practice by an effective system of checks and balances. Sovereignty was no longer vested in the king, but rather in the "King-in-Parliament." In 1776 this sovereign was dethroned insofar as its jurisdiction over the revolted colonies was concerned. In its place the newly independent states sought to establish constitutional systems consistent with their understanding of the basic human right to reign of law. The American Whigs generally admired the British theory of the separation of powers with its practical embodiment in a system of checks and balances. In the American states British parliamentary institutions were no more, but the theory remained and the practice might even be improved upon.

The Virginia Declaration of Rights recognized the theory and recommended the practice. It formally declared "that the legislative and executive powers of the state should be separate and distinct from the judiciary." But it did not specify how separate and distinct the first two should be from the third, nor did it make altogether clear whether they should also be separate and distinct from one another. Beyond calling for frequent elections and suggesting rotation in office, the practical arrangement of the checks and balances was left to the legislature, in which the governor's influence would be small. Consequently, the system of checks and balances established in Virginia in 1776 left a great deal to be desired.

In short, the form of government provided by the first Virginia constitution can be best described as a system of legislative supremacy. The legislature made the constitution, put it into effect, and presumably could amend or repeal it at pleasure. It not only elected the governor but encumbered him with an executive council to be chosen by itself. The constitution provided for a further check on the executive by dividing the legislature into two branches, one of which was designed to represent more particularly the larger property owners in the state. This upper legislative house, to be sure, would also act as a check upon the somewhat more popular lower house, but its members should possess greater personal prestige than members of the more numerous lower legislative branch and thereby balance more effectively the personal influence of the chief executive. A few years later Jefferson criticized these arrangements as not being the kind of government the revolutionary patriots had fought for. In his celebrated *Notes on Virginia* he remarked: "One hundred and seventy-three despots" (the number of members of the legislature) "would surely be as oppressive as one." He could not consent permanently to a form of representative government in which the actual supremacy of an aristocratic legislature cast doubt upon the theoretical sovereignty of the people.

A majority of the original states were content, at least for a time, with constitutions affording no greater assurance than that of Virginia that governmental powers were derived from the consent of the governed or would actually be exercised with their approval. Legislative supremacy was most complete in Georgia, where the legislature consisted of but a single house, and the positions of the chief executive and judiciary were of extreme dependence. In general the upper houses of the original state legislatures were designed to represent the larger property owners, betraying their derivation from the aristocratic colonial councils which had helped the provincial governors keep the representatives of the colonial populaces in their place. Now the new state senates would help the larger property owners keep the smaller property owners in their place. Legislative supremacy was not to mean a system of representative government marked by unchecked majority rule. There was to be a proper balance between the different classes of people. The American Whigs, despite their acceptance of the principle of popular sovereignty, did not generally desire the embodiment of that principle in governmental institutions characterized by what they would have described as an excess of democracy.

An outstanding exception to the general practice was offered by the state in which the influence of the frontier in 1776 was greatest. In Pennsylvania the revolutionary convention which framed the first state constitution was not dominated by the big Philadelphia merchants. On the contrary, delegates from the back country and frontier held sway. Franklin was the most prominent Philadelphian to be elected, and he represented the spirit of the American West rather than the mercantile interests of the Pennsylvania East. The Declaration of Rights failed to mention the separation of powers, though the Frame of Government provided that the supreme legislative power should be vested in a single house of representatives and the supreme executive power in a president and council.

There was no attempt to establish a balance between them, however. There were twelve councillors, representing twelve electoral districts, and the president had no greater power than any other councillor. In order to preserve the supremacy of the constitution, and thereby hopefully the sovereignty of the people, a special council of censors was to be elected every seven years, charged with the duty of examining the conduct of government during the preceding septennium and submitting to the people for their approval any amendments to the constitution which might seem necessary to correct errors in its application or to improve the form of government in the light of experience. The legislature was denied power to alter the constitution, but otherwise its lawmaking power was unlimited. This was an original plan to combine popular sovereignty with an actual reign of law. It was the most democratic of the original state constitutions and, next to that of Georgia, the one with the least effective system of checks and balances. It was also, next to that of Georgia, the first to be abandoned in favor of a better balanced system.

The states which made the most purposeful and systematic efforts to combine the theory of the separation of powers with an effective system of checks and balances were New York and Massachusetts. In both states there was provision for a bicameral legislature in which the upper house was designed to give special representation to the larger property owners, for an independent chief executive, and for an independent judiciary. The New York constitution of 1777, of which John Jay was the chief architect, provided that the governor and the state senators should be chosen for four years by a special electorate limited by a high property qualification for voting. It provided that the governor should be further limited by a Council of Appointment, consisting of four senators elected by the lower house, which should approve his selections for public office, and by a Council of Revision, including with the governor the principal members of the state judiciary, which should share his power to veto legislative enactments, subject to re-enactment by a two-thirds majority in each branch of the legislature.

Later, in the Constitutional Convention of 1787, several features of this

New York constitution, particularly the joint executive-judicial veto vested in the Council of Revision, were strongly recommended for inclusion in the federal Constitution by two of the leading framers, James Madison of Virginia and James Wilson of Pennsylvania. But the system of separate and independent executive and judicial vetoes, contained in the Massachusetts constitution, was eventually preferred by a majority of the framers. The Massachusetts constitution of 1780, of which John Adams was the chief architect, differed from that of New York in some other important respects. It specified a uniform property qualification for voters and annual elections for the governor and the members of both branches of the legislature. It vested the power of appointment and veto in the governor alone, subject in the former case to the approval of an executive council, and in the latter to legislative re-enactment as in New York. The Massachusetts constitution also provided an improved process for its own amendment and revision. First, the electorate should authorize the election of a constitutional convention; next the delegates should be elected in a manner to be determined by the legislature; and finally all proposed constitutional changes should be referred to the electorate for its approval. This was the most complete process devised anywhere for keeping the fundamental law under the control of the people themselves. It represented the climax of the revolutionary efforts to combine the theoretical sovereignty of the people with an actual reign of law.

The constitutions adopted by the original states, when independence gave them the opportunity to reconstruct their colonial institutions, show a variety of forms which presumably were deemed compatible with the basic principle that governments derive their just powers from the consent of the governed. Doubtless the representatives of the people in the various states in many cases acted hastily under the impact of a rapidly developing revolutionary situation. Two states, Connecticut and Rhode Island, took no action but continued to govern themselves under their colonial charters. Under the circumstances of the time these governments were as nearly democratic in their practical operation as those of any other of the original states. But they did not contain any of the checks upon governmental and particularly legislative power which conservative Whig political philosophers regarded as essential for an effective system of constitutional government.

In general the governmental processes established in the original states called for some sober second thoughts on the science of government, when the progress of the war for independence and the accumulation of experience in self-government should produce a more convenient opportunity for applying the revolutionary principles of government to the problem of state constitution-making. John Adams, in his *Thoughts on Government* published in 1776, and Thomas Jefferson, in his *Notes on Virginia* published in 1783, supplied nutritious food for thought both on the science of government and on the lessons of experience. But most of the original state governments would not be put into a form which could stand the test of at least a generation's time until the revision of the continental system of government in

1787 should supply a generally acceptable model of a political system fully measuring up to the standard called for by American Whig principles.

THE GOVERNMENTAL PERFORMANCE

The third of the essential propositions in the American Whigs' program of political reconstruction related to the governmental performance. It consisted of the maxim that the people should be recognized as possessors of a right of revolution to be asserted when their rulers fail to protect their other rights and persist in exercising governmental powers without the consent of the governed. "Whenever any form of government becomes destructive of these ends," Jefferson wrote with characteristic felicity in the Declaration of Independence, "it is the right of the people to alter or abolish it, and to institute new government, laying its foundation on such principles and organizing its powers in such form, as to them shall seem most likely to effect their safety and happiness." In order to make his meaning doubly clear, Jefferson restated this most important of the revolutionary principles of government in different words: "When a long train of abuses and usurpations, pursuing invariably the same object, evinces a design to reduce them under absolute despotism, it is their right, it is their duty, to throw off such government, and to provide new guards for their future security." This is the classic statement of the right of revolution as understood by the American Whigs.

The right of revolution comprised both a right and a duty, a right to discard a despotic government and a duty to replace it with one more responsive to the general will and more likely to be operated in the public interest. The facts, which Jefferson submitted "to a candid world" in justification of his charge that the king of Great Britain sought to establish "an absolute tyranny" over the people of the colonies, may seem to the present world, shocked by recent spectacles of far greater tyranny than any suffered by the American people in the eighteenth century, "light and transient causes" for so drastic a remedy as revolution. The weightiest "fact" was not noticed, but it may well have been that the British Empire was then beginning a gradual evolution from the monopolistic mercantilist empire, which it had been, to the modern Commonwealth, which it has now become. Its government is now dispersed among constituent states as independent in practice as the Dominion of Canada and the Republic of India. The Queen may still reign over some of these states within the Commonwealth, but the Parliament does not govern outside the limits of the United Kingdom itself and its few remaining and comparatively unimportant dependencies. Such an arrangement in 1776 would doubtless have made the American Whigs happier. But evolutions take longer than revolutions, and the strong urge of the Americans to hold a less dependent position in the Empire than was practicable, or perhaps conceivable, in 1776 made separation from the British people a natural consequence of the circumstances of the time.

The decision to "dissolve the political bands" which had connected the American and British peoples called for an immediate effort to prepare a form of government for the new United States. Whether the existing Continental Congress was merely an intercolonial organization or an actual government is a problem in semantics of no great importance except to antiquarians who wish to rehearse the ancient arguments concerning the priority of the Union over the states or vice versa. In fact, the first Continental Congress, which met in 1774, conducted an active correspondence with the colonial committees of correspondence, issued several addresses and declarations of varying degrees of importance, and sent a petition to the king. The second Continental Congress, which first met in 1775, conducted a wider correspondence, sent another petition to the king, adopted additional addresses and declarations, including eventually the Declaration of Independence, appointed George Washington Commander-in-Chief of the Continental Army, and appointed sundry committees to supervise the conduct of the war and the negotiations with allies. It also recommended to the colonies, when faced with the dissolution of the established colonial governments, that they establish new governments of their own. This and other recommendations were generally followed by those to whom they were addressed. If this Continental Congress was not theoretically a continental government, it certainly acted like one.[4]

The first effort to form a general government for the former British subjects in North America succeeded in establishing a continental confederation, which was excessively imperfect, and in supplying an example of the practical operation of the right of revolution, which was as nearly perfect as any revolutionary philosopher could desire. The Articles of Confederation and Perpetual Union, which were derived from a plan bearing that name submitted by Franklin in the summer of 1775, were prepared by a committee appointed immediately after the appointment of the committee that prepared the Declaration of Independence. This committee reported its draft shortly after the adoption of the Declaration, but controversy over details of the new plan delayed its adoption until the defeat of Burgoyne at Saratoga more than a year later cleared the way for the French alliance and called for an immediate decision on a more efficient form of government. The articles then adopted, however, were not ratified by the last of the original states until 1781, too late to exert an important influence on the conduct of the war, and immediately after Yorktown talk began of its supercession by a new form of government for a more perfect Union.

The government under the Articles of Confederation was built upon the foundation of the Continental Congress. The principal problems that confronted the framers of the Articles were to define the powers of the Congress and to fix the bases of representation and of taxation. The protracted debates over the details of the plan made it clear that in 1776 and 1777 the American Whigs were not ready for a strong continental government, but wanted a loose confederation of states entrusted with no more power than necessary to transact such business relating to the conduct of the war, the regulation of relations with foreign countries, and the making of peace as could not be conveniently transacted by the individual states. These powers, such as they were, were vested exclusively in the Congress. In lieu of an executive branch of the government there was General Washington at the head of the Continental Army, and in lieu of an independent judiciary there was an elaborate arrangement for arbitrating interstate disputes over boundaries and other matters by special commissioners selected under the direction of the Congress.

The essential character of the new government is reflected in the second of the Articles. "Each State retains its sovereignty, freedom, and independence, and every power, jurisdiction, and right," the Article reads, "which is not by this Confederation expressly delegated to the United States in Congress assembled." The Confederation is further described in the next Article as "a firm league of friendship," binding its members "to assist each other against all . . . attacks made upon them, or any of them. . . ." Each state was to have an equal vote in the Congress regardless of differences in population and wealth, but the expenses of the continental government were to be apportioned among the states in proportion to the value of the lands and improvements thereon in the several states. Important matters required the assent of at least nine of the thirteen states, and amendments to the Articles required unanimous assent in the Congress and confirmation by the legislatures of all the states.

In the language of the time this new continental government was a federal government. Ten years later one of the first topics to be discussed in the federal Convention which framed the Constitution of the United States was the difference between a federal government, which the government under the Articles of Confederation was understood to be, and a national government, which some leading members of the Convention of 1787 wished to put in its place. Gouverneur Morris, an outstanding Nationalist, speaking in the Convention on May 30, 1787, explained the difference most succinctly. A federal government, he declared, was "a mere compact resting on the good faith of the parties," whereas a national government had "a complete and compulsive operation." Any system of government for the United States, he contended, must be one or the other, since the supreme power, according to his understanding of the idea of sovereignty, could not be divided between the States and the nation.

George Mason of Virginia, who held a different opinion concerning the nature of sovereignty, tried to make the distinction more clear. "The present confederation," he declared, was "deficient in not providing for coercion and punishment against delinquent States." He argued cogently, according to Madison's report of the debates, that "punishment could not in the nature of things be executed on the States collectively; and therefore that such a government was necessary as could directly operate on individuals." He contended that the kind of government needed for the United States "would punish those only whose guilt required it." A federal government, according to this view, was one without power to enforce its laws directly against the individual citizens of the member states of the Confederation, and the grant of such power to the government of the United States, which all the Nationalists in the Convention of 1787 believed to be necessary, would transform it into a national government. A federal government and a confederate government, according to this view, were political organizations of the same order. If the people of the United States were a nation, the argument ran, they should have a national government capable of acting on the whole body of people as directly as the government of a state acted on the people of the state.

The nature of the government of the United States under the Articles of Confederation suggests a comparison with some of the international organizations established in the present century in the pursuit of international peace. The documents which bear the closest comparison with the Articles of Confederation are the League of Nations Covenant and the United Nations Charter. Both possess some striking resemblances to the Articles, notably, the explicit limitation of the powers delegated to the respective organizations, an equal vote in the principal representative body for all member states (or in the case of the Charter all member states except the five privileged powers holding permanent membership in the Security Council), and the apportionment of expenses among the members on the basis of relative property or production values. The theoretically vital power of amendment is also similar in the Articles and in the Covenant, but in the Charter the power to amend does not require unanimity on the part of all the members. In this important respect the Articles fall into a category closer to the Covenant than to the Charter.

There are also some significant differences between the Articles of Confederation and the other two documents. The former granted more extensive lawmaking powers than the latter two. The Covenant and the Charter, however, distributed important powers between a general assembly and a more select council. They established a much stronger executive branch and provided for an independent judiciary. The Covenant, like the Articles, limited the jurisdiction of the organization to its members, but the Charter purports to extend its jurisdiction over nonmembers as well. The League, like the Confederation, was definitely an interstate organization, but the United Nations seems to be, at least potentially, a world organization. All three are alike, however, in their reliance on the governments of their member states. They possess no direct authority over their several peoples. But the administrative branches of the two modern international organizations were more elaborately constructed and more capable of energetic action than was the administrative branch of the government under the Articles of Confederation.

An important practical difference between the Articles of Confederation and the fundamental laws of the two modern international organizations flows from the provisions regulating the relations between the peoples of the member states. The Articles provided that the free inhabitants of each of the states should be entitled to all the privileges and immunities of free citizens in the several states, that the people of each state should move freely from one state to another, and that they should enjoy in each state the same right as its inhabitants to engage in trade and commerce. The purpose of these provisions was to secure and perpetuate mutual friendship and good relations among the peoples of the different states of the Union. No such intimate relationships between the peoples of the member states were contemplated by the framers of the Covenant or the Charter. Thus the relations between the peoples of the two modern international organizations are much more distant than those between the peoples of the American states under the Articles of Confederation.

Moreover, the restrictions imposed upon the governments of the member states in the interest of peace were more stringent under the Articles of Confederation than under the Covenant or the Charter. No state was allowed to send ambassadors abroad, to receive foreign ambassadors, or to enter into any alliance with a foreign power without the consent of the Congress; nor were any two or more states allowed to enter into any treaty, alliance, or confederation with each other without similar consent. The states were also forbidden to maintain navies and standing armies in time of peace, except such forces as should be expressly authorized by the Congress, but they were specially encouraged to keep up a well regulated and disciplined militia. These provisions for the limitation of armaments went far beyond anything to be found in the Covenant or Charter. Thus the power relationships established by the Articles between the state governments and the Continental Congress put the union of states under the Articles of Confederation in a more advanced stage of development than the associations of nations under the Covenant or the Charter.

Another difference between the Articles of Confederation and the later League of Nations Covenant and United Nations Charter is more fundamental. Supporting the government under the Articles was a body of people already united by a strong and growing sense of common interests and purposes. The American people were an evolving community with a government, though an excessively weak one, of their own. The peoples of the League and of the United Nations fell far short of constituting a true community and found greater difficulty in thinking of the international organization which their governments supported as an organized body of people including themselves. The strengthening and improvement of the government under the Articles of Confederation, though difficult, was an easier task than the strengthening and improvement of the government under the United Nations Charter is likely to be. American statesmen quickly recognized that the government under the Articles of Confederation was too weak for a people in whom the sense of community was as strong as in the United States at the close of the War for Independence. The more perfect Union already existed in public opinion before it received a suitable form at the hands of the framers of the Constitution of 1787.

The Continental Congress under the Articles of Confederation encouraged efforts to revise the Articles with a view to the establishment of a stronger continental government. But the federal Convention of 1787 ignored its instructions to improve the government under the Articles of Confederation and proceeded resolutely with its revolutionary purpose to discard the despised document and replace it with more acceptable articles of union. The complaint against the government under the Articles of Confederation, however, was not of a design to abuse its powers and establish a tyranny but rather of a persistent incapacity to gain for itself adequate powers and to make itself equal to the demands upon it.

The deliberate destruction of the continental government under the Articles of Confederation by its tacit condemnation at the federal Constitutional Convention of 1787 was a genuine revolutionary act. If the American people took little or no notice of the manner of the Continental Congress' end, it does not follow that their right of revolution was not involved in its destruction. But it does follow that there was a duty to put something better in its place. The federal Convention recognized this duty under the third of the revolutionary principles of government. The framing of the Constitution of the United States in 1787 may rightly be regarded, therefore, in terms of the social compact political philosophy, as the lawful continuation and conclusion of the constitution-making process begun by Franklin in 1775 when he introduced into the second Continental Congress his first draft of the Articles of Confederation and Perpetual Union.

CHAPTER THREE

Toward a More Perfect Union

The leadership of the campaign for a more perfect Union fell naturally into the hands of George Washington. While the War for Independence continued, the Commander-in-Chief of the Continental Army was the principal executive officer under the Articles of Confederation. There was no one chief executive, but there was for a time a Superintendent of Finances who operated, like Washington himself, under the direct supervision of the Congress. When this office was filled by the leading Philadelphia merchant Robert Morris, there was good coordination between these two important executive officers, but the success of the arrangement depended heavily upon harmonious personal relations between the two men. There was also a Secretary for Foreign Affairs, but the conduct of diplomatic negotiations with foreign countries was largely in the hands of Benjamin Franklin and his associates in Paris. Throughout the war the Congress jealously guarded its supreme authority in the conduct of public business, giving both Washington and Morris ample cause to lament the weakness of the constitutional system under which they labored. The greater distance and more imperfect communications between Philadelphia and Paris gave Franklin and his associates greater independence in the conduct of their offices. But there could be no doubt in the mind of any of these executive officers that the organization of government under the Articles of Confederation was excessively imperfect.

A NEW MODEL OF POLITICAL PLANNING

Washington devoted his last official communication to the governors of the states, when peace finally seemed to be assured, to a program of policies which he deemed necessary and proper for securing the fruits of victory. This communication, which came to be called Washington's "Legacy"—a precursor of his Farewell Address—was the eighteenth-century equivalent of a modern political party platform. It consisted of four planks. The first plank demanded "an indissoluble Union of the States under one Federal Head." The second and third planks called for "a sacred regard to public justice," that is, the payment of the war debts, and "the adoption of a proper peace establishment," that is, adequate provision for the future national defense. The final plank called for the preservation of a "pacific and friendly disposition among the people of the United States" suitable "to the interest of the community." Clearly Washington was already thinking of the American people as a single body politic, animated by a general consciousness of common interests.[1] But most immediately important was the first demand, that for a more perfect Union.

There were other causes for dissatisfaction with the constitutional system under the Articles of Confederation besides those felt most keenly by the chief strategist and the chief financier of the Revolution. The Congress itself was painfully aware of the gravest of these causes, its own lack of indispensable lawmaking powers. It could not properly control the relations between the states of the Union and foreign countries, it could not even regulate interstate commerce, and above all it could not provide itself with adequate revenues for carrying on its own business. Neither could it remedy these defects in the distribution of powers between the states and the Union. All attempts at amending the Articles of Confederation were frustrated by the requirement of unanimous consent by the thirteen states to any change in the constitutional system.

Though the Congress had shown its incapacity to improve the organization of the Union, it was slow to allow any other body to undertake the necessary task. The Revolutionary War had ruined the national currency and raised a mountainous debt. The war had also disrupted long-established channels of trade, and peace had not restored the prewar markets. Independence would eventually bring better opportunities for foreign trade and better access to overseas markets than had existed while the colonies remained within the British Empire, but time was required for the profitable exploitation of these new opportunities. Meanwhile, business was depressed and suffering was widespread. Meanwhile also, Virginia was taking the lead in direct negotiations among the states for the relief of the most urgent difficulties. These efforts culminated in the Annapolis Convention of 1786, which issued a call for a national convention to meet at Philadelphia in 1787 and consider what might be done to improve the state of the Union. Shays' Rebellion in Massachusetts came at the right time to shock the Congress into giving a reluctant blessing to this unauthorized proceeding.

The Virginia Plan for a more perfect Union was a gradual development.[2] Its various components had doubtless been germinating in the minds of Virginia statesmen since the end of the war. Washington himself seems to have had a firm grasp on the major objectives of the campaign for a more perfect Union, but to have kept an open mind concerning the choice of measures for reaching the end in view. Much of the private correspondence between public men at that period has been preserved, and Washington was a favorite confidant of the more thoughtful among his former military and later political companions. Suggestions for dividing the Union into parts—three seems to have been the preferred number—in the hope that strong central governments could be organized more satisfactorily on a regional basis met with no approval from him. Proposals for establishing a continental monarchy with himself as king were resolutely put aside as untimely. The Virginia leaders were aware, however, that specific proposals of some sort would be expected from them at the Philadelphia Convention, and their correspondence with one another before their departure for Philadelphia reveals their intention to meet the responsibilities of leadership.

The framers of the Virginia Plan were political architects charged with putting a new roof over an existing foundation. The foundation had been well laid, but the walls were weak and the old roof was far from weatherproof. Lawyers might object on the ground that the framers' method of proceeding was unconstitutional, since they had no intention of permitting their efforts to be frustrated by the legal requirement of the unanimous consent of the states for changes in the Articles of Confederation. Historians, however, could reply that their project was a continuation of the political revolution begun in 1776 and, if also revolutionary, was protected by the law of historical continuity. It too would be justified by the consent of the people of the Union. The important matter would be, not technical compliance with the text of the Articles of Confederation, but the practical capacity of the planners to bring about changes which would be sanctioned by a strong and preponderant majority of the people. Support by popular consensus rather than technical legality would be the decisive proof of the validity of their proceedings.

There were indeed many provisions in the Virginia Plan which related directly to the fundamental principles of 1776. Four of the fifteen points in the plan dealt in different ways with the basic principle of popular sovereignty. Four others dealt with the coordinate principle of the reign of law. There were differences of opinion within the Philadelphia Convention concerning the application of these principles, but none concerning the acceptability of the principles themselves. Less attention was paid to two of the three auxiliary principles, those concerning the purpose of government and the governmental performance. It was the improvement of the governmental process which caused the greatest contention in the Convention. How should powers be distributed between the states and the Union and between the different branches of the government of the Union, and how should this government be constructed?

The framers of the Virginia Plan recognized that the first problem to be solved by the architects of a new constitution is to enable the government to control the governed; the second is to compel it to control itself.[3] The Virginia Plan contained proposals for solving these problems but, for the new constitutional structure, the planners necessarily relied upon materials which were more controversial—the diverse experience of the different states, the example of foreign countries, and the teachings of the far from perfect general science of government. There has been much talk by American historians about the compromises of the Constitution, and rightly, for they were numerous and important. Without these compromises the new roof could not have been put in place. But the compromises must be set in their proper perspective. It was a great merit of the Virginia planners that they were ready, able, and willing to compromise, when compromise was necessary and proper, but it is also greatly to their credit that they planned to build the new roof on the old foundation, for the old foundation was sound and durable.

The Constitutional Convention of 1787 was called to meet on Monday the fourteenth of May.[4] The Virginia delegation was present, but no other state was represented by a delegation competent to act except Pennsylvania, whose delegates happened to reside in Philadelphia. In fact no quorum appeared until Friday the twenty-fifth, and the Convention was not completely organized until the following Monday. Thus the Virginia delegates had a full fortnight in which to put their plan in shape for presentation to the Convention.

The Virginia delegates made good use of their free time. They met daily and formed their plan into fifteen specific proposals. It would be interesting to study the development of the plan, if we possessed a record of their discussions. The Virginia delegation was the strongest in the Convention, and the ideas of its members became the point of departure for the actual framing of the Constitution. But the rules of the Convention were designed to ensure the secrecy of the proceedings, lest public knowledge of differences among the delegates should increase the difficulty of agreement upon the changes to be made in the constitutional system. It was a wise precaution, but the consequence was that the American people had to wait many years for the post-mortem publication of private notes on the debates by a few of the delegates in order to learn what went on at Philadelphia in the summer of 1787 and in some cases what the Constitution was intended to mean. Of these private notes the most accurate and complete were Madison's. But Madison left no record of the discussions within the Virginia delegation during that first fortnight.

Many important discussions in all deliberative bodies take place off the floor. It is not only in the closed sittings of committees that great decisions are reached. Members, and especially leaders, hold informal conferences, entirely off the record, to discuss tactical moves of various kinds, and there is much casual discussion around dinner tables and in members' rooms. Many of the delegates to the Philadelphia Convention lived together at the City Tavern or the Indian Queen or the nearby private boarding houses. Washington himself resided throughout the Convention at the hospitable house of his good friend Robert Morris, and his diary discloses many an evening at home with no explanation of how the time was spent. Washington was not the man to sit alone in his room engaged in idle reverie, when his political aides were free to come and go without public notice. The fact that he is known to have spoken only once on the floor of the Convention, and that once on the last day of its sittings, is no measure of his actual influence on the making of the Constitution. He and Robert Morris may well have been content to leave the speaking on the floor to their lawyers and business associates and political advisers, who were present in the Virginia and Pennsylvania delegations. The identity of the masterminds of the Philadelphia Convention is not to be determined by tangible evidence.[5]

There is no doubt, however, concerning the leadership of the Virginia and Pennsylvania delegations in the actual framing of the Constitution. They had the scene all to themselves throughout the first period, when the final touches were being put on the Virginia Plan. At all stages of the proceedings Madison and Randolph and Mason among the Virginians, Wilson and Gouverneur Morris among the Pennsylvanians were among the most frequent debaters on the floor and among the most active workers in the committees. These able delegates represented two of the most powerful forces in the Convention, the great plantation owners and tobacco growers of the Upper South and the great merchants and ship owners of the Maritime North. Only Benjamin Franklin, who had been added to the Pennsylvania delegation as an afterthought on account of his great personal prestige, could speak with real authority for the common man in both town and country. Patrick Henry, who could have spoken with equal authority for the man in the backwoods and on the frontier, had been appointed to the Virginia delegation but refused to serve. He suspected the great planters and merchants of planning to put their special interests ahead of those of the more numerous classes of people for whose interests he felt a particular responsibility. But the influence of class interests cannot be measured by what politicians say when out of office. It must be estimated in the light of what they do, when they have power to act.

The second period in the work of the Constitutional Convention began with the presentation of the Virginia Plan by Edmund Randolph, the youthful governor of the Commonwealth and nominal head of the delegation.[6] Randolph described it as a plan to establish a national government, consisting of a supreme legislature, a supreme executive, and a supreme judiciary.

The Convention immediately resolved itself into a Committee of the Whole for a preliminary examination of the Virginia Plan and of other plans presented for its consideration. Of these others the most important was a plan presented by the New Jersey delegation on behalf of itself and certain members of other delegations, who wished to support a plan based more directly on the Articles of Confederation and the instructions of the Congress than was the Virginia Plan. It contemplated the establishment of a genuine federal government, as that term was then understood, rather than a national government and, though providing for a supreme court, carefully avoided mention of a supreme legislature or executive.

There was an early discussion of the difference between a federal and a national government. The prevailing opinion was that theoretically the essence of the former was a union of states and of the latter a union of people. But the Committee of the Whole was not dealing with theories; it was dealing with plans. Between the two it preferred that supported by the leading Virginians and Pennsylvanians. First, it made some important changes in the Virginia Plan and added four specific proposals to the original fifteen. Then it reported the plan as amended out to the Convention as the basis for its further deliberations.[7] Three weeks had passed, plus a day allowed to the proponents of the New Jersey Plan for the purpose of putting their plan in shape for consideration by the other delegates.

The supporters of the New Jersey Plan came from the smaller states and represented a variety of interests. Prominent among them were William Paterson of New Jersey, who presented the plan to the committee, Roger Sherman of Connecticut, Luther Martin of Maryland, and Robert Yates of New York. They were mostly lawyers from small towns and largely dependent upon the local merchants and farmers for professional success. They were no match as a group for the aristocratic Virginia and Pennsylvania leaders, but they could speak with confidence for the independent farmers and village handicraftsmen who constituted the bulk of the population in these states and gave to local politics a strongly middle-class character. This middle-class character would have to be respected by statesmen who planned constitutional changes which would need the sanction of consent by a strong and preponderant majority of the American people. Several of these small-town lawyers were judges with a natural preference for a kind of law and order in which the judicial power could hold its own against the legislative and executive branches of government. Though defeated in this first encounter with the great planters and merchants, some of them were destined to play an important part in later stages of the struggle to improve the American constitutional system.

In the third of the five periods into which the work of the Convention was divided, the Virginia and Pennsylvania delegations lost control of the Convention. During this period, which covered five weeks in June and July, the delegates went through the Virginia Plan, as amended in the Committee of the Whole, proposal by proposal. It greatly altered some of them, made more modest changes in others, and added four more new proposals, bringing the total to twenty-three. The sharpest dissensions developed over the composition of the Senate and the apportionment of members of the House of Representatives among the states. Two Grand Committees, one to deal with the Senate and the other with the House of Representatives, were appointed, each consisting of one delegate from each state represented in the Convention. During this period the majority of the New York delegation left the Convention on account of their dissatisfaction with the Convention's disregard of the Congress' instructions to confine their recommendations to changes in the Articles of Confederation, and the minority delegate from New York, Alexander Hamilton, discontinued regular attendance since his state no longer possessed a vote. The belated arrival of a delegation from New Hampshire maintained the total number of delegations present at eleven. Rhode Island continued until the end to ignore the Convention and all its works.

The leadership of the Convention in this period of its work was seized by the delegation from Connecticut. This state was at the time a middle-sized state, and a majority of its delegation refused to support the New Jersey Plan when it was presented to the Convention. This majority, consisting of Oliver Ellsworth and Dr. William Samuel Johnson, together with Roger Sherman, made the delegation, though small in number, one of the ablest and most influential in the Convention. Though ready to make the Virginia Plan the basis of the Convention's work, these Connecticut delegates were unwilling to support it without important changes. Under their leadership the Connecticut Compromise, the first of the great compromises and the one which more than any other made possible the continuance of the Convention and the ultimate success of its labors, was adopted. Ellsworth, the son of a small but independent Yankee farmer, was intended for the ministry but eventually trained for the law and made himself the leading lawyer in his state and the outstanding spokesman in the Convention for the kind of people who dominated the Rural North. Like Sherman, he had already become a respected state judge and later was to be raised by President Washington to the high office of Chief Justice of the United States. Dr. Johnson was the son of an early president of King's (now Columbia) College and himself became president of Columbia in the year of the Convention. He enjoyed a wide reputation for scholarly learning and literary skill. The third period ended with the Convention taking a ten-day recess, while a five-man Committee of Detail was preparing a first draft of the Constitution on the basis of the Virginia Plan, as amended in the Committee of the Whole and further revised and amended by the Convention itself.[8]

The Committee of Detail was well chosen for its purpose. Its five members were outstanding spokesmen for the five major regions represented in the Convention—the Maritime North, the Rural North, the Middle States, the Upper South, and the Lower South. John Rutledge of South Carolina, chairman of the committee, was the most prominent revolutionary leader in his section of the country, a leader at the bar as well as in politics, and well qualified to act for the great plantation owners whose luxuriant crops of rice and indigo laid the foundation for this region's early prosperity. Edmund Randolph, a brilliant young scion of one of Virginia's first families, also a successful lawyer, was well qualified by his political experience to represent the smaller farmers as well as the great tobacco planters who dominated this leading section of the country. James Wilson, a penniless immigrant from Scotland who had begun his American career as a country lawyer on the Pennsylvania frontier and worked his way to the leadership of the Philadelphia bar, was well qualified to speak both for rich Philadelphia merchants and for plain citizens anywhere in this rapidly developing grain-growing region, the original corn and wheat belt in American politics. Oliver Ellsworth had already made himself the most authentic spokesman for the interests of the Rural North in the Convention, and Nathaniel Gorham, a Boston merchant with valuable political experience in the state convention which framed the Massachusetts constitution and the most recent president of the Congress, was amply qualified to represent the Maritime North. These five men must be included in any list of the principal makers of the American Constitution.

The Committee of Detail was responsible for changing the name of the document from the Articles of Union, the name chosen by the Virginia planners, to the Constitution of the United States, a name embodying the essential substance of the new constitutional system. But the committee's most important contribution to the new constitutional system was its explicit description of the powers to be granted to the central government of the Union. The Virginia Plan had proposed to grant legislative powers in the most general terms, leaving to the discretion of the members of the national legislature the interpretation of its lawmaking competence in particular cases as they might arise. This cavalier treatment of a problem of the first importance in practical constitution-making had never set well with many of the delegates, but their attention had been preoccupied with more urgent problems. Now a majority of the Committee of Detail insisted on limiting the legislative powers of the Union to specific grants which might meet the special needs of the different regions without unduly prejudicing the general interests of all. This was the beginning of the sensational alliance between Massachusetts and South Carolina, an alliance which greatly influenced the action of the Convention upon the report of the Committee of Detail. The Connecticut member of the committee had his own reasons for preferring that the legislative powers of the central government should be separately enumerated and clearly expressed in the written constitution, but the Virginia and Pennsylvania members saved a portion of the implied powers which they wanted for the more perfect Union by adding the provision that the Congress should also possess all the powers which might be necessary and proper for carrying into effect those expressly granted.

The fourth period in the Convention's work was devoted to a thorough discussion of the report of the Committee of Detail. This period also lasted five full weeks and witnessed a confused struggle over the proposed grants of legislative power to the new central government. This struggle threatened to drown the national interest in a turbulent sea of conflicting sectional and local interests. Four Grand Committees were appointed to explore the possibilities of compromising the antagonistic positions of the various regions and sections. Their deliberations were not unfruitful. Nevertheless, in the general scramble for special advantages, responsible leadership seemed lost from view.

The last of these Grand Committees was that on Postponed Matters and Unfinished Business. Several of the ablest politicians in the Convention served on this committee. Among them Madison of Virginia, Gouverneur Morris of Pennsylvania, and Rufus King of Massachusetts were outstanding. John Dickinson of Delaware, Dr. Johnson of Connecticut, and Judge Brearley of New Jersey were also important. The committee succeeded in reaching agreement upon a series of compromises which produced a frame of government that left only barely recognizable traces of the original Virginia Plan. It also left some of the original planners deeply disgusted with the fruits of their toil. But all the delegations present at the close of the Convention were able to give it their approval. Among the delegates the conviction was general that no better results could be expected from another convention, for, as Franklin put it, "they had many interests to reconcile."

In the fifth and final period of the Convention's work General Washington and the remnants of the original Nationalists regained the leadership of the Convention. They now called themselves Federalists, and many of the original Federalists who had not abandoned the Convention in disgust with the trend of the proceedings joined with the former Nationalists in making the finished draft as generally acceptable as possible. A second committee of five, called the Committee of Style and Arrangement, was appointed under the chairmanship of Dr. Johnson of Connecticut to put the draft in the most attractive form.[9] The other four members were all comparatively young men who had taken an active part in pushing forward the plans of the original Nationalists. James Madison, Gouverneur Morris, Rufus King, and Alexander Hamilton—these were the men who put the finishing touches on the Constitution. None of them was altogether happy with the results of the Convention's labors, and Hamilton at least was frank in admitting that the finished Constitution was very remote from his idea of the proper basis of a satisfactory constitutional system.

The discussion of the report of the Committee of Detail lasted one week and ended on Monday, September 17, with the signing of the draft Constitution by thirty-nine of the forty-two delegates still in the Convention. Altogether the drafting of the Constitution required eighteen weeks. Almost a quarter of the fifty-five delegates who attended the Convention at one time or another had dropped out before the end, some because they did not like what was being done, others because they regarded other duties as more important. But at the end Washington's leadership seemed fully restored. On the last day, when he took the floor for the first time to address the delegates in support of a minor change in the text of the Constitution, a change designed to make it more acceptable to the friends of a more democratic frame of government, his suggestion was adopted unanimously without debate.

THE FUNDAMENTAL PRINCIPLES OF FREE GOVERNMENT IN THE FEDERAL CONVENTION OF 1787

The Constitutional Convention of 1787 was well pleased with the idea of popular sovereignty expressed in the Preamble to the Constitution, as finally adopted. "We the People of the United States," the expression ran, "do establish and ordain this Constitution. . . ." The phrase "We the People" extricated the framers from an awkward dilemma. The Preamble originally suggested in the report of the Committee of Detail used the expression "We the People of the States of New Hampshire, Massachusetts, etc." The practical difficulty was that the new Constitution would not require the approval of all the states in order to go into effect, and it could not be foreseen which states would provide the necessary number of ratifications. To cite the authority of the people of the United States for the establishment of the new central government in place of the government under the Articles of Confederation sounded well. But did the expression mean the people of the whole Union, regarded as a single body politic, or the separate peoples of each of the ratifying states, regarded as distinct bodies politic? If sovereignty be defined as supreme political power, unlimited by man-made law, then by definition it cannot be divided between different bodies of people. It must have resided in the people of the Union, regarded as a unified independent state, or in the peoples of the original states, regarded as independent components of the constitutional system. On the other hand, if sovereignty be differently defined so as to be theoretically divisible, what becomes of the sovereign people? The framers of the Constitution did not clearly say.

The theoretical problem is important. If sovereignty resided in the people of each of the states, then any of them, having freely joined the new and hopefully more perfect Union, would be equally free to withdraw from it at pleasure and resume an independent position outside the constitutional system. But if sovereignty resided in the people of the whole Union, then the Union must have been indissoluble, as General Washington recommended in his "Legacy" of 1783, except by a revolutionary act which would be unlawful under the Constitution. Under the circumstances of the time the framers of the Constitution naturally wished to discourage discussion of further revolutionary acts. Their own proceedings represented as much revolutionary action as they deemed desirable. It is not surprising that they left theoretical discussion of the nature and location of sovereign power to the future.

The text of the Virginia Plan throws some light on the framers' concept of sovereignty. Number eleven of the proposals called for an explicit guarantee of the republican form of government to the states. If sovereignty was to reside in the states, each state should have been free to adopt any form of government desired by its people. If the government of the Union was to have the responsibility for maintaining republican governments in the states, the implication is that sovereignty was located in the people of the Union. This interpretation of the intent of the Virginia planners is consistent with Washington's plea that the Union be indissoluble. Since this provision of the Virginia Plan was adopted by the Convention without reservations or qualifications of any kind, the Virginia planners would seem to have spoken acceptably for all the framers. On the other hand, the Convention did not approve Randolph's description of the government planned by the Virginians as a national government with supreme legislative, executive, and judicial organs. The answer to the theoretical question about sovereignty was evidently not entirely free from doubt.

The Virginia Plan also called for a new process of constitutional revision and amendment which would not require the unanimous consent of the states to change the fundamental law, as did the Articles of Confederation. If the individual states were to surrender their power to block changes in the general constitutional system to which they might be opposed, it is impossible to maintain the view that they would retain the essential attribute of sovereign power in the proposed new constitutional system. This view of the location of sovereignty is supported by the further proposal that new states might be admitted to the Union by a process not requiring the unanimous consent of the existing members of the Union. Yet this proposal does not leave the theoretical question wholly free from doubt. The people of the new states were to be admitted as states and not merely as additional people.

The clearest evidence concerning the intent of the framers is afforded by the fifteenth and last of the Virginia planners' original proposals. This proposal dealt with the procedure for superceding the Articles of Confederation and called for referring changes in the constitutional system agreed upon by the Convention first to the Congress for its approval and then to specially elected conventions in the states for final ratification. These state ratifying conventions would speak for the people as directly as was deemed feasible at that time, but for what people—the people of each state, regarded as a sovereign body politic, or collectively for the people of the whole Union? The answer to that question seems to be implied in the decision that the new Constitution should become operative when ratified by conventions in at least nine of the thirteen states. The more perfect union was apparently a national union, as the Virginians had originally planned, and not a strictly federal union.

Madison's *Debates in the Federal Convention of 1787* show that when the Virginia delegation was polled on the question, what number of states should be required to put the new Constitution into effect, General Washington favored seven, a bare majority of the total number of states. Washington's view was consistent with the nationalistic attitude shown in his "Legacy" of 1783. In fact the new Constitution was put into operation by eleven of the thirteen states, leaving two of them temporarily outside the new and hopefully more perfect Union. The exclusion of these two states, North Carolina and Rhode Island, from the new Union was technically a revolutionary act. Such an act was competent to complete the transition from the old Union to the new, but it could not dispel all traces of doubt concerning the answer to the theoretical question about the location of sovereign power.

All doubt could have been dispelled by the Convention if it had adopted a declaration of rights, as most of the original states had done when establishing new constitutions. But the Convention refused to adopt a declaration of rights, though repeatedly urged to do so by several delegates. The Virginia planners had said nothing about a declaration of rights in their original proposals, although one of their number, George Mason, author of the influential Virginia Declaration of Rights, prefixed to the first Virginia state constitution, was most urgent in calling for such action and gave the failure to do so as one of his principal reasons for refusing to sign the finished Constitution. The matter came up near the close of the Convention, when the delegates were tired and impatient to put an end to their labors. They accepted the view that a federal declaration of rights was unnecessary, since the state declarations seemed to serve adequately to remind the people and their representatives of their respective rights and duties.

This view was not acceptable to the state ratifying conventions. The Massachusetts ratifying convention consented by a narrow majority to the new Constitution, but it also adopted a strong recommendation that a federal declaration of rights be added at the first opportunity. Thereafter, most of the states which ratified the new Constitution adopted a similar recommendation. The prevailing view clearly was that a federal bill of rights was as necessary to protect the people against the abuse of power by a federal government as were state bills of rights to prevent the abuse of power by state governments. One of the early acts of the first Congress under the Constitution was to submit to the states, in lieu of a federal declaration of rights, the proposals which became in 1791 the first ten amendments to the Constitution. Those amendments, because of their importance in the new constitutional system, may be regarded as an integral part of the fundamental constitutional document.

The first ten amendments were of three kinds. Some of them were substantive limitations on the legislative powers of the Congress, others were procedural limitations on congressional powers, and still others were merely good advice to the people of the United States, including of course congressmen. The best illustration of the first two kinds of amendments is that relating to the quartering of troops upon the inhabitants, should suitable barracks not be available. The amendment provided that this should not be done under any circumstances in time of peace, and in time of war only in a manner to be prescribed by law. The former part of the amendment was a substantive limitation on federal power, the latter a procedural limitation. The most important substantive limitations were provided by the First Amendment, which forbade the Congress to make any law respecting an establishment of religion or prohibiting the free exercise of a religion, or abridging the freedom of speech or of the press, or the rights of assembly and of petition. The most important procedural limitation was the Fifth Amendment, which forbade the Congress to deprive any person of life, liberty, or property without due process of law.

The first Congress, which framed the First Amendment, did not attempt to define more precisely what it meant by religious freedom or by the freedoms of speech, press, assembly, and petition. At that time there were established state churches in most of the original states, and a strong movement was already under way to disestablish them and put all religions on an equal position before the law without special legal privileges of any kind for any of them. The Virginia Statute of Religious Freedom, the drafting of which Jefferson considered one of the three most important acts of his life, had been adopted shortly before the Philadelphia Convention, and most of the delegates doubtless expected that similar legislation would be generally adopted by all the states in due course. In fact, however, the last of the original state churches to be disestablished, that of Massachusetts, was not deprived of its special privileges until 1833. Recognizing that different religious conditions in different states made uniform national legislation on the subject undesirable, the framers of the First Amendment agreed that the choice between the policies of union and of separation of church and state should be made by the peoples of the several states, each acting for itself alone. This most important decision of a sovereign people was denied to the people of the United States and reserved to the peoples of the states.

The effect of the denial to the Congress of power to abridge the freedoms of speech, press, assembly, and petition, constituting collectively the basic freedom for the communication of ideas, is more difficult to determine. This freedom is the essential foundation of popular government. In England and colonial America the important feature of the freedom of thought and its communication had been procedural. In prosecutions for the abuse of this freedom, and generally in actions at law involving alleged slander or libel, the judge had declared the law and the jury had been restricted to the comparatively narrow function of determining the fact of utterance or publication of the language alleged to be slanderous or libelous. At about this time Fox's famous libel act, a landmark in the growing expansion of liberties under the British Constitution, broadened the power of juries and restricted that of judges in adjudicating such actions. There was doubtless also a growing interest in the United States in the improvement of judicial procedure in libel cases. But this was a procedural rather than a substantive right.

Of course no one contended that freedom of speech meant an unqualified right to say anything one might be pleased to say at any time regardless of the circumstances or presumable consequences. On the other hand, no

American Whig could have been satisfied at the time of the Revolution with a concept of free speech and a free press no more substantial than a prohibition against official censorship of speeches or newspapers prior to utterance or publication. The abolition of prior censorship was doubtless generally understood as an indispensable part of the freedom of communication of ideas, but how much more substance resided in the revolutionary concept of freedom of speech and of the press? No clear answer to this question was to be found either in the federal or in the state bills of rights. Revolutionary statesmen deliberately refrained from embodying explicit definitions in their bills of rights, lest by so doing they impede a desirable expansion of the basic concepts under the influence of the growing liberalization of the American way of life under the new free institutions. The framers of the Constitution intended to secure for the people of the Union as effective protection of these basic rights as existed in any of the states, but they did not presume to impose a uniform concept upon the peoples of the several states. They wished to leave the field clear for experimentation by the states which were most hospitable to liberal ideas.

The procedural rights, provided for by the second kind of amendments constituting the federal Bill of Rights, were generally more important than the substantive rights. Among them, the most significant for the future development of the revolutionary concept of freedom was bound in the nature of things to be the requirement that there be no deprivation of life, liberty, or property by the federal government without due process of law. Many of the elements of due process of law were explicitly enumerated in the federal Bill of Rights, and others had been specified in the main body of the Constitution. But the specification of some was not intended to exclude the existence of others. Moreover, the framers did not define precisely what they meant by liberty and property, as these words were used in the Fifth Amendment. Those framers who were familiar with Blackstone's *Commentaries on the Laws of England*, which had once been the favorite reading of American Whigs, were acquainted with his explanation of the meaning of these terms, but they naturally did not wish to restrict their countrymen forever to the interpretations of fundamental concepts favored by the English Tory jurist. They preferred to leave to future American judges and juries the task of applying the recommended principles to American problems under the fresh American conditions, and of thereby giving them fruitful significance to the American people and their posterity. The federal courts would finally ascertain what was meant by due process of law for the people of the Union, but due process of law for the peoples of the states would be determined, at least in the first instance, by state courts and juries. Which, if either, represented sovereign power?

More light on the location of sovereignty in the new and hopefully more perfect Union is to be found in the Ninth and Tenth Amendments, those containing the provisions which must be classified under the heading of good advice to the American people. The Ninth Amendment provided that the enumeration in the Constitution of certain rights should not be construed to deny or disparage others retained by the people. The Tenth provided that the powers not delegated to the United States by the Constitution, nor prohibited by it to the states, were reserved to the states respectively or to the people. But who were these mysterious people? If the Ninth Amendment had specified that these people were the people of the United States, or the people of the states respectively, the location of sovereignty would have been less controversial than it became in later years. Or if the Tenth Amendment had concluded with the additional word *thereof*, a right of secession might have been claimed with greater persuasiveness. Seventy years later, when the Constitution of the Confederate States of America was drafted, the word *thereof* was appended to the language of the Tenth Amendment, which was incorporated in that Constitution. But by then the appeal to arms had ended the dispute over the location of sovereignty under the federal Constitution. The victor in the trial by battle dictated its own interpretation of the essential character of the American constitutional system.

The second of the two basic principles of the constitutional system was that of the reign of law. Neither the Virginia Plan nor the finished Constitution added much to the popular understanding of this principle. The Virginia Plan called for due respect for established legal rights during the transition from government under the Articles of Confederation to that under the proposed Articles of Union, and the Philadelphia Convention made the necessary provision for the continued operation of the laws during the transition. The Virginia Plan also called for binding all state officers by oath to support the new constitutional system, and provision for this means of assuring the supremacy of the new system was duly made by the Convention. But neither the Virginia Plan nor the finished Constitution called for further explanation of the nature of law or of a constitutional system in which the law is supreme and the government is one of laws and not of men.

Under the Articles of Confederation there was an attempt to protect the people of a state against unfriendly treatment under the laws of other states. One of the Articles expressly provided that the citizens of each state should enjoy all the rights and privileges of citizens of the several states, and the Constitution of 1787 added the provision that each state should show proper respect for the official acts of other states. But nothing was said in the new Constitution about the privileges or immunities of citizens of the United States. Doubtless it was a reasonable inference from the nature of the new constitutional system that there were some special rights adhering to United States citizenship. Among them, for instance, there must have been a right to travel freely throughout the Union regardless of differences in local institutions and ways of life. But could the master of slaves take his slaves with him into a state in which slavery had been abolished and continue to hold them there in the bondage authorized under the laws of his own state? To this question there was no clear answer. The new Constitution did not even say who were citizens of the United States.

The proper treatment of the status of Negroes was a vexatious problem for the framers of the Constitution. It is clear that this problem troubled the consciences of most of the delegates to the Philadelphia Convention. They would not permit the word *slave* to be used in the text of the Constitution, and whenever the institution of slavery had to be referred to, some awkward circumlocution was employed. Some of the delegates were obviously embarrassed by the necessity of tolerating slavery in the states where it still existed, and others were outspoken in their condemnation of the institution. When the question was under discussion of permitting under the Constitution, for a limited time, the importation of slaves from abroad, Judge Ellsworth of Connecticut remarked that the morality of slavery was an issue for the states, and that, if it were to be considered as a national issue, it would be necessary to abolish slavery everywhere. Most of the delegates were manifestly determined that responsibility for the maintenance of the institution should remain as definitely as possible with the peoples of the particular states in which it existed.

The deliberate evasion of responsibility for the institution of slavery by the majority of the Convention raises the question, what was their understanding of the "self-evident" truth, proclaimed in the Declaration of Independence, that all men are created equal? The debates in the Convention ignored the question. The framers, regarding themselves as practical statesmen, found no time for such theoretical disquisitions. Not even when discussing such questions as the right to vote and hold public office did the delegates consider the implications of this basic political axiom. They did not confuse the electorate with the people. The electorate was merely the agent of the people, and the qualifications for voting were to be determined in the light of the duties of the agency. There was much talk about the people, but precisely who they were and in what sense of the word all of them could be regarded as actually equal nobody bothered to say.

Years later, when the question became important in American politics, politicians sought to vindicate the intelligence and character of the Founding Fathers by arguing that all that was meant by the claim that all men are created equal was that British subjects in America were entitled to equal rights with Englishmen at home. This argument, however, was unconvincing. The most acceptable answer to the question was supplied by Abraham Lincoln, speaking at Springfield, Illinois, June 27, 1857:

> I think the authors of that notable instrument [the Declaration of Independence] intended to include all men, but that they did not intend to declare all men equal in all respects. They did not mean to say that all were equal in color, size, intellect, moral development, or social capacity. They defined with tolerable distinctness in what respects they did consider all men created equal—equal in certain inalienable rights, among which are life, liberty, and the pursuit of happiness. This they said and this they meant. They did not mean

> to assert the obvious untruth, that all men were then actually enjoying that equality, nor yet that they were about to confer it upon them. In fact, they had no power to confer such a boon. They meant simply to declare the right, so that the enforcement of it might follow as fast as circumstances should permit. They meant to set up a standard maxim for free society which should be familiar to all and revered by all—constantly looked to, constantly labored for, and even, though never perfectly attained, constantly approximated; and thereby constantly spreading and deepening its influence and augmenting the happiness and value of life to all people, of all colors, everywhere.

The framers of the Constitution may not have added much to popular understanding of the basic political ideas of the American Revolution, but what they did was consistent with those ideas. There was a genuine consensus among them that the more perfect Union should be built upon the solid foundation of the sovereignty of the people and the reign of law. The establishment of the new constitutional system was not essentially an independent revolutionary proceeding but rather a continuation of the original Revolution. The framers left some important questions unanswered: the American Revolution would not be completed until years later, and not even then without a sanguinary struggle. It was unfortunate that the framers in 1787 could not answer all the unanswered questions of 1776. Nevertheless, their high place in history rests securely upon their skill and success in answering the questions they actually tried to answer, despite sharply conflicting interests and deep differences of opinion and much contention among them.

THE REVOLUTIONARY PRINCIPLES OF 1776 IN THE FEDERAL CONVENTION OF 1787

The framers of the Constitution had more to say about the purpose of government than Jefferson felt called upon to say in the Declaration of Independence. Jefferson mentioned only one purpose, to secure the inalienable rights of men, because that was the primary purpose of the Revolution. But by 1787 there were other matters to be attended to. Already the framers of the Articles of Confederation had recognized that there were other purposes which constitution-makers must keep in mind, if their work is to be justified by its fruits. The authors of the Virginia Plan were not unmindful of their predecessors' contribution to the constitutional system.

Point number one in the Virginia Plan was that the Articles of Confederation ought to be so corrected as to accomplish the objects of the Confederation—namely, the common defense, the security of liberty, and the general welfare. The framers of the Articles put the common defense first, because they relied upon the states to safeguard the security of the people's liberties. It was the security of the states themselves that would be the primary concern of the Confederation. Since the framers of the Constitution quickly turned their attention away from the correction of the Articles of

Confederation to the preparation of something better to put in their place, it is not surprising that they took little notice of the Virginia planners' first point. In fact, the Virginia planners' hope was to provide for the whole body of the American people a government capable of serving their common needs as effectively as the best of the state governments served the particular needs of the peoples of the states.

The Preamble to the Constitution in its final form supplied a statement of the purposes of government which is a matchless justification of the existence of a political community founded upon the separation of church and state. To establish justice, to insure domestic tranquillity, to provide for the common defense, to promote the general welfare, to secure the blessings of liberty for all the members of the community: this is a formulation of high purpose which cannot fail to strengthen the foundations of the more perfect Union as long as it continues to express the true intent of the American people. But this formulation was the work of the Committee of Style and Arrangement at the close of the Convention. It was not the fruit of any comprehensive and systematic discussion of the basic axioms of a free society.

Nor did the delegates to the Philadelphia Convention ever get around to defining the fundamental concepts of a serviceable science of politics. Of justice and liberty there must necessarily be much talk in a constitutional convention, but if its members do not already possess a working knowledge of the meaning of these concepts to their fellow citizens, their efforts are not likely to be enduring. The task of precise definition might be somewhat simplified by defining one concept in terms of the other. Liberty might be defined as a right to do as one pleases within the limits imposed by just laws, but the problem of defining justice would still remain. It is a mark of wisdom to leave the completion of the task to each generation that lives in the particular political community, to the end that constant striving for a more satisfying meaning may give greater vitality to the life of the community.

Discussion of the purposes of government by the delegates at Philadelphia was strictly incidental to the consideration of specific proposals for incorporation into the Constitution. The problem of the qualifications for voting and officeholding was the chief stimulant to such discussions. There were numerous delegates who thought that there should be at least a low property qualification for voters eligible to choose representatives in the more popular branch of the Congress and a high property qualification for membership in the less popular branch. Young Charles Pinckney of South Carolina, a wealthy member of an exceptionally wealthy delegation, once suggested that a President of the United States should possess an estate of at least one hundred thousand dollars' value and that senators should be proportionately endowed with worldly goods, but these figures were too high to be taken seriously by most of the delegates.[10] John Rutledge, head of the South Carolina delegation, was foremost among those who contended that the chief purpose of government was the protection of property, but he gave no support to this idea of the young Pinckney.

Other delegates were men of humble origin and, though prosperous in private life as well as successful in politics, were by no means convinced that superior wealth was acceptable evidence of superior qualification for important public offices. Rutledge's contention for a privileged position of property provoked James Wilson to an elaborate defense of the political capacity of the common man. "All men wherever placed," he declared, "have equal rights and are equally entitled to confidence." He insisted that "the majority of people wherever found ought in all questions to govern the minority." He could not agree with Rutledge that "property was the sole or the primary object of government and society." On the contrary, "the cultivation and improvement of the human mind was the most noble object." Madison's *Debates* do not record which of the two speakers was greeted with the more impressive signs of approval by the members on the floor.[11]

Outstanding among the delegates who spoke in defense of the common man, regarded as a political animal, was Benjamin Franklin.[12] Franklin was himself an aristocrat in the true sense of the word. Though of humble origin, he had been a sensationally successful printer and publisher and had acquired sufficient wealth to qualify for President by any plutocrat's test. He could also qualify for leadership in theoretical and applied science, and as a founding member of the American Philosophical Society could hold his own in the academic world. In theoretical and practical politics, however, he was as good a democrat as was to be found in the Convention. Speaking in the same debate as Rutledge and Wilson, Franklin reminded his fellow delegates that "the virtue and public spirit of our common people . . . contributed principally to the favorable issue" of the Revolutionary War. It was important, he asserted, to treat them with due respect. The Convention evaded a clear answer to the proposals to establish property qualifications for voting and officeholding by referring them to the states.

A final answer to the question, what did the framers of the Constitution add to the understanding of the purposes of government gained from the Declaration of Independence, will have to wait for a study of what the framers did in the Philadelphia Convention as well as of what they said. It is clear from the record of the debates, however, that they did not commit themselves to the proposition that the primary purpose of government is to protect property. It is clear also from the debates that there would have to be some protection of property in order to insure domestic tranquillity and promote the general welfare. Further, there would have to be some effort to secure the rights of men by promoting the development of an educated citizenry, capable of knowing their rights and maintaining them effectively by making good use of their opportunities as voters and jurors. Meanwhile, the Preamble to the Constitution would stand as the most authentic and instructive statement of what the framers believed to be the purposes of such a government as they were striving to establish.

The improvement of the governmental structure and processes, as established by the Articles of Confederation, provoked much greater conflict of opinion within the Convention than the development of the basic principles. But the details of the debates over the governmental process remained what we now call highly classified information until the self-imposed secrecy of the Convention's proceedings was removed by the death of the last of its members. Madison's *Debates* was not published until 1840, and meanwhile the public was compelled to rely on imperfect reports of debates in the state ratifying conventions and on argumentative literature produced by the struggle over ratification for its knowledge of differences of opinion within the Convention. Of the argumentative literature, far the most important was the collection of papers written by Hamilton, Madison, and Jay and published under the title, *The Federalist*. Hamilton was the principal author, but the new Constitution, as he candidly confessed at the close of the Convention, was radically different from his idea of a suitable frame of government, and his explanation and defense of the Constitution is an able lawyer's argument rather than a candid statement of a personal creed.

Madison's contributions to *The Federalist* were more philosophical in tone. He was not a lawyer but rather what we would now call a political scientist, one of the first great political scientists in American politics. His speeches in the Convention rank with his contributions to *The Federalist* as commentaries on the thinking behind the written Constitution, and his *Debates* have been since their publication our principal source of knowledge concerning the actual making of the Constitution of the United States. That Madison was the father of the Constitution is claiming too much for him, as his own record of the debates clearly shows, but he may perhaps be rightly described as the father of the Virginia Plan. It is a just tribute to a great American as well as a convenient introduction to the study of the framing of the Constitution to take Madison's exposition of the Virginia Plan in the Convention as the point of departure for the development of the structure and processes of government in the more perfect Union.

The redesign and improvement of the governmental process proved to be the principal business of the Convention. It was not accomplished without protracted argument between the advocates of different plans and much give-and-take in matters of detail on the part of the most effective leaders. The spirit of the dominant leadership is reflected in two letters written by Washington, one before the Convention was called and the other after its work had been approved by the necessary number of states. Writing to John Jay on August 1, 1786, he declared: "I do not conceive that we can exist long as a nation without having lodged somewhere a power, which will pervade the whole Union in as energetic a manner as that of the state governments extends over the several states." Writing to Thomas Jefferson on August 31, 1788, he confessed: "For myself, I was ready to have embraced any tolerable compromise that was competent to save us from impending ruin. . . ."

The principal business of the Convention was so complicated and exacting that its analysis requires a separate chapter. It must suffice here to emphasize the conditions which made eventual success possible. The superior ability and practical experience of the majority of the delegates, whom Jefferson, writing from Paris while the Convention was at work, described in a pardonable burst of enthusiasm as "demi-gods," contributed greatly to the happy result. But the temper of the Convention, under the skillful management of the leaders, contributed greatly also. It was well illustrated by Franklin's little speech on the last day, when he made his memorable plea for harmony. He did not claim that he liked every detail of the final text then before them for adoption. But, having lived long and learned by experience that he was often forced to change opinions, once formed, in the light of later and better information, he was not sure that he would not think better of it in the future. He wished that every delegate who might have objections to any part of the proposed Constitution would, like himself, "doubt a little of his own infallibility." One skeptical delegate confided to his private notebook that Franklin's little speech was well designed to protect his own reputation, whatever might be the ultimate fate of the proposed Constitution. Be that as it may, Franklin, like Washington, set an impressive example of devotion to moderate measures for terminating political controversy and in general to the middle way in practical politics.

The last of the revolutionary principles of government, that which sought to justify a right of revolution in cases of an unacceptable governmental performance, received no consideration whatever by the members of the Philadelphia Convention. The delegates were content to let their work, whether revolutionary or not, speak for itself. There is no evidence that they rejected the theory of revolution which Jefferson had presented to his fellow Americans in the Declaration of Independence. But neither did they explicitly endorse it. They intended to obtain the consent of the governed to the establishment of a more perfect Union by an appeal to reason, and to discountenance by their example, if not by their precept, any further resort to violence in the manner of the Shaysites for the redress of grievances.

Eventually the American people would learn how to use political parties as a substitute for revolutions in bringing about changes in the control of government. Under a two-party system, the party in power can be turned out of office, and the "outs" can take their turn at the helm of the ship of state whenever the "ins" lose the confidence of the voters. What is necessary to make the change without resort to violence is a reasonably fair election with an honest count of the votes and a full return of the results. There must also be acceptable assurance that general elections will be held at suitable intervals. Under the American form of the two-party system the frequency of elections is strictly controlled by the calendar; under the British form there is more room for the manipulation of election dates by the party in power. Each system possesses its particular advantages and disadvantages, and each works well enough to command the support of public opinion. Both systems of revolution by ballot should under favorable circumstances make the original right of revolution by violence as obsolete as muzzle-loading firearms, lead bullets, and black powder.

It would be necessary, however, that the conditions be favorable. First, it is desirable that the two parties divide the voters not too unequally, so that the "outs" can ordinarily hope to gain enough recruits at the next election by exploiting the mistakes or the misfortunes of the "ins" to secure a plurality at the polls. Secondly, the balance of power should lie in the hands of voters who are ready, able, and willing to shift from one side to the other, as the normal vicissitudes in the conduct of public affairs enhance or diminish the prestige of the party in power or the credit of the opposition. Thirdly, there should be general acceptance by both parties of the basic principles of the constitutional system so that the great bulk of the voters will ordinarily consent to make their choice between the candidates of the two major parties. Fourthly, the differences between the two parties respecting the controversial issues of the day should not be so great that the voters will ignore the differences between the personal qualifications of the major party candidates, or so little that the results at the polls will furnish inadequate guidance to the victors. Finally, the major parties, or at least one of them, must be capable of adopting new policies which have been brought forward by minor parties or factions and shown to possess durable capacity to attract popular support.

Whether the necessary conditions for an efficient two-party system, capable of making the right of revolution superfluous, are easy or hard to maintain depends on the nature of the parties. Ambitious and realistic politicians do not ordinarily organize political parties in order to perpetuate a constitutional system. They take the established constitutional system for granted and use their parties in order to win elections and gain the power to govern. There is doubtless a natural tendency under ordinary conditions in a free society for the system of parties to become a two-party system, since politicians with limited opportunities for rising to the leadership of a large and strongly preponderant major party may hope to better their chances of personal success by joining the principal opposition party. Nevertheless, the nature of the parties as well as the temper of the politicians is important for the development of a durable two-party system.

Major political parties exhibit both a realistic and an idealistic character. If a party exists primarily to nominate candidates and promote their success at the polls and in office, its durability will depend largely on the personalities of the leader and his most active associates. Charismatic leadership can bring and hold together a wide and diversified body of followers who value the services of vigorous and spirited leaders above the particular policies and measures which they may adopt from time to time to meet the exigencies of the moment. If, on the other hand, the bulk of the membership of a party is deeply concerned about particular measures and policies, the choice of leaders will be regarded rather as a means to an end than as an end in itself. If a major party is to possess the durability that is essential for a serviceable two-party system, neither the personality of the leader nor the importance of the paramount issue must be so great as to outweigh all other considerations in the minds of loyal partisans. Evenness of temper and moderation of purpose on the part of both leaders and other members of the major parties are indispensable concomitants of a durable two-party system. Yet either of these excellent qualities, if carried to excess, can produce a degree of indifference to the results of elections and the management of public affairs that will be ruinous to a two-party system.

The alternatives to a two-party system of representative government are one-party and multi-party systems. The one-party system is most appropriate in a time of widespread and intense devotion to a single all-important issue, as during a period of violent revolution. At such a time violent opposition will be put down by force, if possible, and peaceful opposition either does not exist or will not be tolerated. It is not surprising that in an age of universal and profound change such as our own, one-party systems of government flourish in many parts of the world. The necessary conditions for the two-party system do not exist in most newly independent countries, to say nothing of those older countries where the waves of change roll high, and cannot quickly be established.

Multi-party systems make lesser demands both upon party leaders and upon the ordinary members of the parties. Their leaders need not possess either the breadth of view in the selection of measures or the dexterity of technique in the management of elections and of governments that are indispensable for successful major-party operations under a two-party system. Under modern systems of representative government the organization of parties on a geographical basis is particularly easy where a multi-party system exists. But under such conditions almost any kind of conscious difference among the people of a state is sufficient for the organization of a party, so great is the inducement to the formation of parties in an open society, where there is free competition for public offices and for the power and perquisites that go with them. The most frequent and substantial bases for the organization of parties, however, as James Madison argued with persuasive lucidity in the celebrated tenth number of *The Federalist*, are the unequal distribution of property and the unequal effects of the possession of property of different kinds. The significance and importance of the general theory of the economic basis of politics need not distract us here. But there can be no doubt of the importance, direct or indirect, of particular economic interests in the organization of parties under a multi-party system.

In 1787 the party system in the United States was extraordinarily fluid. The Revolution had produced a sharp conflict between the American branches of the two great English parties, the Whigs and the Tories. To the everlasting credit of the revolutionary leaders, the greatest extremes in revolutionary conflict had been avoided. There were no punitive executions of antirevolutionary leaders or other sanguinary reprisals against members of the defeated party such as have marred the history of revolution in many lands. Many Tories abandoned their country, however, and there was much confiscation of Tory-owned property. The victorious Whigs remained masters of the political scene, and a one-party system of national politics was the ineluctable result. There was purposeful and systematic opposition to the men in power in many of the original states, but no organized nation-wide opposition to the leadership of the Virginians in the Philadelphia Convention.

The Virginia Plan contained no proposal concerning a system of parties. There was indeed little discussion of possible party systems in the Convention. There was a good deal of discussion of the economic basis of politics and of the undesirability of the organization of parties, or factions as the delegates generally preferred to call them, on a geographical basis. Several delegates disclosed by casual remarks in the course of the debates their expectation that under the proposed Constitution, if put into effect, the "outs" would combine their strength to oppose the "ins" and that factiousness, or partisanship, would surely come into existence. But what its role might eventually be in the operation of the planned constitutional system nobody ventured to predict.

The hope obviously was to continue, if possible to complete, the great revolution begun in 1776. Nevertheless no one suggested that the work of the Convention was a task of the Whig party. The Virginians' leadership was not directed toward the achievement of a Whig triumph over an opposition party of any kind. It is clear that the purpose of General Washington, whatever may have been in the minds of some of his colleagues, was to reach a consensus in support of a more perfect Union on the part of the delegates from as many states as possible. It was not to be a victory for any fixed combination of state factions. It was to be an act of the people of the United States. Under such leadership, animated by such a purpose, there was no point in further discussion of a natural right of revolution or of the possible role of an organized system of parties in making the exercise of a right of revolution forever unnecessary.

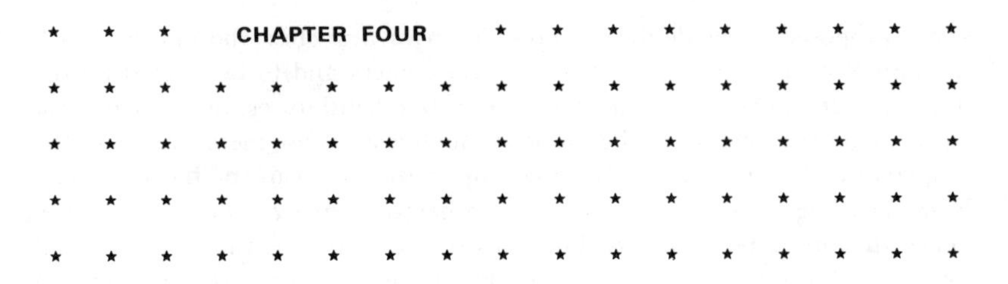

The Constitutional Principles of 1787

The Virginia Plan was designed to provide a general government for the whole body of people in the United States which would do for the more perfect Union what well-ordered state governments were expected to do for their respective states. To this end all necessary powers were to be granted to a new central government dependent for support directly on the people of the Union and not at all, or as little as possible, on the state governments. The Congress under the Articles of Confederation was to be replaced by a new national legislature, representative of the people and responsible to them, which would be supreme in its proper sphere. There was to be also a supreme executive, as independent as possible of the legislative branch of the central government, and a supreme court. This was what the Virginia leaders meant by a national government and was their justification for calling themselves Nationalists.

FEDERALISM

The details of the plan were somewhat indefinite. The members of the Virginia delegation were not agreed upon the qualifications of the voters who would elect representatives to the proposed national legislature nor upon a formula for the apportionment of representatives among the states.

They proposed to divide the Congress into two branches, the upper branch to represent the more substantial property owners and to be elected by the lower out of candidates nominated by the state legislatures, but they did not agree upon the amount of the property qualification for membership in the upper branch. They were not agreed upon the structure of the executive, some favoring a single chief executive, others preferring a plural executive. They did not agree upon the functions of the Supreme Court, though all seemed to favor giving the judges, like the executive, some part in the making as well as in the interpretation of the laws.

The debates later in the Convention disclosed that the differences of opinion within the Virginia delegation on some of these points were serious. But there seemed to be at the beginning no important differences among the Virginians concerning three basic features of their plan, to which great opposition promptly developed within the Convention. This opposition resulted in the eventual abandonment of these features by the Virginians or in their defeat by the Convention. The first of these was a proposal for the coercion of the states by military force, if necessary, to secure their compliance with the decisions of the national government. The second was a proposal to endow the supreme legislature with a general grant of lawmaking power, the extent of the national authority in particular cases to be defined by the national government. The third was a proposal for legislative guardianship of the supremacy of the national government rather than the assertion of a judicial supremacy such as might have been expected from statesmen devoted to the principle of a reign of law

These proposals, if adopted, would have established a highly centralized form of government, which in the light of later events can now be seen to have been unacceptable to the American people. It is difficult to understand the original support of these proposals by the Virginia delegation, unless the Virginians expected the government of the more perfect Union to be dominated by the representatives of a state as great and powerful as was Virginia at that time. Virginia then included the present states of West Virginia and Kentucky, comprising a share of the total population of the United States equal to that of the present states of New York and California together. It is not surprising that the great Virginia planters, producers of the country's principal money crop, should have thought of themselves as the leading interest in national politics. Naturally the Virginians were Nationalists.

The proposal for military coercion of the states was perhaps consistent with the view that under a nationalistic constitutional system the states were to be reduced to the level of mere organs of local government. But a large majority of the delegates were unwilling to accept such a view of the future status of the states and refused to sanction this proposal for their forcible coercion. There are federal systems in Latin America, based originally on the United States Constitution of 1787, in which provision is made for forcible intervention by the federal chief executive for the purpose of removing state governors in order to maintain the supremacy of a national government. But the Philadelphia Convention would not hear of such a use of force; the proposal was dropped by the Virginians without thorough discussion on the floor, and nothing was proposed by them in place of this manifestly unpopular project.

Years later, when South Carolina adopted its ordinance of secession, President Buchanan took the position that, although a state had no constitutional right to secede from the Union, the government of the United States had no right to compel a state to remain within the Union. President Lincoln, however, adopted the view that public officers, like private persons, are personally responsible for their acts, both official and unofficial, and should be dealt with accordingly when charged with unlawful resistance to the authority of the central government. He waited for officers of the Southern Confederacy to commit themselves to the forcible seizure of fortifications and other property belonging to the government of the United States and then employed all necessary force to put an end to their unlawful proceedings. According to this view of the legal nature of the Civil War, the states which presumed to join the Southern Confederacy were never out of the Union and could resume their places in it whenever peace-loving and law-abiding citizens could be found to take office under the state constitutions. The constitutionality of the reconstruction acts adopted by the Congress of the United States after the end of active military operations, however, involves other considerations, and its discussion must be deferred.

The lawmaking powers which the Virginia delegation proposed for their supreme legislature were suitable for such a national government as they had in mind. These powers were to include all the powers of the Congress under the Articles of Confederation, and in addition the power to legislate "in all cases to which the separate States are incompetent, or in which the harmony of the United States may be interrupted by the exercise of individual legislation." This comprehensive grant of vaguely defined legislative power was accepted by the Committee of the Whole and once by the Convention, despite considerable expressed misgiving. The Committee of Detail struck it out of the first draft of the Constitution and substituted an itemized list of specific powers. This important part of the committee's report was accepted by the Convention without recorded objection by the Virginia delegation. Thus ended a scheme of lawmaking power which, if adopted, would have had the effect of making the proposed national legislature the judge of its own legislative competence.

The third basic feature of the Virginia Plan, to which great opposition developed in the Convention, was a proposal that the supreme legislature have the power to disallow or veto state legislation which it should find to be in conflict with the Articles of Union under which the national government would be formed. A few of the Nationalist delegates were not satisfied with this legislative guardianship of the new constitutional system and wished to extend the power to disallow state legislation to cover legislative acts which in the opinion of the supreme legislature would conflict with national legislative policies. But this was too much centralization for serious consideration by the Convention. The more limited project for legislative guardianship of the constitutional system collided with the views of delegates who preferred to look to the judiciary for guardianship of the Constitution. The majority of the delegates clearly distrusted a political guardianship of the constitutional distribution of power between the states and the Union, such as would presumably result from giving a supreme legislature any direct control over state legislation.[1]

At least one of the Nationalist delegates would have gone even further with the consolidation of power in the proposed national government. Alexander Hamilton, in a long and brilliant address delivered when the report of the Committee of the Whole was under consideration in the Convention, proposed that the supreme executive should have power to remove state governors, when such action was deemed necessary in order to carry into effect duly authorized national policies.[2] But this proposal was not taken seriously by the Convention. If adopted, in addition to the other proposals for establishing the supremacy of the national government, it would have brought about a relationship between the states and the Union closely resembling that before the Revolution between the British colonies in North America and the imperial government in London. Hamilton and those few Nationalists who may have agreed with him might be described as Imperialists, if there were any point in dignifying with a name a faction without influence in the development of the federal system ultimately adopted by the Convention.

In the Committee of the Whole the Nationalists controlled only two delegations, those from Virginia and Pennsylvania. Four other delegations, however, that from Massachusetts and those from the three states to the south of Virginia, supported the leadership of the Nationalists without subscribing to all their political theories. They were ready to abandon the Articles of Confederation and to oppose all efforts to maintain equality of representation for all states in the Congress, or in any branch of it, if the bicameral system should be adopted. They made no attempt to draft a plan of their own and probably could not at this stage have agreed upon such a plan if they had tried. Delegates from three of these states, however, were to play important parts in the parliamentary maneuvers which later culminated in the rejection of the Virginians' plan for a nationalistic upper branch of the proposed supreme legislature.

At the opposite end of the scale for measuring the distribution of power between the states and the Union were those delegates who advocated unlimited sovereignty for the states. Among them Luther Martin of Maryland was the most vocal and the most dogmatic. This doughty foe of centralized government claimed that each of the former colonies had acquired sovereign power with its independence from Great Britain and had surrendered no part of this power under the Articles of Confederation. According to this view the Congress was a mere conference of ambassadors rather than the principal organ of a genuine government, and the Confederation was no true state but rather a voluntary association of sovereign states organized primarily to implement a military alliance. An impressive number of the delegates showed unrestrained impatience both with Luther Martin's long-winded exposition of his political theories and with his particular brand of opposition to the formation of a more perfect Union.[3]

Another faction among the opponents of the Virginia Plan consisted of those delegates who based their opposition on strictly practical considerations. They argued, first, that the Convention was not authorized under the call issued by the Congress to do more than revise and strengthen the Articles of Confederation; and secondly, that the people of the United States would not accept a form of government so highly centralized as that proposed by the Virginia Nationalists. The case against the Virginia Plan was set forth on these grounds by William Paterson of New Jersey, when he presented the New Jersey Plan to the Committee of the Whole.[4] Paterson, an able lawyer and later a justice of the Supreme Court by appointment of President Washington, did not discuss at length the details of this plan upon their merits, preferring to play the role of an opportunist in Convention politics. The members of this faction showed little interest in the doctrine of state sovereignty and in general seemed to be governed more by expediency than by principle. To distinguish them from the strict states' rights faction, these delegates might be called Confederationists. Among them Judge Sherman of Connecticut was the most active participant in the debates on the floor of the Convention and in the work of the committees.

These Confederationists were the original Federalists in national politics. At the end of the Convention, however, all the supporters of the finished Constitution were calling themselves Federalists, and the word had lost its original meaning. This change of meaning is a principal clue to what really happened in the federal Convention of 1787. The Philadelphia Convention was in fact a national convention as well as a federal convention. The acceptance of the appellation Federalist by all factions except the states' rights dogmatists marked the formation of what we would now call a national political party. This party led the fight for ratification of the Constitution. Their defeated opponents became known in history as Antifederalists.

A third faction among the supporters of the New Jersey Plan consisted of delegates from small states who objected to all Nationalist schemes that threatened to submerge their states in one centralized leviathan. They were not necessarily opposed to plans for forming a more perfect Union by substituting a new central government for the old Congress under the Articles of Confederation; but the new Union, in order to meet their criticisms of the Virginia Plan, would have to be a union of states as well as a union of the American people. Prominent among the members of this faction was John Dickinson of Delaware, formerly of Pennsylvania. As the celebrated author of the *Letters of a Pennsylvania Farmer*, an early and outstanding statement of the colonial case against King George III's government, Dickinson had been a national leader before the Revolution, and, as chairman of the Annapolis

Convention which had first issued the call for the Constitutional Convention of 1787, he had become an outstanding advocate of a more perfect Union. He was an admirer of the British Constitution and liked many features of the Virginia Plan, but he could not give it his support until it was modified so as to allay the fears of the delegates from the small states.[5]

Despite the diversity of reasons for supporting the New Jersey Plan in the Committee of the Whole, the plan contained some important features which proved of general interest in the subsequent development of the Federalist constitutional system. Instead of building the new system around a new national house of representatives, as the Nationalists proposed, the authors of the New Jersey Plan proposed to keep the Congress as it was, adding to its powers those deemed necessary to correct the weaknesses of the government under the Articles of Confederation and establishing a separate federal executive and federal judiciary. The proposed federal executive was to be a plural executive, elected for fixed terms by the Congress and restricted to the enforcement of the laws, without any participation in their making, by means of a veto power or otherwise. The federal judiciary was to consist of a single supreme court appointed by the executive to serve during good behavior and vested with final authority to interpret the laws and presumably also the new Articles of Union. This federal executive would obviously have been a comparatively weak organ of the new government, but the new supreme court would have had a stronger position than that proposed in the Virginia Plan.

By proposing no direct representation of the people in the new constitutional system, the New Jersey planners misjudged the temper of the Philadelphia Convention. The combination of state-rights dogmatists, state Confederationists, and delegates from small states could control only four state delegations—New York, New Jersey, Delaware, and Maryland. The other seven states rejected the New Jersey Plan, and the Committee of the Whole reported to the Convention that further proceedings should be based upon the proposals of the Virginians, objectionable though their plan was in several important respects. But the New Jersey planners had presented a scheme for maintaining a reign of law to which the Convention would return. When a way should be found for combining this scheme with another for establishing the sovereignty of the people in some suitable form, the first task of the Convention would be achieved.

This achievement was accomplished under the leadership of the delegation from Connecticut. Judge Ellsworth and Dr. Johnson cast the vote of Connecticut for proceeding under the Virginia Plan, because they shared the Virginians' desire for a national House of Representatives to protect the national interest as understood by a majority of the people. But they could not share the Virginians' desire for an upper branch of the supreme legislature dedicated to the protection of the special interests of property owners, especially the owners of large amounts of property. They believed that the state governments were the best servants of the people within their proper sphere of action. They were not interested in forming a highly centralized national government in order to protect the people of the states against the abuse of power of their own state governments. They were more concerned with preserving sufficient authority in the states to protect their peoples against the abuse of power by a strong national government. To effectuate this purpose it was essential to utilize the upper branch of the proposed national legislature as the special agent of the states in the government of the more perfect Union.[6]

History has no particular name for these Connecticut delegates, who were the principal contributors to the solution of the problem of distributing power between the new and stronger central government and the existing state governments. In default of a name sanctioned by ancient usage we may most conveniently call them Unionists. Their special contribution rested upon their belief that sovereign power could be divided in a properly designed constitutional system between the central government and the local governments in the states. In the nineteenth century the so-called positive school of jurists convinced themselves that sovereignty is indivisible and hence must be located either in the central government or in the state governments. But in the eighteenth century, when belief in the ultimate supremacy of a law higher than any man-made law was widespread and deeply rooted, there was no difficulty in accepting the doctrine that sovereignty in the realm of man-made law is not absolute but limited and hence divisible. The more perfect Union, therefore, should be both a union of states and a union of people. Instead of a national government or a federal government in the original sense of the term, there should be a general government of a national-federal union.

The Connecticut delegation, as experienced parliamentarians and skillful political tacticians, accepted the Virginia Plan as a point of departure in designing a stronger and more suitable central government for the more perfect Union, because they also believed that they could more easily get agreement upon the kind of union they wanted by amending the Virginia Plan than by substituting for it an alternative plan based upon a radically different principle. Their first tactical move was to substitute for the expression, *national government*, the more equivocal but also more politic expression, *government of the United States*.[7] But their main emphasis lay upon the importance of making what came to be known as the Senate of the United States a body in which the states should be represented in their corporate capacity as separate bodies politic. The Connecticut delegates, since they represented a state which at that time was not strictly speaking a small state but one of the middle rank, were not greatly concerned whether the states were represented in the Senate equally or in proportion to some rough measure of their relative importance. In either case, being an average state, Connecticut would get the same representation. But the Connecticut delegates preferred equal representation of the states in the Senate, because equality would be more consistent with their view that the states should be represented as separate bodies politic and not as divisions of the whole body of the American people. They believed in popular government for the more perfect Union, based upon the concurrence of majorities both of the whole nation and of the peoples of the several states.

The concept of the new constitutional system held by the Connecticut delegation may be further defined by comparison with the positions of the other factions which were critical of the Virginia Plan. The Unionists rejected as excessively unrealistic the dogmatic devotion to the doctrine of state sovereignty best represented by Luther Martin. They rejected as untimely opportunism the extreme caution exhibited by the Confederationists. They rejected as unseemly un-Americanism the extreme devotion of the small-state faction to the interests of the small states. They could not go along with the authors of the New Jersey Plan when the latter were supporting a plan which made no provision for a national House of Representatives.

The so-called "Connecticut Compromise" was not a true compromise. The original supporters of the Virginia Plan were unwilling to surrender their project for an aristocratic Senate. The then great states of Massachusetts, Pennsylvania, and Virginia, together with the three more southerly states of North Carolina, South Carolina, and Georgia, stood together through a protracted debate in which Connecticut was supported by the four states that had earlier supported the New Jersey Plan. When at last a vote was reached, it happened that only two of the Georgia delegates were present, one of whom, Abraham Baldwin, had been born and educated in Connecticut, having moved south after the Revolution in search of better opportunity for his talents. Baldwin voted with the Connecticut leaders, thus deadlocking the Convention.

Franklin, Sherman, and others strongly recommended search for a suitable compromise. The first of the Grand Committees was appointed, which brought in a report endorsing the Connecticut Plan with the addition of the Franklin proviso. This was a provision that money bills, including bills to establish public offices which would be a charge upon the treasury of the United States, should originate in the House of Representatives and should not be amended in the Senate, though the Senate would be able to reject them. The provision was designed to make the proposed bicameral legislative system more attractive to those who wanted a strong as well as popular House of Representatives but had the effect also of making it still more objectionable to the Virginians and their allies. When the latter objected that the proposed compromise, if adopted, would result in an excessively weak Senate, Franklin replied that he would be willing to dispense with the Senate altogether.[8]

After further debate the so-called compromise was adopted by a vote of five states against four. On the final vote a full Georgia delegation supported the Virginians, but the Massachusetts delegation was divided by the switching of two of its four delegates from the Nationalist to the Unionist side, and the North Carolina delegation went over to the opposition. The result was a stunning defeat for the Nationalists, to which they were never fully reconciled. Later in the Convention the Franklin proviso was weakened by restricting it to bills for raising revenue and by providing that these bills, like others, might be amended in the Senate. Franklin and some others felt that this retroactive alteration of the compromise was somewhat unfair, but by then the Virginians themselves had become "Federalists" and were beginning to regain their leadership of the Convention.

The triumph of what American history has called federalism was not of course a victory for federalism as the term was understood at the beginning of the Convention. But it was a victory for the spirit of moderation in politics, for even-tempered leadership, and for that opportunistic sense of what is possible that has usually characterized the most successful American politicians. So close were the votes in the Convention which led to the adoption of the Connecticut Compromise that a superficial critic might ascribe the outcome to accident or chance rather than to sound political judgment and astute tactical leadership. But it is clear that the final result was more acceptable to the American people than the alternative would have been, and that the delegates were moved by a subtle perception of popular sentiment more potent than formal arguments on the Convention floor. Washington's intervention on the last day of the Convention, for the purpose of giving a somewhat more popular cast to the arrangements for establishing the bicameral legislative system in the new Constitution, shows his awareness of the essential character of the American way in politics. But the American way put an end to the use of the word *federalist* to describe a specific category in a logical classification of forms of government. For Americans, federalism means simply that special mixture of original federalism and nationalism which is embodied in the actual constitutional system. It is not a rational but an empirical concept.

CHECKS AND BALANCES

If the first purpose of sound constitutional planning is to create a government capable of controlling the governed, the second, the authors of the Virginia Plan believed, is to oblige the government to control itself. This way of thinking inclined a large majority of the delegates toward the favorite political idea of the eighteenth century in the English-speaking world. It is the experience of the ages, the French political philosopher Montesquieu had written in his celebrated work, *L'Esprit des Lois*, that every man is capable of abusing power and, if he attains it, is likely to do so. He presses forward until he finds his limit. If power is not to be abused, Montesquieu concluded, then in the nature of things it is necessary that power be made a check to power.[9] The authors of the Virginia Plan were convinced that American experience was in harmony with that of the ages. They agreed with Montesquieu that the political maxim which he derived from universal experience was indeed consistent with the nature of things.

The Virginia planners allowed no exception to this maxim for governments based on the principle of popular sovereignty. A majority of the people in a popular government, like lesser portions of mankind, they believed, were capable of abusing their power and were likely to do so unless restrained by suitable constitutional limitations. Most of the framers, though born loyal subjects of a king, had come to believe in popular government. Few believed, however, that the representatives of a sovereign people would be wholly free from the natural faults which they associated with all possessors of governmental power. As Madison put it, "a dependence on the people is, no doubt, the primary control of the government, but experience has taught mankind the necessity of auxiliary precautions."[10]

The Virginia planners proceeded upon the assumption that the most important "auxiliary precaution" would be an efficient system of checks and balances. They proposed, therefore, that the danger of the abuse of power by a supreme house of representatives should be met by three different kinds of checks which they hoped would keep the national government in a durable state of balanced equilibrium. The first of these would be produced by a division of the supreme legislature into two branches, one of which would be designed to represent that particular minority of the nation which they deemed most likely to be the victim of the abuse of power by the representatives of a majority of the people. The second would be produced by the creation of a strong and independent executive branch of the government. The third, by the creation of a strong and independent judiciary.

The Virginia planners' belief, that the minority of the nation most in need of special protection against the abuse of power by the representatives of a majority of the people would be the larger property owners, was expressed by several of the Nationalist delegates with astonishing candor. Foremost among the advocates of special representation for property owners in the proposed bicameral Congress was Alexander Hamilton. Expounding his personal political philosophy in an elaborate speech on the floor of the Convention,[11] he declared, according to Madison's *Debates*, that "in every community where industry is encouraged there will be a division of it into the few and the many. Hence separate interests will arise. . . . Give all power to the many, they will oppress the few. Give all power to the few, they will oppress the many." According to another record of the secret proceedings and debates in the federal Convention, kept by Robert Yates of New York, Hamilton was more explicit. "All communities," Judge Yates reported Hamilton as saying, "divide themselves into the few and the many. The first are the rich and well-born, the other the mass of the people."[12] Gouverneur Morris was equally candid and explicit. In a long speech a fortnight later Morris committed himself to the same two-class system of politics. "The rich," he declared, "will strive to establish their dominion and enslave the rest. They always did. They always will."[13]

The bicameral legislative system advocated by these aristocratic Nationalists was based with consistent logic on the proposition that this social dichotomy into the upper class and the masses was the basic fact of politics. The proper security against the abuse of power by "the rich," Morris declared, would be "to form them into a separate interest. The two forces will then control each other." The representatives of "the masses" in the popular branch of the legislature would check the representatives of "the rich" in the upper house, and vice versa. Thus a balance would be established between them. "The aristocratic body," Morris asserted, "should be as independent and firm as the democratic. "To this end he urged that its membership should possess "great personal property," that it should have "the aristocratic spirit," and that "it must love to lord it through pride."

This aristocratic theory of the relations between the upper class and the masses must not be confused with the Marxist version of the doctrine of class struggle. The Marxists, like these aristocratic Nationalists in the Philadelphia Convention, believed in an economic interpretation of politics, but, unlike these aristocratic Nationalists, were convinced also that in the long run the masses were destined to defeat the upper class and gain the supreme power for themselves alone. Hamilton and Morris rejected this view of destiny. The "rich and well-born," they did not doubt, could protect themselves against political destruction, if the system of checks and balances were properly designed and maintained with proper determination by the upper-class representatives in their branch of the supreme legislature. To this end they intimated that the members of the upper-class body might well hold office for life, or at least during good behavior, whatever that might mean, and thereby be in a stronger position to defend the interests of the wealthy minority in the perennial competition with the representatives of the poor.

The Virginia Plan did not go as far in the direction of a privileged position for the "rich and well-born" as Hamilton and Morris would have liked. The proposal for the election of the members of the Senate by the national House of Representatives from candidates nominated by the state legislatures was to be coupled with further proposals for high property qualifications for senators and more modest qualifications for members of the more popular branch of the Congress. But a difficulty arose through the uneven distribution of wealth among the thirteen states and the impossibility of finding uniform tests that would not be too high in some states or too low in others. This difficulty was overcome by the Committee of Detail, when it reported that the whole problem of property qualifications for voting and officeholding should be left to the several states for action in keeping with local conditions in the different parts of the country. Thus the principle of federalism came to be recognized as a second, though lesser, "auxiliary precaution."

The representatives of the rich in the Convention of 1787 were apparently in a position to frame a government which would assure them of protection against the poor, if they had deemed it right and proper to do so. Two thirds of the delegates were wealthy planters or merchants, or professional men connected with the families of wealthy planters or merchants and largely dependent upon these groups for clients and professional success. They composed a majority of the delegations from nine of the states represented in the Convention. If these delegates had wished to act as Gouverneur Morris asserted that the rich were universally disposed to act, they could easily have dominated the proceedings in their own interest. In fact, the arguments of Hamilton and Morris seemed to fall on deaf ears, and their ideas for the structure of the Senate were rejected by the Convention. Doubtless circumstances conspired against them. Be that as it may, there is no evidence from the record of the debates that the Convention was interested in theoretical speculations concerning the nature of the class struggle.

In the state ratifying conventions there were some discussions of the class struggle among the American people. A view strongly represented in these discussions was that the essential character of the American class system was determined by the existence of three rather than merely two classes. These were the upper class, the lower class, and an intermediate or middle class. The former consisted of the relatively few who were rich; the second class, of the more numerous groups who were poor. But the bulk of the population, the independent farmers in the open country and the more or less skilled handicraftsmen and tradesmen in the towns, formed a middle class which in most parts of the country, the argument ran, was more numerous than the poor and much more influential in local politics. The then recently published book by John Adams, entitled *Defense of the Constitutions of Government of the United States*, which extolled the contemporary state governments and particularly that of Massachusetts, was cited in several of the state ratifying conventions as authority for the view that the most stable and serviceable governments recognized the existence of all three classes of people and gave a strong and preponderant position to the middle class.[14] Adams was not altogether consistent in his formulation of this three-class system of politics, it must be confessed, but his concept of a middle class capable of holding the balance between the opulent and the indigent, and thereby dominating the political scene, won some influential adherents. Nevertheless the idea of class consciousness as an important factor in the politics of a sovereign people was not widely popular in 1787. In general there was much support for the view that the proper basis of American politics was the self-respecting individual American rather than any self-conscious class of Americans.

In the federal Convention there were no small farmers or artisans, although there were more than a few delegates who had begun life in humble circumstances. Approximately one third of the delegates, mostly lawyers, were not directly connected with wealthy landowning or mercantile families and were well qualified to speak for the middle class or for the average man both in the open country and in the towns. Outstanding among them was Franklin, who had left a middle-class home in Boston to seek his fortune in what was then the frontier town of Philadelphia. Franklin's sensational success qualified him for a place in the aristocracy, if he had wished it, but he retained throughout his long life a natural sympathy with the average man which enabled him to speak for that typical American with greater authority than any other member of the Convention. In the debate on the qualifications of voters for representatives in the popular branch of the Congress, he stressed the importance of keeping the requirements low so that the United States would continue to attract the better sort of immigrants from Europe, who liked the country because of its liberal treatment of the common people and who contributed greatly to its prosperity.[15] No delegate ventured to contradict him, and his interposition in the debate brought it to an end. Unspoken awareness of the importance of the middle class in the politics of the states and of the necessity of procuring its consent to the projected new constitutional system was a silent but impelling factor in all the Convention deliberations relating to the principle of checks and balances.

The sense of frustration on the part of the Nationalists, caused by the defeat of their scheme for reciprocal checks in a bicameral legislature, which would enable an aristocratic Senate to balance a more popular House of Representatives, made them all the more eager to carry into effect the other features of their grand design for a constitutional system based on the principle of checks and balances. In order to enable the executive and judicial branches of the proposed national government to check the power of a popular House of Representatives and establish a suitable balance in the whole constitutional system, it would be necessary to make them sufficiently independent of the legislative branch. This, however, was difficult for the Virginia planners to accomplish, since they were handicapped by their habitual support of a system of legislative supremacy in their own state. They could not agree upon a method of choosing the supreme executive and judicial authorities except by legislative election, and the importance of putting fixed limits on terms of office, at least for the chief executive authorities, would compound the difficulties of the task of making them sufficiently independent and strong. The Virginians could not even agree on a single rather than plural chief executive, which tended to increase their sense of frustration.

James Madison of Virginia and James Wilson of Pennsylvania, however, the most active protagonists of the Virginia Plan on the floor of the Convention, were agreed upon the desirability of establishing a single chief executive in as independent and powerful a position as possible. Madison could think of no better way to preserve the independence of the chief executive than to make him ineligible for re-election at the end of his term, and he therefore advocated a long term for that officer. Wilson, with a longer exposure to the more democratic ways in Pennsylvania politics, would have preferred direct election of the President by the people, if practicable, and was more hospitable to novel devices such as their election by special electoral colleges in the several states for a shorter term, with eligibility for immediate re-election. The Convention at first adopted Madison's scheme but eventually came around to the Wilsonian concept of the presidency. Meanwhile, uncertainty and indecision dominated the proceedings relating to this important feature of an efficient system of checks and balances.

The problems of the Nationalists were further complicated by strong opposition to any system of checks and balances. Franklin, who had enjoyed ample opportunity to study the vaunted British parliamentary system of checks and balances at close range and had formed a low opinion of its alleged merits, was an avowed leader of this opposition. He would doubtless have preferred something like the system of ministerial leadership and cabinet government which eventually developed in Great Britain, but no one in 1787 could imagine such a system, though it was actually beginning to develop at that very time under the inspired guidance of the younger Pitt. Judge Sherman, another active leader of the opposition to the checks and balances system, would apparently have preferred something more like the present Swiss system of a plural executive. But he and other leading Confederationists contented themselves at this stage of the proceedings in the Convention with advocating an important rival principle of government, that of the separation of powers.

The principle of the separation of powers was embodied with exemplary logic in the New Jersey Plan. Each of the three kinds of power—legislative, executive, and judicial—was to be vested in a separate branch of the proposed general government. No one of these branches was expressly endowed with any portion of the power of the other branches. There was no question of a balance between them. The New Jersey Plan would have led directly to a system of legislative supremacy. The chief protection against an abuse of power by the Congress would have been a strict interpretation of the law-making authority to be expressly delegated to it by the revised Articles of Confederation. Presumably the framers of the New Jersey Plan relied on patriotic jurymen, encouraged and guided by suitable declarations of rights, to refuse to convict persons prosecuted under federal legislation which in their opinion might be unconstitutional.

There has been much controversy down through the years concerning the role of judges in the maintenance of the constitutional system. The debates in the Committee of the Whole, when the Virginia and New Jersey Plans were under consideration, indicate that the power of judges to declare questionable legislation unconstitutional was widely recognized. The Massachusetts delegates intimated that such a power definitely existed in their state under the well-balanced state constitution of 1780. David Brearley of New Jersey had been a member of a state supreme court which had actually declared a legislative enactment to be unconstitutional. The power followed logically from the first principle of constitutional government, namely, that ordinary laws must give way when they conflict with the supreme law embodied in the written constitution. The reason is clear. Ordinary laws are legislative acts, but constitutions come nearer to being acts of the sovereign people. Public officers of all kinds, legislative, executive, and judicial, would be bound by oath to support the Constitution, which implied a duty to interpret the supreme law in a manner acceptable to men of good conscience. The great advantage of judicial over legislative and executive interpretations would be that in the ordinary processes of a government of laws the judges spoke last.

The authors of the Virginia Plan lacked confidence in the practical capacity of judges to maintain the balance of the constitutional system. Judges did not seem to them to be different from other men in public life, and the influence of liberal and fixed salaries for judges and of tenure of office during good behavior in encouraging independence of thought and action in the judicial branch of government was yet to be demonstrated. Judges in Rhode Island, who ventured to set aside popular state legislation which in their opinion impaired the obligation of contracts in an unconstitutional manner, promptly failed of re-election to their offices by the legislature. If politics were to rule the action of the judiciary it would be better, the Virginian planners were convinced, to treat judges like other politicians. So they proposed to strengthen the executive and judicial branches of government, which they believed to be in greatest need of more power to protect their interests in a well-balanced constitutional system, by giving them jointly a power to veto legislative acts deemed to conflict with the fundamental law, subject to a right of the legislative branch to re-enact them by a two-thirds majority.

Some of the more extreme Nationalists would have preferred a form of joint executive-judicial veto in which state legislative acts contrary to the policies of the national government could be set aside by the Congress, subject to a veto by concurrent action of executives and judges. But this proposal would have involved the judges in politics too deeply for approval by the authors of the Virginia Plan. It ran counter to their conception of a sound system of checks and balances and also, as has been shown, to the requirements of a generally acceptable form of federalism. Eventually, though not at first, the Convention rejected the idea of a joint executive-judicial veto, insisting on a clearer and more definite separation of the executive and judicial powers. Madison and Wilson were not happy over this decision, until a consensus had been reached concerning an acceptable scheme for strengthening the independent positions of chief executives and judges and for enabling them to check and balance one another as well as the legislative branch of the projected new government.

The propriety of a separate judicial veto was discussed briefly on the floor of the Convention, when the report of the Committee of Detail was under consideration. J. F. Mercer of Maryland, a brash young man who had only recently joined the Convention and who withdrew shortly afterwards, expressed the opinion that the judges should have no authority to refuse to enforce an act of Congress on the ground of a conflict with the Constitution. He thought statutes should be carefully framed and then respected.[16] No delegate agreed with him. John Dickinson, who felt some misgiving concerning the judicial veto, confessed he could think of no better arrangement for maintaining the supremacy of the fundamental law. Neither could any other member of the Convention. No other delegate ventured an opinion concerning the danger of judges abusing this novel and imperfectly understood power of judicial veto. Recognition of such a potentially important and peculiarly American function of the judges was a leap in the dark.

The propriety of a separate judicial veto received more attention during the struggle over ratification of the Constitution than in the Convention. Jefferson, writing from Paris whither a copy was promptly forwarded to him by Madison, while deploring the absence of a bill of rights, expressed the opinion that competent judges could make good use of such a power. They could presumably make an even better use of such a power if their authority were fortified by a suitable bill of rights. Among the Antifederalists, however, there was considerable opposition to the judicial veto on the ground that judges would be likely to be governed in their use of such a power by what they might be pleased to consider the spirit of the Constitution and, being naturally more conservative than ordinary people, would tend to give the Constitution a more conservative cast than would be agreeable to the general public. Hamilton regarded this objection to the new Constitution as sufficiently serious to require a special refutation. In the eighty-fourth number of *The Federalist* he argued that, though of course the judicial veto was implied in the nature of the judicial power under the Constitution, the likelihood of its abuse was negligible. But, while professing to repudiate a power to disallow acts of Congress on the ground that they violated the spirit of the Constitution, Hamilton succeeded in leaving the impression that the constitutional system might be improved by the existence of such a power. He clearly put greater trust in judges than in popularly elected legislators for protecting the Constitution against the infusion of an improper spirit. Whether Jefferson or Hamilton was the better prophet would be an interesting question in the later evolution of the system of checks and balances.

The immediate question was, will the Convention give the judicial branch of the new central government a sufficiently independent and strong position to enable it to make effective use of its novel power? To provide an acceptable answer to this question was the task of the Committee on Postponed Matters and Unfinished Business, the last of the Grand Committees appointed to work out suitable compromises between the contending factions in the Convention. Judge Brearley was the chairman of this committee, Judge Sherman was an active member, and John Dickinson was also present. The original Nationalists, as well as the original Confederationists, were also strongly represented. The result was a compromise which was warmly supported by these two leading factions. It was equally acceptable to the leading Unionists. Its adoption cemented the union of all those delegates who now agreed to call themselves Federalists.

The independence of both the executive and the judiciary was made as secure as was possible under the conditions of the age. Instead of being named by the Congress, the President was to be elected by a novel and complicated process intended to reduce the influence of the Congress to a minimum. Since direct popular elections in a single nation-wide constituency were deemed impracticable under the then existing conditions, the committee devised a scheme for choosing state electoral colleges with a membership equal to the total number of a state's representation in the Congress in a manner to be determined by each state for itself and authorizing them in turn to vote for two candidates for President. The electors were forbidden to vote for two candidates from the same state, thus insuring a wide distribution of the electoral votes. The candidate receiving the greatest number of votes would become President, provided he received a majority of the total number of votes cast, and his nearest rival would fill the newly created office of Vice-President. If no candidate for President should receive a majority of the votes, the President and Vice-President would be chosen by the Senate from the candidates with the five highest numbers of votes. (This arrangement was subsequently changed by the Convention so that the President, if not definitely chosen by the electors, would be elected by the House of Representatives, each state delegation casting one vote, regardless of its size. This was to make the arrangement more palatable to the delegates who thought the Senate was already too greatly superior to the popular branch of the Congress, while not making it less palatable to the original small-states delegates and Confederationists. Obviously there were many different interests to conciliate.)

In the language of modern American politics this scheme was a combination of a presidential nominating system and an election system. Unless some arrangement could be devised for concentrating the votes of the state electors on one candidate for the presidency, there was likely to be no definite election at that stage of the proceedings. The election would go to the Congress, and the final choice would be made by senators (or representatives) elected at least two years earlier. This undemocratic arrangement would not have escaped serious criticism, if the delegates by then had not been beginning to show the effects of exhausting toil during a long hot summer, and if there had not been a universal expectation that Washington would be the successful candidate at the first election. No delegate ventured to look ahead to a time when the rivalry of factions (or parties) would create a demand for a more efficient nominating system (or when the need for a more responsible nominating system would create a demand for a more efficient party system).

The committee was more happily inspired in providing for the independence of the judiciary. Instead of the election of the Supreme Court by the Senate, the judges were to be appointed by the President, subject to the approval of the Senate. Thus a firmer foundation was supplied for the development of the judicial veto. On the other hand, the Supreme Court was deprived of its previous jurisdiction over impeachments. This potentially political exercise of the judicial power was transferred to the Congress, where it might serve to counterbalance the potentially political exercise of the power of judicial review of legislative and executive acts. These changes were obvious departures from the principle of the separation of powers.

They were, however, potentially important contributions to an effective system of checks and balances.

The Convention, impatient as usual with theoretical discussions, gave little attention, when the report of this last of the Grand Committees was under discussion, to the comparative merits of the two great principles, that of the separation of powers and that of checks and balances. The former was embodied most emphatically in the text of the Constitution. The executive power was vested in the President of the United States. The judicial power was vested in the Supreme Court and in such inferior courts as the Congress might establish. All legislative powers granted to the new central government were vested in the Congress. But portions of the executive and judicial powers were also in fact granted to the Congress. The Senate, for instance, was authorized to advise the President in the matter of appointments to office and to veto (by withholding its consent) those it should deem inadvisable, and both branches of the Congress were made judges of the elections and qualifications of members.

On the other hand, the exercise of legislative powers by the Congress might be checked by the separate executive and judicial vetoes. Whether an effective balance would result would depend on the way these potentially important powers should be used. Doubtless the Convention thought of them primarily as weapons for the defense of the executive and judicial branches against trespasses on their independence by aggressive Congresses. But they might be used as offensive weapons by ambitious and vigorous chief executives and judges bent on enforcing their own views of sound public policy. Washington and his leading associates in the Convention did not try to pierce the mysteries of a distant future. They seemed content that the new Constitution should have good prospects of lasting long enough to give the reconstructed constitutional system a fair trial. This, they believed, would be a reasonable expectation, if the Constitution were ratified by at least nine of the thirteen states.

There was one significant feature of the system of checks and balances that has received less attention from commentators than its manifest importance would seem to require. This was the radically different treatment of the executive power in the conduct of the country's foreign relations than in the handling of domestic affairs. The checks upon executive power in the former field of action were much less extensive than in the latter. Treaties with a foreign power would require the approval of two thirds of the Senate, and of course money could not be used in the promotion of a President's foreign policy without an appropriation by the Congress. But the President could make executive agreements with foreign governments at his own discretion, and his supreme command of the armed forces of the United States would enable him to create situations in which a patriotic Congress would find great difficulty in withholding from him all necessary support. The President of course could not bind his successors in their conduct of foreign affairs, except by procuring the enactment of laws by the Congress or by negotiating treaties, which if ratified would have the force of laws. But he could commit the country to foreign policies which reluctant successors might be constrained by circumstances to accept as their own.

The dual nature of the presidency was calculated to exert an important but unpredictable effect on the operation of the system of checks and balances. The Nationalists, who wished the President to take the lead in the normal governmental process, could foresee that at times when foreign affairs dominated the political scene the influence of the executive branch of government would be at a maximum. The Confederationists, who wished to build the government around the Congress, could foresee that the predominance of domestic affairs would be more favorable to that result. But, though these experienced politicians could be sure that the future would bring many vicissitudes in the business of government, no one could predict how the course of events would affect the relations between foreign and domestic affairs. No one could be sure either that the executive would not overbalance the legislative branch of the government or that the legislative would not overbalance the executive branch. But the complexities of the checks and balances system, it might be hoped, would enable the balance eventually to be restored, if at times tipped too far in the direction of either legislative or executive supremacy. Then, too, there was always the unpredictable influence of the judicial veto to prevent the constitutional system from getting too far off center.

In view of all these uncertainties the framers of the Constitution could not be sure how the system of checks would operate in practice or whether an effective balance between the principal constitutional officers would be established. On the whole, nevertheless, the protagonists of the principle of checks and balances seemed to have put their mark on the finished document more heavily than those of the principle of the separation of powers. The original Nationalist leaders together with their new allies, operating under the name of Federalists, succeeded in procuring support for the new Constitution by accredited spokesmen for all the states represented in the Convention at its close, and, subject to the implicit promise of an eventual bill of rights, they managed to obtain its prompt ratification by conventions in eleven of the thirteen states. They won for themselves the opportunity to make a fair trial of its merits. It was a magnificent performance in the art of practical politics which has justly earned for them a high place in the history of the science of government.

PLURALISM

The third of the "auxiliary precautions," which Madison, writing in *The Federalist* in support of the new Constitution, considered necessary for preventing the abuse of power by popular majorities in a government of a sovereign people, involved a reliance upon a principle which we would now call *pluralism*. Madison's primary "precaution" against what he considered a dangerous preponderance of power in the proposed national House of Representatives was of course the system of checks and balances. A secondary "precaution," namely federalism, had been forced on the Nationalists by the exigencies of the struggle in the Philadelphia Convention to form a more perfect Union. The final "precaution," to which Madison gave no particular name, was more agreeable to his way of thinking.[17]

Pluralism, regarded as a constitutional principle, is based on the observation that there are natural limits to the power of numerical majorities of the people in a popular government. These natural limits spring from the natural differences among the people in a population large enough to constitute a durable sovereign state. The larger the state, the greater the variety and importance of these differences will normally be, and the greater also, therefore, will be their limiting effect on the formation of popular majorities capable of exploiting their power for the advancement of their own special interests. In general their effect, Madison believed, would be to put substantial obstacles in the way of organizing popular majorities into factions or parties capable of dominating representative bodies. Thus he reached the comfortable conclusion that in a state the size of the more perfect Union this "precaution" would be more effective than in any single state or combination of states within the Union.

This argument for forming a more perfect Union may be tested by the struggles in the Convention over the granting of legislative power to the proposed bicameral Congress. When the report of the Committee of Detail was under consideration, the principal problem before the Convention was the specific definition of the lawmaking powers to be substituted for the general grant of power originally proposed in the Virginia Plan and provisionally accepted by the Convention. Different sections of the country possessed radically different interests which could be helped to prosper by favorable combinations in the legislative bodies or seriously injured by unfavorable combinations. The major sections of the country were of course the North and the South, which were divided against each other by the different distribution of slaves. Great efforts had been made in the Convention to prevent a direct conflict between these two sections under the new Constitution. The basis of representation in the national House of Representatives had been adjusted by the compromise which counted a slave as the equivalent of three fifths of a free person in apportioning representatives among the states. The compromise had been facilitated by coupling it with the proviso that direct taxes should be apportioned among the states in the same manner. This compromise disposed of the problem of representation, but it left unsolved the problems of the tax power and the power to regulate commerce between the states and with foreign countries.

These two problems lay at the heart of the struggle between the minor sections of the country over the lawmaking powers of the Congress. The Lower South wanted no power in the Congress to tax the export of its leading products, rice and indigo, and also no power to put an end to the importation of slaves from Africa. The Upper South wanted to put an end to the importation of slaves and to be protected against the taxation of its leading export, tobacco. The Maritime North wanted the Congress to have unrestricted power to regulate interstate and foreign commerce, especially to pass a navigation act, which all the states exporting raw material would find objectionable since it might increase the cost of transporting their produce to market. The Maritime North also wanted no restriction on the power to tax exports. The entire cost of the central government might be defrayed by a tax on exports, even perhaps by a tax on tobacco alone, leaving the other special interests free from federal taxation. Thus there was a powerful incentive for a combination of factions against the Virginians and their planter-allies in the Upper and Lower South. But the Maritime North could not count on the support of the Rural North and Middle States for such a program, since the small independent farmers in these sections had cause for conflict with the big merchants as well as with the big plantation owners.

The process of compromise between these various sectional and local economic interests began in the Committee of Detail. This committee's report recommended that the power to regulate commerce be limited by the provisions that the importation of slaves was never to be restricted by federal legislation and that no navigation act was to be passed except by a two-thirds vote in each branch of the Congress. These provisions reflected the influence of the Massachusetts and South Carolina members of the committee but were so distasteful to other special interests in the Convention that they were sent back to a Grand Committee for reconsideration and revision. This committee was headed by Governor William Livingston of New Jersey, a big landed proprietor and strong antislavery man, and brought in a new version of the compromise under which the importation of slaves might be prohibited by the Congress after the year 1800 and a navigation act might be adopted by an ordinary majority like other legislation. A bitter fight by the Lower South on the floor of the Convention succeeded in extending the period for the unrestricted importation of slaves to twenty-one years, but in other respects this committee's version of the compromise was approved by the Convention.

The Committee of Detail proposed that the power to tax be limited by the provision that no tax should be imposed on exports from any state except by a two-thirds vote in each branch of the Congress. This modest limitation of the tax power left the proposed compromises over the commerce power still unpalatable to the Upper South, which found the committee's recommendations concerning navigation acts and the slave trade particularly objectionable. Within the Virginia delegation there was a split over the proposed limited protection of its major export. General Washington was willing to consent to the taxation of exports by a two-thirds vote in the interest of general harmony, but a majority of the delegation disagreed and so eventually did the Convention. The whole proceedings in connection with these compromises showed how right Madison was in thinking that the variety of special and local interests in a country as large as the United States would offer formidable obstacles to the formation of durable combinations of factions capable of dominating the legislative process in the national House of Representatives.

Nevertheless the timely and impressive success of the Committee on Postponed Matters and Unfinished Business made General Washington the leader of the first national political party in the more perfect Union. The original Nationalists contributed two states to the support of his leadership. The original Confederationists and their small-state allies contributed four more. The Unionists of various kinds contributed the other five states which composed the Convention at this stage of its proceedings. It was a masterly performance in the rare art of making a revolution without resort to physical force and violence.

Washington's Farewell Address, published in 1796, showed how dubious he was at the end of his political career concerning the role of parties in the governmental process. He solemnly warned against the excessive development of party spirit and against all partisanship based on geographical distinctions. This critical attitude toward parties was doubtless influenced by his experience in the presidency, but it reflected a point of view which he had formed early in his political career. At the beginning of the Philadelphia Convention he would certainly have endorsed Madison's principle of pluralism as an important component of a set of rational constitutional principles. Yet he had welded the Lower South, the Upper South, the Maritime North, the Rural North, and the Middle States into a harmonious political coalition capable of presenting a radically new Constitution to the people of the United States with encouraging prospects of securing their approval. He had achieved this impressive result despite the powerful array of factions based on geographical distinctions which had resolutely pursued their various special interests during the months of debate on the floor of the Convention. It was an achievement which might be the harbinger of a serviceable party system in national politics.

The formation of the Federalist party put an end to organized opposition within the Philadelphia Convention. But the proceedings in the state ratifying conventions showed that it had not put an end to vigorous opposition in the country. In the small states, where satisfaction with the work of the Convention was almost universal, there was little opposition to the new Constitution. But in the larger states formidable opposition arose, which made the struggle for ratification close and the outcome for a time doubtful. It soon became clear that the Federalist chieftains had underestimated the strength of the interests which had been underrepresented in the Convention.

The distribution of the votes opposed to the new Constitution in the state ratifying conventions discloses the nature of the opposition and the location of its strength. The negative votes were cast by members who had been elected mainly from rural districts and who were in general representative of farmers and planters less favorably situated for marketing their crops and other produce than the population represented by the affirmative votes in the

Conventions. They included many settlers located away from the navigable rivers and improved roads and pioneers on the frontier. These less favorably situated settlers and pioneers were distrustful of a powerful new central government which would be far away and out of sight and might easily get out of popular control, and which was highly recommended by aristocratic politicians on the ground that the influence of majorities of the people, as reflected in the national House of Representatives, would be effectively checked and balanced by senators and Presidents and Supreme Court judges in whose selection they would have no direct part. It was not a case of the indigent against the opulent, for these underprivileged groups formed an important part of the great middle class, the average men and women who constituted the bulk of the American people at this time. The votes in the ratifying conventions in the important states of Massachusetts, New York, and Virginia were very close, and the supporters of the new Constitution prevailed in the end because they included the greater part of these same average men and women. The influence of national figures, particularly Washington and Franklin, who stood high in the esteem of middle-class Americans, may well have been decisive in bringing about ratification. The result was a triumph, not only for the moderate measures and even-tempered leadership of the Federalist chieftains, but also for the good sense and public spirit of middle-class Americans.

The successful fight for ratification of the Constitution confirmed the ascendancy of the Federalists, but it did not lead immediately to a two-party system in national politics. Many of the necessary conditions for a two-party system were present at the time, but one important condition was lacking. The opposition to Federalist leadership and policies was not a national opposition but rather an unorganized group of state oppositions. Those oppositions represented the first appearance of the great American West in national politics, but it appeared in the form of local factions which may be described as uncoordinated "state wests." Their time would come with the arrival on the national political scene of leadership capable of organizing them into a single national party.

In the Philadelphia Convention there was little consideration of national party systems. The principle of pluralism encouraged the belief that durable national parties would be exceedingly difficult to organize and the hope that the organization of more than one at a time would be impracticable. A few imaginative members of the Convention, notably Gouverneur Morris and Oliver Ellsworth, speculated on the prospects for national parties. They observed that the "outs" would strive to combine against the "ins" in order to take their places in the government, but they did not venture to predict the kind of party system that might emerge from such factious strife. No delegate, as has been noted, foresaw the effect on factiousness and partisanship of the novel scheme finally adopted for nominating and electing Presidents. No one indeed seems to have anticipated the commanding role which presidential nominations and elections would eventually play in the organization of parties. With the advantage of hindsight it is clear that the peculiar system which was provided for choosing the chief executive made a two-party system of national politics inevitable. But at the time, the Federalist chieftains were preoccupied with the task of making a success out of an improvised one-party system. An unplanned party system of this kind formed an indispensable component of the new constitutional system.

The truth is that the framers of the Constitution of 1787 did not contemplate a system of party government for the more perfect Union. They looked forward to government by superior persons, a natural aristocracy, rather than to a constitutional system which they would have called democratic. They gave little thought to the eventual development of an unwritten constitution, which would supplement and in part transform the written Constitution which they had produced with so much effort and—it must be recognized—skill. But they did produce a national political party as well as a national-federal Constitution. It was a major, though unplanned, contribution to the development of the American constitutional system.

CHAPTER FIVE

The Development of the Constitutional System

The Federalist chieftains never expected their new Constitution to last long without change. Their hope was that it would soon be improved in the light of experience. An early decision of the Supreme Court, taking jurisdiction over suits against states by citizens of other states, precipitated a general demand for an amendment which would protect the states against such suits. The Eleventh Amendment soothed the feelings of jealous states' rights men without greatly diminishing the practical capacity of the Supreme Court to maintain its authority under the established constitutional system. By holding state officials personally responsible for their actions in the name of their states, the federal courts were able to preserve a reign of law in all justiciable controversies. But the treatment of political controversies in courts of law remained a problem for the future.

THE UNPLANNED PARTY SYSTEM

The unplanned party system was the first important component of the government process to create serious difficulties in the operation of the new constitutional system. The party chieftains became aware of these difficulties as soon as they faced the problem of selecting a successor to President Washington. Under the original plan for presidential elections the members of the electoral colleges were to vote for two persons, only one of whom could be a citizen of the same state as the individual elector. This arrangement was devised primarily in order to get a wide distribution of candidates for consideration by the House of Representatives in the final election. In fact, at the first election all the electors were expected to vote for General Washington, and the immediate problem was to select a suitable Vice-President. Since Washington was a Southerner, the general opinion was that the candidate for the second place should come from the North. "Honest John" Adams was the first national statesman of New England, if not of the entire North, and was an easy winner of second place among the presidential candidates. This made him Vice-President. It was a hollow victory for Adams, who found the office excessively unimportant, but it put him in the lead for the succession to Washington.

Some of the Federalist chieftains, particularly Alexander Hamilton, did not like Adams or considered him unsuitable for the presidency. They deemed him too independent in thought and action for the leadership of the party, a position which obviously would go to the head of the administration. Nevertheless, in 1796 they felt obliged to recommend him for one of the two votes to be cast by each Federalist elector. Their problem was to procure a concentration of the Federalist electoral votes on a second presidential candidate who might perhaps run ahead of Adams in the electoral colleges and eventually gain first place in the election. They selected Thomas Pinckney of the South Carolina Pinckneys, thus reverting to the Constitutional Convention alliance between Massachusetts and South Carolina. Pinckney, however, ran poorly, and Thomas Jefferson, the prime favorite and natural leader of the opposition to another Federalist administration, was an easy winner of the second place and the vice-presidency.

The lessons of this election were not lost on the national party leaders. In 1800 the Federalist electors cast all their votes for Adams and all but one for the second party candidate, General Charles Cotesworth Pinckney of South Carolina, Washington's successor in the presidency of the veteran officers' organization, the Society of the Cincinnati. Their Republican opponents, however, cast all their votes for both their candidates, Thomas Jefferson and Aaron Burr, and, since both gained a small lead over Adams, the House of Representatives, elected two years previously and still controlled by the Federalists, had the awkward task of deciding which of the Republicans would be President and which Vice-President. At first the Federalist congressmen yielded to the temptation to put party advantage before the public interest and voted for Burr over Jefferson, but eventually better counsels prevailed and Jefferson was awarded the place to which he was entitled as leader of the Republicans. It was plainly evident that an election system in which the defeated party could determine which of the victorious party's two nominees would become President was intolerable. So the Twelfth Amendment to the Constitution was duly proposed by the necessary two-thirds majority in each of the two branches of the Congress and promptly ratified by three fourths of the state legislatures.

This constitutional amendment, by requiring presidential electors to vote separately for a candidate for the presidency and for a candidate for the vice-presidency, prevented a recurrence of the baleful Jefferson-Burr contest. But it did nothing to cure the other defects in the method of choosing a chief executive. The excessively undemocratic practice of leaving a final choice, if no candidate received a majority of the electoral votes, to a House of Representatives elected two years previously and voting by states, was partly corrected by the so-called Lame Duck Amendment a century and a quarter later. This amendment, the twentieth, moved up the dates of the inauguration of the President and the opening of Congress from March 4 to days in January so arranged that, if no President were elected by the electoral colleges, the new Congress would have time to make the final choice of the new President before inauguration day. This was a great improvement over the original practice. The Lame Duck Amendment, however, did nothing to correct the method of voting in the House, by which Delaware and Nevada possess the same weight as California and New York in a presidential election. In a democratic age the possibility that such a method of election may defeat the choice of a majority of the voters increases the need for a system which will surely keep presidential elections out of the House of Representatives.

The Twelfth Amendment created a new problem of the vice-presidency. No party leader, qualified for the presidency, wanted the vice-presidency for its own sake. The temptation was strong to select party candidates for the inferior office primarily on the basis of their potential contributions to the campaign rather than for their qualifications to preside over the Senate and, in case of a vacancy in the presidential office, to act as chief executive and party leader. The ability of a vice-presidential candidate to "balance the ticket," by holding the support of those factions within a party least satisfied with the presidential candidate, became a prime consideration in the making of nominations. This practice meant that the accidental succession of a Vice-President to the presidency would bring the threat of a radical change in the policy of the administration and thereby would introduce a deplorable element of chance into the government of the nation.

Growing popular interest in presidential elections created a strong demand for party institutions capable of nominating candidates who could be elected by the electoral colleges without appeal to the House of Representatives. In the early presidential campaigns the Federalists arranged their tickets by private correspondence among the party leaders. This aristocratic practice was consistent with the aristocratic political ideas of that party but not helpful in arousing popular support for their candidates. The Jeffersonian Republicans employed a more efficient method of nomination, the congressional caucus. This method increased the dependence of partisan Presidents upon the party leaders in the Congress but also increased their sense of responsibility to members of their party everywhere. It helped give a desirable continuity to the Republican administrations, but it put serious obstacles in the way of the emergence of new and more vigorous party leadership from outside the Congress. In an increasingly democratic age this practice also could be discredited as excessively undemocratic.

The swift development of national party nominating systems favored the establishment of the two-party system in national elections. But the party leaders were slow to recognize the necessity and propriety of such a system in American politics. Washington's antipathy to such a system is well known. In his Farewell Address he deplored the "alternate domination" of one "faction" over another. If there must be party government, he naturally preferred a one-party system under which the friends of the Constitution could keep the supreme power in their own hands. Jefferson was equally devoted to the one-party system. "We are all Federalists, we are all Republicans," he hopefully declared in his First Inaugural Address. That was actually the way the first national party struggle under the Constitution ended in the "era of good-feeling" during the administration of his long-time friend, neighbor, and fellow Republican, James Monroe. The Federalists, who ran a candidate for the presidency for the last time in 1816, either joined the Republicans or retired from the field.

The two-party system, regarded as a recognized component of the constitutional system, is a product of the age of Jackson.[1] Effective control of the nominating process by the congressional caucus broke down in 1824. Three members of Monroe's cabinet, the Secretaries of State, the Treasury, and War, together with the Speaker of the House of Representatives, aspired to succeed the President. The congressional caucus was unable to make its choice acceptable to the Republican party, and the ensuing "scrub race" for the presidency destroyed the party's unity and its effectiveness as a political organization. When everybody was a Republican, nobody could gain by appropriating to himself the party label. Moreover, there was an outsider, also a Republican, General Jackson, who aspired to the highest office in the land, and a large portion, though not at first a majority, of the voters regarded him as a natural choice, like General Washington, for the presidency. Jackson gained a plurality of the electoral votes, but John Quincy Adams, with a strong assist from Henry Clay, won the election in the House of Representatives.

The Adams administration saw the birth of two new parties. The supporters of the administration, calling themselves National Republicans, sought to keep the administration in power in the campaign of 1828 and, after Adams' defeat by Jackson, to return it to power under Clay's leadership in the campaign of 1832. The supporters of Andrew Jackson, calling themselves at first Democratic Republicans and later simply Democrats, succeeded in putting him in office in 1828 and in keeping him there four years later. But the two-party system, regarded as a permanent feature of the constitutional system, was not formally recognized until 1834. In that year Jackson's leading opponents, Clay, Webster, and Calhoun, despite their differing views on the issues of the day, organized a new party to oppose the Jacksonians. To give their party an honorable place in the political scene, they revived the good old revolutionary party name of Whig. The good old Jeffersonian party name of Republican was laid aside, to be revived and put to new uses by the Antislavery Republicans two decades later.

The reorganization of parties in the age of Jackson throws light on the nature of national parties in American politics and on the functions of the two-party system in the constitutional system. Parties are something more than mere conspiracies of politicians to win votes and gain power under the federal Constitution. They are something less than bodies of people organized for the purpose of promoting the public interest upon some principle on which all the members are agreed. They must have leadership and may, like the Jacksonian Democrats, come into existence primarily in order that voters who admire the gift of leadership beyond other qualities in candidates for the high office of President may give the most effective support to a charismatic leader like Andrew Jackson. Parties must also take a position respecting important issues, at least if they possess the governing power, and may be helped into power by a politic choice of measures, if they are in opposition, like the anti-Jackson Whigs.

At first the Jacksonian Democrats seemed to lack issues other than the one purpose to put Jackson in power, and the anti-Jackson Democrats seemed to have too many issues in addition to the common purpose to put an end to his rule. The Jacksonians, faced with the responsibilities of power, rapidly acquired a coherent set of working principles as Jackson in his vigorous way dealt with the issues of the day. The Whigs, struggling with the various more or less conflicting issues sponsored by the heads of their several factions, needed more time to agree on their most suitable leader. Of course both parties possessed some principles from the beginning, but these were the basic principles of the American constitutional system. They could not conveniently serve as paramount issues in presidential campaigns between bodies of voters, all of whom professed unquestionable loyalty to the Constitution as they understood it.

The Jacksonians were not long bothered by their heavy dependence on the power of personality in politics. After coming into power they had to stand on their record or leave the party. The Whigs, being in opposition, found their abundance of fighting issues a heavier burden in their search for winning leadership. The party seemed at first to be a revival of the early coalition between Massachusetts and South Carolina with the addition of an influential section of the American West. But cotton-growing South Carolina under John C. Calhoun was a different political phenomenon from rice-growing South Carolina under John Rutledge and the Pinckneys, and cotton-manufacturing Massachusetts under Daniel Webster was a different political phenomenon from maritime Massachusetts under the contemporaries of John Adams and John Hancock. Furthermore, Henry Clay, regarded as a Western leader, faced a radically different political problem from Thomas Jefferson, who first succeeded in blending various components of the West with his Southern, Eastern, and Northern following into a powerful national party.

Moreover, Clay had to compete for Western support with Andrew Jackson, a veritable personification of the Western spirit.

The character of a national party, however, depends on more than the personal qualities of its original leadership or the popularity of its first winning issues. Leaders come and go, if the party proves to be durable, and issues change with the changing circumstances and conditions of the times. The character of the party, in the long run, springs from the purposes of its membership, and those purposes tend to reflect the members' interests and the capacity of government to protect and promote their interests. If there were no important differences between the two major parties, a two-party system could still serve the people of a democratic republic by presenting them with a suitable choice of candidates for the presidency and helping them choose wisely. But in fact there are important differences between the major parties.

The best evidence of the most significant differences between the Whigs and the Jacksonian Democrats is that afforded by the distribution of the voters between their candidates in presidential elections. During the period of Jacksonian ascendancy in national politics, which extended from 1828 to 1860, the Democratic candidates who followed Jackson were taken from the membership of Democratic administrations or were well-known national party leaders, except in 1852. In that year the candidate was so obscure that, according to an unverified report, one Democratic voter was heard to ask plaintively, "Is there such a person as Franklin Pierce?" However, under the sobriquet of "Young Hickory" he ran very well indeed. It was an extraordinary triumph of political availability, the quality in candidates which puts first their presumed ability to hold the members of the party together through a presidential campaign and to win votes from the opposition. The Whigs, on the other hand, being generally in opposition, were more free to select presidential candidates for their presumed vote-getting capability regardless of political experience or lack thereof. Neither Webster nor Calhoun could ever get the party nomination, and Clay could get it only once. The two Whig victories were won with famous generals at the head of the ticket and little effort to exploit partisan positions on the issues of the day. Both parties, however, were able to carry states in all sections of the country for their candidates, thereby demonstrating their right to be called national parties.

There were significant differences, however, in the distribution of the popular votes between the candidates of the two major parties within the states. In the eastern part of the country, both North and South, the electoral pattern in the1830's and 1840's was strikingly like that in the same sections during the campaigns when the Federalists were contending against the Jeffersonian Republicans. There were of course departures from the pattern in some states on account of exceptional circumstances or special local conditions, but in general the voters living on the more fertile soils or in locations with cheaper and easier access to their markets tended to adhere to the Whigs, whereas the Jacksonian Democrats developed greater strength in less favored localities. The country was still predominantly rural and Jackson, like Jefferson before him, avowedly gave first place to the agricultural interests in the development of administration policies. Only in Massachusetts and Rhode Island did the urban population predominate over the rural, compelling the leaders in state politics to find some way of making a common cause with substantial portions of the agricultural population elsewhere, if they were to exert an influence in national politics.

In the new West, comprised of states which had been admitted to the Union since the adoption of the Constitution, the distribution of votes in presidential elections in the age of Jackson tended to follow a similar pattern. Although fertile soil was more abundant, the less developed state of transportation and communications facilities at first favored the Jacksonians. Trade tended to follow the rivers, which ran from North to South, and the Jacksonians generally preferred to let it run its natural course. Henry Clay's "American System" of federally financed internal improvements, coupled with protective tariffs for the development of domestic manufactures and home markets for agricultural produce, was designed to strengthen the economic basis for a political alliance between East and West that could contend with the Jacksonians in national elections on equal terms. But Clay was ahead of his time. Not till the coming of the railroads and telegraphs would the economic basis of a political alliance between East and West threaten the supremacy of a national party based on an alliance between North and South. Clay made a national reputation as "The Great Compromiser" and displayed superlative political talents which would have assured him a most successful career under something like the British parliamentary system. But under the American constitutional system he could not reach the top.

The economic basis of national politics in the age of Jackson had its ideological counterpart. The Democrats talked more about the natural equality of man and men's equal rights under the constitutional system than did the Whigs. The latter, on the other hand, were more inclined to stress the importance of utilizing the services of the superior man in public affairs. It was the Democrats who first introduced into national politics the idea of rotation in office and keeping the business of government as simple as possible so that the average man could take his turn in public office without too much damage to the public services. The spirit of the Whig party was more aristocratic. There is a passage in the personal correspondence between John Adams and Thomas Jefferson in their old age which makes both the characters of these eminent statesmen and the aristocratic spirit in American politics more intelligible. They agreed that there is an important difference between a natural and an artificial aristocracy. The latter comprises the rich and wellborn, and in their opinion always carries a threat to the peace and good order of the commonwealth because of its insatiable craving for power. The former comprises the intelligent and public-spirited (who might also, of course, be rich or wellborn in particular cases), and there cannot be too much opportunity for their services in the government of a well-ordered republic. But in the age of Jackson the average man was coming into his own in national politics and was little interested in philosophical speculations concerning the nature of natural aristocracy or its place in the government of a democratic republic.

Both major parties solved the problem of selecting their presidential candidates by the same institutional arrangements. Instead of the congressional caucus they established the delegate convention system. Primary meetings of party members in convenient local areas elected delegates to county conventions, which elected delegates to state conventions, which in turn elected delegates to national conventions. The national conventions nominated candidates for President and Vice-President and, usually but not always in the early years, adopted platforms setting forth the principles of the parties or at least the prevailing attitudes toward controversial issues. In an age when democratic ideas were prevailing over the more aristocratic ideas of the framers of the Constitution, this system was a great improvement over the nominating system written into the Constitution. It was manifestly a more popular system than the congressional caucus. But it had its limitations.

In 1844 John C. Calhoun, who had come to occupy the leading position in the Harrison-Tyler Whig administration originally held by Daniel Webster, made his last bid for the presidency. Knowing he could not be nominated by the Whigs, who were determined to make Clay their candidate, he sought the nomination of the Democratic party. He found he could not get it, despite his acknowledged talents and superior experience in national affairs. He lamented that under the delegate convention system the voice of the people became more and more faint at each stage in the nominating process, until at last in the national convention it became inaudible. There was of course some ground for this complaint. The convention system did tend to concentrate partisan power in the hands of the more active local politicians. But it also tended to put the power into the hands of politicians who understood best what the people thought they wanted and who possessed the strongest incentives to win the elections. It thus tended strongly to emphasize the availability of candidates with the best prospects of success in the electoral colleges and thereby to keep the final election out of the House of Representatives. It was a system with sufficient practical advantages to hold its place in the constitutional system until the present time as the standard arrangement for nominating presidential candidates.

The operation of the convention system is best illustrated by the character of the candidates nominated by the major parties at the thirty-two presidential elections since its original adoption. The system operates in substantially the same way for both parties, but quite differently for the party which happens to be in power and for the party in opposition at any particular election. The administration party has nominated the President in office sixteen times and a party leader closely connected with the administration on five other occasions. Five times it has nominated other national leaders, twice it has nominated military heroes instead of party leaders, three times (when it has felt the need of diverting attention from the record of an unpopular administration) state governors, and once a lesser state politician. The opposition party, on the other hand, has nominated a state governor thirteen times and other state politicians four times; it has nominated military heroes eight times, and only seven times has it nominated candidates who could be accurately described as important national party leaders.

It is clear that under the convention system the party in power tends to be committed by its record (unless the record is extraordinarily bad) to a candidate connected with the administration, whereas the opposition tends to unite behind a candidate without important experience in national politics. It is a system with excellent qualifications for facilitating the peaceful transfer of power from the "ins" to the "outs," but it possesses inferior capacity for keeping leadership in the hands of veteran national politicians. Yet, for times of crisis, it has produced Presidents of the stature of Abraham Lincoln, Woodrow Wilson, and Franklin D. Roosevelt, all of whom were nominated by opposition parties over the heads of distinguished national party leaders. It is a system of selecting presidential candidates which seems well suited to the requirements of a two-party system of government in a constitutional system based on the principles of 1776 and 1787. How well suited appears from a closer analysis of the presidential electoral process.[2]

For the purposes of this analysis the United States may be divided into three major regions (which may be contiguous or dis-contiguous). The first is the region in which one of the major parties possesses a substantial and durable superiority in membership over the other. The second is the region where the reverse is the case. In the third region the two major parties are more evenly matched. The first two regions tend to produce the most influential party leaders in the Congress. The third contains the voters who hold the balance of power in presidential elections.

This basic feature of the two-party system explains some of the peculiarities of national politics under the constitutional system. The party leaders in both branches of the Congress tend to come from the strongly partisan regions, since they are more likely to win successive re-elections and thereby to be able to gain national prominence and high seniority on the important congressional committees. Thus partisanship in the Congress tends to reflect the interests and purposes of the people in the strongly partisan regions. But Presidents are the products of successful campaigns in the closely divided region, particularly in the big doubtful states where the largest blocks of electoral votes may be captured by the smallest pluralities of popular votes. They necessarily reflect in greater measure the interests and purposes of the more independent voters in these states. Thus the presidential candidates of both major parties must make a persuasive appeal to the same groups of voters. It is this perennial necessity which under ordinary circumstances tends to keep national administrations from straying too far from the political center of the nation. More extreme attitudes may flourish in the two branches of the Congress, especially in the lower branch. But in the presidency the normal attitudes of average men and women must ever be kept in mind.

The operation of the two-party system has shaped the character of the constitutional system. By its dependence on the average man in the big close states, the system of national parties originally assured the ascendancy of the middle-class inhabitants of rural America. The ambitious and realistic politician could not ignore altogether the interests and purposes of the big planters and merchants and manufacturers, but neither could he go far in national politics without careful consideration for the needs and attitudes of the independent self-respecting farmer. Class consciousness in the Marxist sense of the term had no place in the political thought of the age of Jackson. The domination of the rural middle class was in fact as real as it was rational under the two-party system.

THE NEW NATIONALISM AND THE FREE-ENTERPRISE SYSTEM

The Civil War put the constitutional system to a cruel test. The Constitution of 1787 said nothing about a right of secession, but actions spoke louder than words. The framers of the Constitution, by undertaking to form a more perfect Union, in effect seceded from the less perfect Union under the Articles of Confederation. They agreed that the new Union would be established by the accession of any nine states. In fact the accession of eleven states left North Carolina and Rhode Island to carry on under the Articles, if they were so minded. How much more perfect would the new Union have to be than the old, in order that no right of secession would survive? This was a question which practical politicians preferred not to raise until the controversy between North and South over slavery brought it into the center of the political arena.

The major party leaders found practical answers to practical questions which for many years made an answer to a purely speculative or theoretical inquiry unnecessary. The Missouri Compromise was sustained by an implicit supplementary agreement that the number of slave states should be kept equal to the number of free states, thus enabling the two major sections of the country to protect themselves against unfriendly legislation by their equality of votes in the Senate. The Compromise of 1850 upset this balance by providing for the admission of California as a free state. During the decade of the 1850's the North grew more rapidly than the South, further disturbing the political balance between them. By 1860 the admission of Minnesota and Oregon as free states and the impending admission of Kansas portended the permanent inferiority of the South in the government of the Union. For the effective protection of their "peculiar institution" the slave states would have to rely upon themselves rather than upon special arrangements under the constitutional system. Might they secede from the Union and form a separate Confederacy?

In 1860 this was a political and not a justiciable question. After the Confederate armies had laid down their arms the Supreme Court in the leading case of *Texas v. White* recorded the judgment of history.[3] The more perfect Union was an indestructible Union composed of indestructible states. But the answer came too late to help the politicians. The Southern leaders who ordered the firing on Fort Sumter had committed two grave errors, which together proved fatal to their cause. They misjudged both the political temper and the military capacity of the North and deliberately appealed from the verdict of the national elections to the ordeal by battle. President Lincoln in his First Inaugural Address reminded them in vain that they had taken no oath to destroy the Union under the Constitution of 1787, whereas he had taken a most solemn oath to preserve, protect, and defend that Constitution. The Thirteenth Amendment confirmed what the Emancipation Proclamation ordained. The institution of slavery would never again be a bone of contention between North and South.

This was the first great triumph of the New Nationalism. In the Constitutional Convention of 1787 the Virginia planners had talked of a national government and most of them also had expressed their repugnance to slavery, but none of them had proposed that the national government which they wished to establish should have power to abolish the institution. The prevailing view in the Convention had been expressed by Judge Ellsworth of Connecticut when he remarked on August 21 that "the morality or wisdom of slavery are considerations belonging to the States themselves." The next day there was extended discussion of a proposal to give the Congress power to prohibit the importation of slaves from abroad, and Ellsworth added the thought that "if it [slavery] was to be considered in a moral light we ought to go farther and free those [slaves] already in the country." But nobody suggested that the Convention should consider the institution in a moral light at that time. Now the time had come when the conscience of the nation insisted on national action. In the New Nationalism there was a new spirit that would not stop without putting new institutions in the place of the old.

The framers of the Fourteenth Amendment faced the task of determining the conditions upon which the frustrated Confederates would resume their places among the people of the United States. After some hesitation the framers wisely decided not to leave the relationship of the Southern people to the Union merely implicit in the situation, but to make it as explicit and clear as the text of a constitutional amendment and the circumstances of the time would permit. They agreed that the states which had attempted to form a separate Confederacy should ratify an amendment, embodying the conditions upon which their peoples should again become active members of the whole body of the American people, before their senators and representatives would be received again at Washington and the votes of their electors would be counted in presidential elections. This amendment was prepared with thoughtful care, adopted by the prescribed majorities in each branch of the Congress, and duly ratified by the legislatures of three fourths of the states.

The Fourteenth Amendment completed the unfinished work of the Constitutional Convention of 1787. It contained five sections, of which the first possessed far the greatest permanent importance. This section provided that all persons born or naturalized in the United States, and subject to the jurisdiction thereof, should be citizens of the United States and of the state wherein they reside. It provided further that no state should make or enforce any law which should abridge the privileges or immunities of citizens of the United States. Finally it provided that no state should deprive any person of life, liberty, or property, without due process of law, nor deny to any person within its jurisdiction the equal protection of the laws. These provisions gave the Supreme Court a new authority in reviewing the policy of state legislation, which would have gone far toward reconciling James Madison and James Wilson, if still living in 1868, to the defeat of their original Nationalist program in the Convention of 1787. The provisions thereby inaugurated a new age, the age of the New Nationalism, in the perfecting of the more perfect Union.

The first provision of this section of the Fourteenth Amendment made forever obsolete the ruling of the Supreme Court in the ill-conceived Dred Scott decision, handed down in 1857, that American Negroes were condemned to a position of permanent inferiority under the Constitution of 1787. The spirit of the Constitution, according to the majority of that Court, denied to the Congress, in exercising its power to make all needful rules and regulations respecting the territory belonging to the United States, the power to make American Negroes, previously in a condition of servitude, as free as other Americans. American Negroes, like other Americans, were now to be citizens of the United States and equal to other citizens in respect to their constitutional rights. It was a great triumph for Abraham Lincoln's interpretation of the Jeffersonian principle that all men are created equal, that is, are equally entitled to the enjoyment of the inalienable rights of men. It insured that, if the spirit of the Constitution was to be a guide in its interpretation, the interpretation would be liberal and Jeffersonian.

The second provision of the first section of the Fourteenth Amendment gave no new power to the Congress but established the Supreme Court as the guardian of the rights of all citizens against abridgment by the states. This provision has been less effective than must have been expected by its framers. When in 1875 the Congress tried to take the protection of the rights of the freedmen wholly into its own hands by passing a general civil rights act, the Supreme Court eventually decided that the Congress lacked the power to enact such legislation.[4] That decision left to the Court the responsibility for protecting the freedmen against unfriendly legislation by the states. It proved a heavy responsibility, which was not lightened by the failure of the framers of the amendment to specify what were the privileges and immunities of citizens. It is surprising how little light has been thrown on this seemingly important question by subsequent decisions of the Supreme Court. One view is that the Fourteenth Amendment protects against state encroachment all those rights of citizens which the first ten amendments expressly protect against abridgment by the Congress, as well as certain rights secured in Section 9 of Article I and elsewhere in the Constitution. In addition, of course, there are rights implied in the nature of the constitutional system which have always been protected against abridgment by the states. For example, when the new State of Nevada tried to tax stagecoach tickets, including those for trips outside the state, the Supreme Court held that such taxation was an unconstitutional abridgment of the right of citizens of the United States to travel freely throughout the Union.[5] Many years later, when during the great depression of the 1930's California tried to prevent impoverished citizens of other states from entering California and becoming, it was feared, public charges, a majority of the Supreme Court held that such a restriction on the freedom of travel among the states was an unconstitutional regulation of interstate commerce.[6] A minority of the Court protested vigorously that a Californian's bringing his impecunious Texan brother-in-law into California in his automobile was not commerce, like the transportation of cattle, but rather an exercise of a citizen's right to move about freely within the borders of his country, and that the California statute should be invalidated on this ground. The majority of the Court, however, refused to adopt this view of the rights of citizens and the duty of the Supreme Court.

Justice Douglas spoke for the minority of the judges, who believed they had a better reason than the majority for invalidating the California statute. "I am of the opinion," he declared, "that the right of persons to move freely from State to State occupies a more protected position in our constitutional system than does the movement of cattle, fruit, steel and coal across state lines. . . . The right to move freely from State to State is an incident of *national* citizenship protected by the privileges and immunities clause of the Fourteenth Amendment against state interference." Justice Jackson, in a separate concurring opinion, brought eloquent support to this view of the rights of citizens of the United States. "I think California had no right to make the condition of Duncan's purse . . . the basis of excluding him or punishing one who extended him aid. . . . Rich or penniless, Duncan's citizenship under the Constitution pledges his strength to the defense of California as a part of the United States, and his right to migrate to any part of the land he must defend is something she must respect under the same instrument. Unless this Court is willing to say that citizenship of the United States means at least this much to the citizen, then our heritage of constitutional privileges and immunities is only a promise to the ear to be broken to the hope, a teasing illusion like a munificent bequest in a pauper's will."

The reasons assigned by the minority judges for invalidating the California "Anti-Okie" act seem far more persuasive than those advanced in the opinion for the majority of the Court. If the privileges and immunities of national citizenship are to include anything more than what is expressly stipulated in the Constitution, they should include at least a right to move about freely throughout the country. But the majority judges seemed afraid to open the door for the admission of a more liberal spirit in the interpretation of this neglected clause of the Constitution, lest improvidently they should admit too much. So instead of a salutary expansion of the scope of the privileges and immunities of citizenship clause, there was a greater reliance on the more manageable power of the federal government to regulate commerce. Nevertheless, Americans were looking more and more to their government to improve their way of life, and questions concerning the scope of their privileges and immunities under the Constitution would come up again.

The third provision of the first section of the Fourteenth Amendment has proved in practice to be the most important in the great development of the judicial power which has occurred since the adoption of that amendment. Its two parts, one asserting the right of every person not to be deprived of life, liberty, or property without due process of law, and the other guaranteeing to all persons the equal protection of the laws, have achieved their importance at different times and in different ways. At first it was the due process clause that seemed the more important in the constitutional system. Respecting the equal protection clause, the Supreme Court until recently accepted the view that this did not require identical treatment of Negroes and other persons under state legislation affecting their civil rights. It would be enough, the Court thought, if the treatment of Negroes, though different, were equivalent to that of others.

For example, in public transportation facilities separate accommodations might be provided for the exclusive use of Negroes and whites, respectively, provided that the facilities were substantially equivalent for both races.[8] Racial distinctions under state laws were held to be constitutional, provided the laws did not call for discrimination against either race. What might happen in practice seemed irrelevant to the judges, if the law were above reproach on its face. In fact the facilities were often unequal, but the equal protection clause seemed incapable of reaching the seat of the trouble. It was not a dead letter but an empty promise of meaningless relief.

The due process clause gained its first importance, not from what it did for the Negro, but from its services to other persons, particularly business corporations. The Supreme Court, to be sure, was able to do much for the improvement and standardization of legal processes, particularly in connection with criminal trials. But the actual enjoyment of the benefits of these strictly procedural rights seemed to be slower for Negroes than for others. For instance, this was conspicuously apparent in the case of access by the accused to legal advice before and during trial. Nevertheless the right to due process of law, as understood by the Supreme Court, became a principal foundation of the administration of justice not only in the federal courts but also in those of the states.[9]

The unexpected importance of the due process clause sprang from the gradual introduction of the "rule of reason" into its interpretation. Strictly speaking, the due process clause dealt only with procedural rights, both in civil and in criminal cases. In the latter it meant the right of the accused to his day in court, his right to a trial by a jury of his peers, and the other basic features of the Anglo-American system of criminal justice. But gradually its meaning expanded until it came to comprise elements that were more substantive than procedural. This was accomplished most strikingly by an increasingly broad interpretation of the principal terms of the clause, particularly the concept of liberty.

The Founding Fathers, as has been shown, were familiar with Blackstone's definitions of these terms. Blackstone was writing for a time when the mercantile system was the foundation of British commercial policy and when the public was accustomed to extensive interference by the government with the private management of business affairs in the supposed interest of the sovereign or his kingdom. Adam Smith did not publish his epoch-making treatise on *The Wealth of Nations* until 1776. The new freedoms—freedom of trade, freedom of contract, freedom of enterprise, and the rest—were ideas that were slow to take root on either side of the Atlantic. They were not included among the particular liberties mentioned in the Constitution. They were not even included in the more general concept of liberty mentioned in the Preamble to the Constitution. But they could be read into the Constitution by a Supreme Court bent on putting a new spirit into the fundamental law.

The new spirit was best expressed for thoughtful Americans in such writings as John Stuart Mill's *Essay on Liberty*, first published in 1859, and in Herbert Spencer's *Man Versus the State*, published in the United States in 1884. Freedom of trade actually became a practical policy in the United States as early as 1846, but freedom of contract and freedom of enterprise were ideas of slower germination. In the 1880's in some of the states, notably New York and Illinois, the state courts began setting aside factory laws and labor legislation on the ground that they abridged a constitutional liberty to manage one's own business without state intervention. But the Supreme Court as late as 1898 sustained a state law fixing the maximum hours of labor in coal mines,[10] and it was not until 1905 that it set aside a New York statute limiting the hours of labor in bakeries as unconstitutional interference with the freedom of contract.[11] The New York Bakeries Case definitely committed the Court to the proposition that the due process clause imposes substantive limits on the discretionary authority of state legislatures to regulate the conditions of labor and industry in the public interest.

This decision read the spirit of the free-enterprise system into the Constitution and gave the New Nationalism an unexpected impact on post-Civil War federalism. It evoked an eloquent dissent by Justice Holmes, who declared that the Fourteenth Amendment did not incorporate the social and economic theories of Herbert Spencer into the Constitution, and another by Justice Harlan, who insisted that the state legislature possessed respectable reasons for believing that the limitation of working hours in bakeries would not only protect the health of the workers but also promote that of the general public, and consequently was entitled to protect the public interest in good health by an appropriate police regulation. Nevertheless, a bare majority of the Court held that this regulation unreasonably deprived bakery owners of their constitutional liberty to engage employees for longer hours, and bakery workers of their liberty to work such hours as were agreeable to their employers.

This was the beginning of a practice of judicial review of state legislation, invoking the police power of the states to regulate in the public interest business activities of various kinds, which eventually involved the Supreme Court deeply in politics. This political involvement resulted from the controversial character of decisions concerning the reasonableness and therefore the constitutionality of measures designed to protect the public interest in better working conditions and other improvements in the American way of life. These decisions doubtless saved the public from the enforcement of some ill-conceived and crude legislative experiments in the regulation of labor and industry. However, they also exposed the judges to some well-deserved criticism for substituting their own opinions concerning the expediency of the legislation for the policies adopted by the political branches of the government. One example of the plight in which the Supreme Court might find itself in consequence of its effort to put a new spirit into the Constitution will illustrate the hazards of judicial introduction of the rule of reason into decisions under the due process clauses of the Fifth and Fourteenth Amendments.

The Oregon minimum wage law, enacted in 1913, was one of several similar measures adopted at that time in response to a new popular interest in the legal regulation of the conditions of employment which had been aroused by Theodore Roosevelt's "Bull Moose" campaign for the presidency. This progressive measure applied to women only and raised the question, recently recognized as justiciable, whether fixing a minimum wage for women workers in industry was a reasonable restriction of the freedom of contract of working women and their employers. The Oregon State Supreme Court had no doubt concerning the constitutionality of the measure, but, when in 1917 the case came before the Supreme Court of the United States on appeal, one of the judges, Justice Brandeis, disqualified himself on the ground that he had been counsel in the case before his appointment to the Court, and the other eight judges were equally divided in opinion concerning the reasonableness of such a restriction of freedom of contract. Because of this evenly divided vote, the decision of the state court was allowed to stand as the law of the land.[12] Six years later another case came before the Supreme Court, involving the constitutionality of a similar minimum wage law, which had been enacted by the Congress for the protection of women workers in the District of Columbia. Changes in the membership of the Court since the decision in the Oregon case resulted in a majority of five against the constitutionality of this federal act.[13] Thirteen years later another women's minimum wage law reached the Supreme Court from the State of New York, where a special effort had been made to draft a law which might seem a reasonable limitation upon the freedom of contract. It was declared unconstitutional by a bare majority of five judges, despite a carefully reasoned and persuasive opinion written for the four dissenting judges by Chief Justice Hughes.[14] The next year, however, one of the majority judges in the New York case changed his mind about the reasonableness of minimum wage laws for women in industry; a case under an old law, never repealed, was revived and brought to the Supreme Court from the State of Washington. At last, by a new majority of five to four, such legislation was declared constitutional.[15]

Altogether this kind of legislation had appeared to be reasonable and therefore constitutional for ten years, then unreasonable and therefore unconstitutional for fourteen years, and then, because one judge changed his mind, it became reasonable and therefore constitutional again. During this period of twenty-four years, seventeen different Supreme Court judges passed judgment upon such measures. Eight of them believed the laws to be reasonable and therefore constitutional restrictions upon freedom of contract, five of them found the laws unreasonable, one judge had been on both sides of the question, and three judges had managed to keep their opinions to themselves. Such a record of judicial disagreement, vacillation, and uncertainty cast doubt both upon the usefulness of the rule of reason in the determination of such cases and upon the usefulness of judges in dealing with cases involving highly controversial questions of public policy. It tended to vindicate the sound judgment of the original framers of the Constitution in refusing to give Supreme Court judges any part in reviewing state legislation on grounds of conflict with the policies of the national government.

Decisions of the Supreme Court under the due process clause of the Fourteenth Amendment helped bring about the great collision between the judicial and political branches of the government during the "New Deal" administration of President Franklin D. Roosevelt. Narrow interpretations of the tax power and the power to regulate commerce, resulting in the judicial veto of leading measures of the administration, brought this crisis to a head, but the insistence of the majority faction within the Court in exploiting the "rule of reason" doctrine played an important part in making the alleged abuse of judicial power a political issue. Timely shifts of opinion by members of the majority did not prevent the political branches of the government from resorting to their customary remedy, the appointment of new judges to reverse the discredited judgments of the old, and previous cogent dissenting opinions by Justices Holmes, Brandeis, Stone, and Cardozo pointed out the way in which the rejuvenated Court would go. The due process clause did not lose its importance in the development of the supreme law of the land, but the effort to read into the Constitution the spirit of the laissez-faire school of political philosophy was abandoned. It marked the end of a period in the evolution of the American constitutional system.[16]

The other provisions of the Fourteenth Amendment were of less permanent importance. The second section provided for the apportionment of representatives in Congress among the states and was intended to penalize states which discriminated against Negroes under their election laws by reducing their congressional representation. But the Fourteenth Amendment had hardly been ratified before the Congress in effect superseded this provision by submitting the Fifteenth Amendment, which prohibited the denial of the right to vote to any American citizen on account of race, color, or previous condition of servitude. This amendment possessed the virtue of establishing the principle once for all time that black Americans should have the same rights under the election laws as other Americans. But it tended to create a popular feeling in the North that the problem of Negro suffrage was settled, whereas in fact it had only begun to be a problem. Since the right to vote theoretically gave Negroes the power to protect themselves against adverse discrimination by a state, public opinion in the North tended to oppose action by the federal government for the protection of Negro voters until experience should have demonstrated the need for further federal intervention in elections in the Southern states.

The immediate effect of the Fifteenth Amendment was not to insure the casting and counting of Negro votes but to increase the representation of the Southern states in the national House of Representatives and in presidential elections. These states were able to elect roughly one fifth more congressmen than would have been allotted to them under the rule of apportionment incorporated in the Fourteenth Amendment, if strictly enforced by the Congress. This part of the Fourteenth Amendment would have been easier to enforce than the Fifteenth Amendment, but such a solution would have given the appearance of putting expediency before principle in congressional elections. The apportionment rule of the Fourteenth Amendment would also have put the North in a relatively stronger position in presidential elections. The adoption of the Fifteenth Amendment thus served to complicate the effect of the Civil War upon the structure and composition of the major political parties and upon the operation of the two-party system in national politics. That effect had been immediate and substantial. The Union might be restored, but neither the majority party nor the party of the opposition would ever be the same as in the best years of the Jacksonian Democrats and anti-Jackson Whigs.

What the Civil War did to the two-party system was to put the stamp of sectionalism more heavily than ever before on both the major parties. The Jacksonian Democrats and the anti-Jackson Whigs were both genuine national parties. The Democrats ran somewhat more strongly on the Western frontier than the Whigs, but in the other sections of the country the two parties were evenly matched. The Whig leaders, to be sure, were a coalition of sectional chieftains, but Clay, Webster, and Calhoun were strongly interested throughout the greater part of their careers in national issues and made their party in its prime an effective opposition party in the North, the South, and the West. But the Antislavery Republicans were a sectional party from the beginning and never succeeded in developing formidable strength in all sections of the country. Even when they advanced from their original opposition to the dominant Democrats to the position of dominant major party, they continued to derive their strength from the North and West.

The original impetus to the formation of a new party came from radical antislavery men in the North. The bitter contest over Stephen A. Douglas' Kansas-Nebraska Bill drove into an alliance with them the bulk of the Northern Whigs, who brought to the new party a firm predilection for the economic policies underlying Clay's celebrated "American System," and a substantial portion of the Northern Democrats, bringing with them their traditional democratic attitudes. This sectional party was strong enough to put its candidates in the White House, but its mastery of the Congress depended at first upon the withdrawal of the Southern members. The adoption of the Homestead Act—a measure which the Jacksonian Democrats had rejected on account of its alleged "socialistic" or "communistic" character—as soon as the new party came into power assured to the Republicans the dominant position in the Northwest, where after the Civil War Unionist veterans and great numbers of European immigrants founded new homes on the free lands which the Republican party was credited with giving them. The Antislavery Republicans also made substantial land grants from the public domain to encourage the development of free public education and the construction of transcontinental railroads. These measures, as well as the successful conduct of the war, ensured the durability of Republican power in the North, and particularly in the Northwest and Far West. But in the border states Antislavery Republicanism was originally weak, and in the South nonexistent.

With the return of the Southern members to the Congress, Republican supremacy at Washington seemed to depend on developing some support in the South. Andrew Johnson, on succeeding to the presidency, may have supposed that a suitably moderate policy of reconstruction would win over many of the old Jacksonian Democrats, but, if so, events destroyed this prospect. The Radical Republicans, who eventually controlled the course of reconstruction, convinced themselves that Negro suffrage would provide a durable base for Republican power in the South, but events destroyed this prospect also. Later the Republicans turned toward the Western frontier for the additional support which they needed in order to dominate the political scene at the national capital. They used their temporary control of the central government in the first part of the Harrison administration to admit a half dozen frontier states to the Union in the obvious hope of gaining compensation in the West for their losses in the South. But the rise of Populism and its seizure of control of the Democratic party in 1896 put an end to these hopes. Unexpectedly the "sound money" campaign of 1896, in which the Republican leaders made a virtue of the necessity of combating the "free silver" forces under William Jennings Bryan, brought them fresh accessions of support in the East, inaugurating a new period of supremacy at Washington which lasted, with only one interruption, for more than a third of a century.

The supremacy of the Radical Antislavery Republicans ended with the Panic of 1873 and the ensuing business depression. From the congressional elections of 1874 to the presidential election of 1896 there was only one short period, the first half of the Harrison administration, when the Republicans actually controlled the presidency and both branches of the Congress at the same time. From 1896 to 1930 there was only one period, brought about by the split in the party in 1912 between the Progressive and Conservative Republicans, when the "Grand Old Party," as it now called itself, did not control all branches of the central government. Altogether from 1860 to 1930 Republican administrations ruled with the support of both branches of the Congress during forty years, while the Democrats possessed the power to govern for only eight of these years, two under Grover Cleveland and six under Woodrow Wilson. The Supreme Court contained at least a majority of judges appointed by Republican Presidents from 1865 to 1940. Again Republican supremacy in national politics was ended by a financial panic and business depression. Fortunately for the Republicans the Panic of 1893 came at one of the rare periods when the Democrats were in power, but the Panics of 1873 and 1929 respectively were fatal to the pretensions to power, first of the Radical Republicans and finally of the Conservative Republicans.

The Democratic party after the Civil War was likewise plagued by problems of sectionalism. When the Republicans withdrew all federal troops from the reconstructed states after the disputed election of 1876 and abandoned the effort to enforce Negro suffrage, the South became solidly Democratic and, except for a brief and limited flirtation with Populism in the 1890's, remained the Solid South until the Alfred E. Smith campaign of 1928. The Solid South was not in fact solidly opposed to all the Republican measures at Washington, but it was solidly in favor of federal nonintervention with the Southern way of life. In the growing cities, particularly the large metropolitan areas of the North, there was a parallel situation. The local Democratic bosses were not necessarily opposed to all the national policies of the Republicans, but they were unanimously in favor of federal nonintervention in municipal affairs. In the West, particularly after the Bryan campaign of 1896, the local Democrats were more "progressive" than the national leaders of the Republican party, but they were not able to secure for themselves a monopoly of "progressivism" in their section of the country, particularly not after the rise of the Progressive movement within the Republican party under such leaders as Robert M. LaFollette, George W. Norris, and Theodore Roosevelt. An alliance of the local oppositions in South, North, and West, when added to the heirs of the Jacksonian Democratic tradition, constituted a second major party, which was strong enough to take advantage of Republican mistakes of economic policy or political strategy but not strong enough to seize and hold power for more than a few years at a time.

Nevertheless the two-party system continued to operate in national politics as in the time of the Jacksonian Democrats and anti-Jackson Whigs. The Congress was controlled by the representatives of the sections in which the two major parties, respectively, found their greatest strength. The presidency, however, fell to the party whose candidate could muster a majority of the votes in the closely divided sections, particularly the biggest doubtful states. These states during the whole period of Republican ascendancy were New York in the Northeast and Ohio, Indiana, and Illinois in the Middle West. The Republicans generally took their presidential candidate from Ohio, Indiana, or Illinois, and their vice-presidential candidate from New York. The Democrats tended to favor New Yorkers for their candidate for the presidency and Middle Westerners for the minor place on their ticket. Such political practices tended to encourage moderate middle-of-the-road measures in both parties and to make the way hard for extremists of all kinds.

The tone of the campaigns tended to depend on the section of the country from which the opposition party took its candidate for the presidency. If the Democratic candidate prior to 1928 came from relatively conservative New York, the Republicans were forced to repel an assault from the right. If he came from the more progressive West, the assault was likely to be launched from the left. Of course he never came from the South, since the states of the Solid South were bound to support the Democratic candidate, whoever he might be, or abstain from the election. The South would make its influence felt in the Congress, where the seniority system of filling committee chairmanships would favor its representatives and senators, rather than in the presidency.

The average man in the Middle West was still a farmer or someone more or less dependent on agriculture for his personal success, but in New York the influence of a city-dwellers' world became more important by the end of the century. The urban population of the United States did not exceed the rural population in numbers until after World War I, and the ascendancy of the people in the big metropolitan areas did not arrive until after World War II. The average man in these big doubtful states continued to be the most influential factor in the calculations of national party leaders throughout this period of Republican ascendancy in national politics. Down to World War I, this meant the predominance of agricultural interests in such calculations. Because of the nature of farming in the Middle West and in New York this meant also the predominance of corn belt and dairy belt interests in the Republican party, or at least in the political strategy of Presidents and other national party leaders.

It was such facts and considerations as these that gave character to a party system dominated by the influence of the rural middle class. A novel question, however, began to rise in the minds of the more reflective party leaders after World War I, when the Republicans were once more in power in Washington. The two-party system seemed to have made for both order and progress in national politics, while the balance of power was held by the rural middle class. What would happen when the preponderance of power should fall into the hands of the urban population? Would there be an urban middle class which might perform a function similar to that of the rural middle class? And if the balance of power should not be held by an urban middle class, capable of imparting to national politics a bent toward even-tempered stability and order combined with a moderate degree of progressivism, what would happen to the party system, regarded as an essential component of the constitutional system? On the Continent, communism and fascism contended for mastery in the more advanced industrial states. Was it the destiny of the New World also to be the scene of bitter struggles for power by extreme parties hitherto unknown or negligible in American politics?

And what about the free-enterprise system in the new national politics? This system, though most suitable to the urban businessman unless he was specially interested in a protective tariff, was congenial also to the independent middle-class farmer. In general, both farmer and businessman were pragmatists in national politics and more concerned with specific measures than with general principles and theoretical speculations. But as industrial labor, particularly organized industrial labor, gained influence in partisan political councils, the free-enterprise system began to come under more searching scrutiny and, with the advent of business depression and hard times, under destructive criticism. In the great depression of the early 1930's its credit, like that of some other capitalistic institutions, was virtually destroyed.[17]

THE WELFARE STATE

The third of the constitutional amendments which have played an outstanding role in the development of the constitutional system is the Sixteenth Amendment. This amendment authorizes the Congress to tax incomes from all sources without apportionment among the states according to their respective populations. The theory of this amendment does not suggest its great political importance. There is no mention in the Constitution of an income tax, but there was never any doubt that the tax power originally granted to the Congress included a power to tax incomes. The question was whether an income tax was a direct or an indirect tax. If it was a direct tax, its yield would have to be apportioned among the states according to their respective populations. If it was an indirect tax, it could be levied at uniform rates regardless of the distribution of large income tax payers among the states.

In fact, when the question became politically important in the 1890's, it was expected that income tax payers would not be distributed uniformly throughout the Union. On the contrary, it was clear that the kind of income tax which the Democratic party planned to introduce, to compensate for an expected loss of revenue from its proposed tariff reform law, would fall largely on the heavily industrialized states where the prospective income tax payers were concentrated. The plan called for a tax computed at what would now seem extraordinarily low rates, modeled more or less closely on the contemporary British income tax and providing a comparatively high minimum income exemption, which would leave most farmers and wage earners free of tax. Opponents of an income tax, or of tariff reform, which threatened the established system of protective duties and was alleged to make the income tax necessary, denounced income taxation as socialistic or communistic or otherwise un-American, although a moderate income tax had been imposed during the Civil War without serious criticism as one of the emergency measures for financing that costly calamity. Its supporters cited in furtherance of their program the current arguments for a tax on incomes developed in Great Britain by the leaders of the Liberal party.

The Supreme Court had a hard time determining whether an income tax was a direct or indirect tax. At the first hearing of a test case the Court was divided four against four with one judge unable to make up his mind. After reargument the doubtful judge joined his four colleagues who believed the tax to be indirect, and the tax law therefore to be constitutional, but meanwhile one of these four judges changed his mind and joined the other four judges who believed the tax to be direct. Thus the law became unconstitutional.[18] Like the Dred Scott decision, the income tax decision was a heavy blow to one of the major political parties, and it formed one of the principal grievances of the Bryan Democrats in the superheated presidential campaign of 1896.

Changing circumstances provided both the opportunity to make an income tax law constitutional again and the incentive to exploit its latent possibilities in a developing constitutional system. In 1909 the Republican party found that it could not get its tariff reform measure through the Congress without submitting a proposed constitutional amendment which would do for the income tax decision what the Fourteenth Amendment had done for the Dred Scott decision. The Sixteenth Amendment became part of the Constitution in 1913, just in time for use by the Democratic party after its return to power at the election of 1912. The American people were rapidly changing from a predominantly rural to a predominantly urban people. With the change in the nature of their habitat came a corresponding change in their attitude toward the functions of government. The people of a city-dwellers' world need and expect much greater services from government, not only at the municipal level but also at the higher levels. They likewise need and demand better financed governments, which can afford to offer and maintain the new and improved public services which, despite the theories of the age that has gone before, do come into existence as time marches on.

The transition from the characteristic ideology of an agrarian economy to that of an urban industrialized world was accelerated by the two world wars. The enormous growth of governmental expenditures for military purposes accustomed the people to a burden of taxation which would have been unthinkable under normal conditions of peaceful progress. But the critical event in the transition from the free-enterprise system of the Conservative Republicans to the "New Deal" welfare state of Franklin D. Roosevelt was the stock market crash of 1929 and the ensuing "Great Depression" of the 1930's. Business crises and economic depressions have always caused trouble for the political party in power at Washington; there is nothing under the American two-party system which so surely brings the "outs" into the place of the "ins."

The great crisis of 1929 did more than bring the New Deal Democrats into the place of the Hoover Republicans; it brought about a durable change in the relations between the two major parties. The Republicans had never looked so strong as in the 1920's. Under their extraordinarily successful vote-getting slogans of Americanism (1920), Constitutionalism (1924), and Individualism (1928), they had won unprecedented victories at the polls and seemed destined for an indefinite tenure of office and of power. Yet they won only two of the next eight presidential elections and only two of the next seventeen congressional elections. Only once in this entire period have the Republicans gained control of all branches of the national government simultaneously, and then they held it for only the first half of the first Eisenhower administration. The period since 1930 has been as definitely a period of Democratic ascendancy in national politics as the preceding period was of Republican ascendancy.

The spirit of the new political order was a product of the conditions under which the order came into existence. Under the fresh slogans of Relief, Recovery, and Reform, the New Deal administration improvised an array of novel measures with which to combat the depression. An exhilarating show of self-confident leadership, combined with an unprecedented use of national credit, quickly relieved the most acute suffering from the massive unemployment. Private industry recovered less quickly under the impact of radical remedies of uncertain efficacy. The reform of discredited business practices, particularly in the field of private finance, produced good results more slowly. The outstanding characteristic of the new economic order was the lavish use of government money. The resolute will and practical ability to bring public credit to the aid of private capital and to the advantage of the people of the country gave the new welfare state its enduring character.

The Sixteenth Amendment was the indispensable accomplice of the welfare state. By means of unprecedented rates of levy on the incomes of individuals and corporations the New Deal administration "smote the rock of the national resources and out gushed torrents of public revenue." The actual result seemed easy; the theoretical justification was more difficult. It fell at last to the Supreme Court to justify the legislative foundation of the new economic and political order. This the Court was proceeding to do, once it had been duly reconstructed by the Roosevelt administration, in a series of bold and solid decisions, when World War II brought fresh complications into the effort to express the new spirit of the Constitution. The field of action shifted again from the judicial to the political branches of the national government. Again the question was, what is the role of the party system in the constitutional system?

The pattern of partisanship under the two-party system shifted as definitely in 1932 as in 1896.[19] The Democratic party, which came into power at Washington under Franklin D. Roosevelt, like its earlier predecessors in the leadership of the nation under the two-party system, was a combination of sectional oppositions. First and most significant was the new and frustrated city-dwellers' world, which gained its political importance through its domination of the highly industrialized metropolitan areas of the Northeast. Secondly, there were the depressed farmers, whose political importance rested largely on their predominating influence in the rural areas of the old Northwest. Thirdly, there was the Solid South, whether acutely depressed as in Arkansas and Mississippi or rapidly expanding as in Florida and Texas. These sectional interests were united by a common hostility to the lack of enterprise in dealing with the great depression shown by the then dominant conservative Republican party. They were divided, however, by radically different attitudes toward the spirit of the welfare state, for which the New Deal leadership of the Democratic party was the outstanding protagonist.

The new and more spirited leadership of the Democratic party brought about a durable realignment of the two major political parties. The Democrats made their greatest gains in the Northeast, where the rapidly growing metropolitan areas greatly increased their political influence in the section as a whole. They made substantial gains also on the Pacific Coast, where rapidly growing metropolitan areas likewise produced their characteristic effects on the alignment of parties. In the rural areas of the North and West, on the other hand, after the first impact of the depression had been borne, the appeal of the welfare state proved less attractive and the Republicans regained their traditional ascendancy. In the South the control of the administration by the protagonists of the welfare state put a heavy strain on the bonds of party allegiance. The reaction of that section to the ascendancy of the northeastern section of the party was foreshadowed by the pattern of the presidential vote in the Alfred E. Smith campaign of 1928. In that year five states of the Solid South—Florida, North Carolina, Tennessee, Texas, and Virginia—had preferred Hoover to Smith. Only six Southern states—South Carolina, Georgia, Alabama, Mississippi, Louisiana, and Arkansas—had remained true to their national party allegiance.

Despite the lack of a consensus among the major sectional components of the New Deal democracy concerning the development of a welfare state, the new alignment of national parties continued to serve more than tolerably well the essential purposes of the two-party system. The two major parties succeeded in offering the American people at each presidential election a generally acceptable choice between two leading candidates for the highest office in the land. The demand for third parties during this period of Democratic ascendancy never became strong enough to make serious inroads in the major parties. At least 95 per cent of the voters, in more than one election as many as 99 per cent of the voters, were content to choose between the regular candidates of the Democratic and Republican parties. In the latter part of the period so-called States' Rights candidates or Dixiecrats in the Lower South drew off a few electoral votes from the regular Democratic ticket without causing its defeat. At one election, that of 1948, a faction on the left, under the equivocal banner of Progressivism and the unrealistic leadership of Henry A. Wallace, polled a million and a half votes from discontented minorities in all sections, but without gaining any electoral votes. In general the bulk of the opponents to the rule of Democratic administrations was able to support the regular candidates of the Republican party, as the theory of the two-party system in a democratic constitutional system requires.

Moreover, the two major parties continued to divide the national electorate at most elections into nearly equal parts. If the two-party system is to produce satisfactory results under a constitutional system not originally designed to work as democratically as public opinion has come to desire, the regular opposition party must not be so inferior in strength as to leave its leaders with little hope of getting into power in a not too distant future. It is not necessary in a welfare state that the opposition be united on any issue more substantial than a general distrust of such a state or of the dominant party's management of the kind of welfare state that exists. Of course the major parties must possess some principles, but in modern times these have been the same principles, the fundamental principles of the American constitutional system. The prime necessity for the dominant party in a modern welfare state is to keep unemployment at a minimum. As long as the administration succeeds in achieving this objective, no radical realignment of parties is likely. But there is always the question, what is a reasonable minimum of unemployment, and the administration must be able to give acceptable answers when pressed by the opposition. The test of success is not the annihilation of the organized opposition but merely the maintenance at the polls of a working majority for the administration.

The balance of power between the two major parties also had shifted along with the realignment of parties in the 1930's. During the long period of Conservative Republican supremacy the balance of power had been held by New York and the old northwestern states of Ohio, Indiana, and Illinois. Now with the growth of cities, and especially of the big metropolitan areas in the great industrial states, first California and then Texas moved into the list of big, close, doubtful states, whose interests had to be carefully considered in the nomination of presidential candidates and the selection of party issues. New York, Pennsylvania, Michigan, Ohio, Illinois, California, Texas—these are the states which have come to be most important in the working of the two-party system in national politics. The present test of efficient major party leadership is the practical capacity to carry these states for the presidential ticket.

The campaign strategy of the party leaders must be based primarily on their prospects in these big, close, doubtful states. No candidate can win without carrying several of them. Victory is practically certain for a candidate who can carry almost all of them and is highly probable for a candidate who can carry a majority, including the biggest. The important point in the working of the two-party system is that the balance of power in presidential elections no longer lies with voters who live in rural areas but is now in the hands of voters in big metropolitan areas. The problem, in assessing the value of the two-party system, is to identify the voters in these decisive metropolitan areas and to appraise their influence in the party system. Are they capable of functioning in national politics as the average farmer in the American corn and wheat belts used to function in the formative years of the Jacksonian Democrats and Antislavery Republicans?

The evidence on this point is significant, if not entirely conclusive.[20] Seven of the eight largest metropolitan areas in the country are located in five of the biggest states of the North and West. The division of these metropolitan areas into congressional districts enables the political analyst to classify them into three main categories on the basis of the comparative rental value of residential property. There are the relatively high-value districts, the relatively low-value districts, and the districts dominated by residential property with intermediate rental values. In general, at recent congressional elections the high-value districts have tended to be Republican, the low-value districts have tended to be Democratic, and the intermediate-value districts have tended to be close and to shift more frequently from one side to the other. Altogether under the congressional reapportionment and redistricting after the census of 1960 there were nearly eighty of these metropolitan congressional districts, and the balance of power between the two major parties in these states seemed to be held by the voters in the intermediate districts. The presumption is not unreasonable that the voters who actually held the balance of power in these big, close, doubtful states were middle-class urban or suburban residents.

Of course it does not necessarily follow that a voter's political attitudes and party allegiance are determined by his position on an economic scale measuring the rental value of residential property. Political attitudes and party affiliation may be influenced by a voter's position in the productive processes of the national economy, by his traditional social and cultural relationships, or by his racial or religious associations. In local elections political affiliations known to be dominated by racial or religious associations may tend to drive other racial or religious groups into an opposite political affiliation, and the net effect of a political drive by a nonpolitical group may be difficult to estimate. In national elections racial and religious influences are still more indeterminate. The fact that a particular specialized group may possess more votes than the difference between the total votes cast for each of the major parties in a particular locality does not mean that the group holds the balance of power between the two parties. The two-party system is more complex. Local conditions vary in different sections of the country, but the phenomenon of middle-class predominance remains the same everywhere.

Class consciousness seems to be less manifest in national elections than many kinds of specialized group consciousness. Yet America is middle class, and in the nature of things the known attitudes of normal middle-class voters will exert a compelling influence on the calculations of the major party leaders. The experience of the generations since the formal establishment of the two-party system ensures respect by responsible party leaders for the purposes and interests of their middle-class followers, whether residing in great cities or in the open country. Now that the bulk of the middle class resides in the cities or in their suburbs, and since that part of it which holds the balance of power in the big, close, doubtful states is to be found in their largest metropolitan areas, the political effects should be the same as before. The purposes and interests of the urban and suburban middle class in the age of the welfare state provide the principal clue to the working of the contemporary two-party system. Regarded as an essential component of the constitutional system, the two-party system should function in national politics as the same stabilizing and moderating force as in earlier stages of the developing national economy. Middle-class interests may not always be identical with the general public interest, but they normally approach it more closely than specialized interests of any other kind. The greater the influence of the urban industrialized middle class in the normal operation of the two-party system under contemporary conditions, the more generally satisfying and durable should be the established political order.[21]

Considerations of this kind of course did not consciously influence the Supreme Court in its attitude toward the use of the spending power by the New Deal Congresses. The leading decisions in the Social Security Act and other epoch-making cases rested on acceptable juristic grounds. In this stage of the developing constitutional system, the dominant political party rather than a new majority within the Supreme Court was the prime instrument of the sovereign people.

CHAPTER SIX

A Living Constitution

The Constitution of the United States guarantees to each of the states a republican form of government. It does not define the term, but presumably every state was republican in 1787. Moreover, the new government of the more perfect Union also conformed to that constitutional standard. But how different could a government within the constitutional system be and still be republican? And what does its form of government reveal concerning the nature of the American community?

THE NATURE OF THE AMERICAN COMMUNITY

A simple answer to this question was offered by Roger Sherman in a letter written in 1787 to his old revolutionary friend, John Adams.[1] A republican government, he wrote, was a government without a king. This negative definition satisfied neither Adams nor other leading political scientists of the day. James Madison, writing in *The Federalist*, defined republican government as representative government. In a republic, he declared, the laws are made by elected legislators.[2] This definition, however, raises another question. How unrepresentative can a so-called representative government be and still be republican?

More than a half century later Dorr's Rebellion in Rhode Island put this question to the Supreme Court. The Rhode Island rebels denounced as excessively unrepresentative the long-established government under the royal charter of 1663, because it was not based on the principle of manhood suffrage. Since the men in power resisted all attempts to modernize it by suitable amendments, the rebels declared their intention of replacing it with a new state constitution based on acceptable democratic principles. Failing to make effective use of their natural right of revolution and being convicted of treason, they appealed to the federal courts for justice.[3] But the Supreme Court refused to decide the appeal on its merits, declaring that the question was political rather than justiciable. Pointing out that the Congress had not refused to admit representatives and senators, elected under the old charter, and that the President had not refused to recognize the governor under the charter as competent to speak for the state, the Court declared that it would abide by the decision of the proper political authorities. A fair inference was that an undemocratic representative government was not necessarily an unconstitutional government.

Early in the twentieth century the question arose again in Oregon, where the established system of representative government had been modified by the adoption of a system of direct legislation by the people through the use of the initiative and referendum. In this instance a telephone company objected to paying taxes which had been imposed upon it by a majority of the state electorate.[4] Again the distinction between a political and a justiciable question was utilized by the Supreme Court to avoid a direct answer to the question whether Oregon possessed a republican form of government. The political branches of the national government ignored the question, and the final result was the same as in Dorr's Rebellion. There is still no judicial determination of the nature of a republican form of government.

A different treatment of this question was offered by John Adams in correspondence with Roger Sherman. His definition of a republic called for the distribution of the lawmaking powers under a system of checks and balances. It was best illustrated at that time by the original constitution of the Commonwealth of Massachusetts, in the making of which he had taken a leading part. Adams confused the issue by declaring in his *Discourses on Davila* that a government with a king, like that of Great Britain, might still be republican in form, if the power to govern were distributed among the different kinds of officers, legislative, executive, and judicial, so that there would be a proper balance between them. With an effective system of checks and balances, he argued, the British monarchy would be a true republic. This exercise in semantics was too much for most plain Americans at the end of the eighteenth century, though no well-informed American today would object to calling Britain and the Scandinavian monarchies republics, if anybody cared to raise the question. But Adams' aristocratic republican notions were unpopular, and the Jeffersonians gained votes for themselves by associating their party with more democratic republican ideas. No influential public man at that time risked his career by identifying himself with "pure" democracy, that is, a government of the people without either a king or a representative body of lawmakers. Practical politicians generally preferred to stand on the fundamental principles of the revolutionary Whigs and define a good republic as a body politic based on the theoretical sovereignty of the people and striving to maintain an actual reign of law by a suitable system of checks and balances.

In recent years both the principle of popular sovereignty and the practice of a reign of law have proved troublesome. Concerning the place of the sovereign people in the constitutional system there are three questions of major importance. First, who are the people? Second, how free are the people to express their opinions in public speech and in print and to get the attention of public servants for public opinion? Third, have the people the same freedom to use the most modern means of communication, particularly motion pictures, radio, and television?

The framers of the Fourteenth Amendment tried to give a definitive answer to the first of these questions. They were concerned particularly with the problem of the newly emancipated slaves and wished to secure for them a suitable position in the body politic. By this they did not mean at first an equal right to vote, but it did mean to them an end to discrimination against the freedmen respecting their civil rights on account of their race, color, or previous condition of servitude. So the Fourteenth Amendment defined the people in terms of citizenship and declared that all persons born or naturalized in the United States were citizens of the United States and of the state in which they resided. This made the freedmen a part of the sovereign people but did not determine what should be their actual role in the practical exercise of popular sovereignty.

The framers of the Fourteenth Amendment were aware that a legal right is not the same as a practical capacity to make effective use of the opportunity which the right is designed to secure. Some of them pointed out that personal liberty would not be enough to secure real independence for the freedmen and urged that economic freedom should be fostered by a redistribution of property. "Forty acres and a mule" was a current formula for the kind and amount of economic aid that in their opinion would be desirable for an able-bodied freedman. Others insisted that education was more important than property to secure a workingman's independence and was indispensable to the stability of a free state. In their opinion a democratic system of public education was a necessary and proper feature of a democratic constitutional system and should be developed with a special concern for the education of the freedmen. Emancipation itself had effected a radical redistribution of property in the former slave states, and interest in a further redistribution of property in this suddenly impoverished section of the country rapidly faded away. Interest in the education of the freedmen continued.

Traditional habits of thought in a section which had hailed the Dred Scott decision as the right solution of the race problem stood in the way of the development of a theoretically democratic system of education. The

Southern way of life called for the development of separate educational systems for the two races. Eventually the Supreme Court adopted the view that separate but equal accommodations expressed an acceptable formula for adjusting the aspirations of the freedmen to the needs of Southern society.[5] Despite Justice John Marshall Harlan's cogent dissent on the ground that the Constitution since the adoption of the Fourteenth Amendment was color-blind, and despite the awkward fact that the colored schools, as generally administered, tended to give unequal educational opportunities to their pupils, this formula prevailed for more than a half century. In 1954, in the sensational School Desegregation Cases, the Supreme Court reversed itself and made the original Harlan view the law of the land.[6]

The Supreme Court's decision in the School Desegregation Cases provoked widespread and bitter criticism in the South. The sociological evidence, on which the Court relied for its opinion that there could not be equal educational opportunity for the two races in public schools unless they were integrated, was challenged on the ground of its alleged inadequacy. Moreover, the critics argued, the Court had been gradually raising the standards of the colored schools by its handling of successive cases involving the application of the separate but equal formula. In dealing with a problem of constitutional interpretation growing out of a conflict between a legal principle and the long-established mores of a substantial part of the sovereign people, the Court, in its critics' opinion, would reach the desired goal of a color-blind system of public education more surely and quickly by adhering to this empirical formula than by trying to solve the problem at once and for all time by substituting what might seem to be a more rational interpretation of the Fourteenth Amendment. The Court, they urged, was really engaged in the highly controversial business of revising a part of the fundamental law. This was an experiment in lawmaking which should be left to the political branches of the government. They were in a better position to perform work of this kind. In short, such important political questions should be left to the politicians.

The Supreme Court happily had been unanimous in its opinion that separate public schools for the two races could not give colored pupils equal training for citizenship in a democratic republic, and that their maintenance involved a denial of the equal protection of the laws to one of the races. It announced in a later decision that reasonable time would be allowed to the public school authorities to make the necessary readjustment to the new interpretation of the Constitution and that reasonable discretion in the choice of proper methods for making the readjustment would also be allowed.[7] Thus the Court hoped to preserve the important advantages of a gradual process of readjustment, as under the separate but equal formula, while obtaining the solid gain of avowed adherence to political principles suitable for a democratic republic. The principle of popular sovereignty, it believed, could not be maintained by a people divided against itself. Under the Fourteenth Amendment, eventually if not immediately, a single body of citizens, properly instructed in the rights and duties of citizenship, regardless of race or color, would constitute a sovereign people.

These decisions, signalizing Chief Justice Warren's arrival at the head of the Supreme Court, finally put the seal of judicial approval on the doctrine that the right system of public education is the crowning glory of the American version of democratic republicanism. Negro resentment at enforced submission to second-class citizenship, long smoldering, flared up at enforced participation in World War II, a war fought for the purpose, among others, of discrediting the Nazi dogma of racial superiority. The involvement of the Japanese and Chinese prevented it from being purely a white man's war, and the involvement of the American Negro forcibly reminded such Americans that theirs was a Negro's country as well as a white man's country. The School Desegregation Cases not only were an outstanding landmark in the development of the American form of republican government, they constituted also a decisive victory for the American faith in the power of the law to expedite the triumph of reason over tradition in the evolution of a way of life.[8]

The question, how free are the sovereign people to express their opinions and to get for them the attention of public servants, is one which the Founding Fathers tried to answer in the First Amendment to the Constitution. Congress shall make no law, according to this amendment, abridging the freedom of speech or of the press, or the right of the people peaceably to assemble and to petition the government for the redress of grievances. This positive injunction would seem to secure a constitutional right of communication between the sovereign people and their public servants. But this amendment protected the people only against the abridgment of their rights by the government of the United States. The framers of the Fourteenth Amendment sought to extend this protection to cover abridgments by the state governments. No state shall make or enforce any law, this amendment reads, which shall abridge the privileges or immunities of citizens of the United States, nor shall any state deprive any person of life, liberty, or property, without due process of law, nor deny to any person within its jurisdiction the equal protection of the laws. The two amendments together should give effective protection to the rights of communication among the citizens of the United States and between the sovereign people and their public servants.

Of course no reasonable person would claim an unlimited right to speak and publish whatever he pleases regardless of its impact on others. No one, for instance, would claim a right to slander his neighbor with impunity or to publish false, malicious, and defamatory statements about a public servant for purely private ends. Nor does the good citizen disturb public tranquillity without due cause, as by crying fire in a public meeting house where there is no fire for the pleasure of seeing how those present will behave in a moment of panic. There are other public interests besides the freedom of communication which the public authorities are bound to protect by appropriate measures. In addition to insuring domestic tranquillity, the authorities must provide for the common defense, which in time of war may involve necessary restraints on the communication of military intelligence and even on public discussion of the conduct of the war in such a manner as to give aid and comfort to the enemy. The First and Fourteenth Amendments to the Constitution were designed to protect the people in both war and peace, but the enforcement of constitutional rights need not be identical under different kinds of circumstances. The various and sometimes competing needs of the public must be balanced against each other, and the balance cannot be struck at the same point under all circumstances. The essential aim in protecting the public interest in freedom of communication would seem to be to give the public maximum scope in all cases involving popular grievances and to make honest efforts to get them redressed by governmental action.

Of course there can be no guarantee that freedom of communication will not result in the dissemination of error as well as truth. There have always been some persons who have believed that error should not have the same rights as truth and have contended that suitable measures should be employed to insure to the latter a preferred position. But this contention raises the difficult questions, how shall the guardians of the truth be found, and who shall declare their competence for their exacting duties? The framers of the Fourteenth Amendment were acquainted with John Stuart Mill's then fresh and widely read exposition of the reasons for leaving to the market place for ideas the competition between truth and error. The reasons were set forth in his best-selling essay *On Liberty,* in which his reflections "On the Liberty of Thought and Discussion" occupy a prominent place. His conclusion, that the public needs access to all kinds of opinion in order to insure the acceptance of the best, made a strong appeal to a democratic people.

The framers of the First Amendment adopted a different justification of the freedom of communication under a republican form of government. They started with the assumption that the people possessed a natural right to such a freedom and should exchange it for a civil right, to be defined by man-made law, only insofar as restraints on the natural right would serve some public purpose. Thus the burden of proof that restraint is needed in the public interest would be thrown on the advocates of a particular restriction. Before the American Revolution the principal restriction had been the royal censorship of the press, and the paramount issue had been the abolition of such censorship. Censorship of the press by the federal government was effectually precluded by the First Amendment. This amendment, however, did not provide a clear definition of the freedom of speech or the other components of a general freedom of communication. The framers generally looked to the right of trial by jury for protection against an arbitrary and oppressive enforcement of such sedition laws as might be enacted to meet the expected crises of an unpredictable future. But when the first crisis came in 1798, trial by jury proved a frail shield against the abuse of power under the Sedition Act of that year.

Longer acquaintance with the ways of juries led to a greater reliance on the judges, especially those on the Supreme Court, for the final balancing of the competing public interests involved in a particular situation, which constitutes the essence of the constitutional freedoms protected by the First and Fourteenth Amendments. The judges were free to choose between two different methods of justifying the weighting of the various public interests competing for consideration in a freedom of speech case before the Court for decision. They could resort to the clause protecting the privileges and immunities of citizenship, in which case they would have to define more precisely what they meant by freedom of speech or of the press or the rights of assembly and petition. This is difficult to do, since these freedoms are something less than a right to say or do what one pleases under any and all circumstances and something more than a right to say or do what the authorities who make and enforce the law are pleased to permit to be said or done. But how much less and how much more? The answer seems to depend on the personal attitudes of the particular men who interpret and apply the laws and thereby give them their practical significance.

Nevertheless a government of law is something more than a government of men. The essential difference lies in the concept of due process of law. This means that the men who interpret and enforce the law are bound to perform their official tasks in strict compliance with established rules which prescribe how their tasks shall be performed. The purpose of the rules is to insure as far as is humanly possible that action in a particular case will not be taken without full knowledge of the facts in the case and due consideration of the reasons for action. Thus the second method of justifying the assignment of weight to competing public interests, which consists in not depriving any person of liberty without due process of law, seems to be more objective than the first. But the appearance is deceptive, since it is still necessary for the judges to say what they mean by the kind of liberty involved in a particular case. Does freedom of the press, for instance, mean the absence of censorship prior to publication and the determination of the character of the matter printed, whether libelous or not, by the jury rather than by the judge? Or does it mean a right to print any opinion, right or wrong, that may reasonably be supposed to be capable of helping the sovereign people, or their representatives, reach a right decision concerning a controversial matter without too much injury to some other public interest, such as protection of the government against subversion by agents of a foreign power?

The Supreme Court has not yet succeeded in formulating an acceptable definition of any of the freedoms composing the general right of communication or even in finally determining which of the two methods of dealing with such questions is preferable. The favorite formula in the early years of the republic was to consider the tendency of an alleged unlawful speech or other communication. If the tendency was bad—that is, if the communication seemed to bring the government into hatred or contempt or otherwise impair its capacity to accomplish its purpose—the communication was not regarded as privileged under the Constitution. This was the attitude of the courts during the prosecutions under the Sedition Act of 1798, when even a congressman was sent to prison for his critical remarks about President John Adams. During the prosecutions under the Sedition Act of 1917, Justice Holmes introduced a more discriminating formula, in order that a critic of the war effort might not be sent to prison unless his remarks caused a "clear and present danger" of interference with the successful conduct of the war.[9] But this formula did not secure the liberty of Eugene V. Debs, the perennial Socialist candidate for President, who was convicted of obstructing the draft, to say nothing of more obscure and reckless agitators as well as comparatively harmless pacifists whose conscientious objections to war got them into trouble with zealous public prosecutors.

The subsequent adoption of the Smith and McCarran Acts (the Sedition Act of 1940 and the Internal Security Act of 1950) gave the Supreme Court further opportunities to explain the meaning of the fundamental freedoms protected by the First and Fourteenth Amendments. But these acts were directed against conspiracies by organized groups of malcontents, particularly against the Communist party, as well as against individual persons, and can more conveniently be discussed in connection with the natural right of revolution. The Court has only recently gotten around to considering an order that the officers of the Communist party register with the Subversive Activities Control Board, and a decision on the merits of the principal issues presented by this litigation is still to come. It is enough to emphasize here that the protection of the fundamental freedoms of communication under the rapidly changing conditions of the nuclear age involves new efforts at striking a rational balance between the conflicting public interests involved in conventional free speech cases. The Constitution is indeed a living constitution.

A final question concerning the power of the sovereign people to control their constitutional rulers through the expression of public opinion is, do the people have the same freedom of expression through the new means of communication—motion pictures, radio, and television—as through public speaking and the printing press? A short answer is that they do not. However, as in the case of freedom of speech and of the press, the Supreme Court judges have been closely divided in their opinions in the leading cases brought before them, and there seems to be a definite trend in recent years toward a more liberal view of the public interest in freedom of communication among the people as the cornerstone of the American version of democratic republicanism.

The treatment of the right to exhibit motion pictures has been affected by the traditional attitude toward the theater as a place of public entertainment rather than public instruction. As long ago as 1915 the Supreme Court decided that motion-picture exhibitors might be required to submit their films to official censorship before showing them to the public and that the freedoms of speech and the press would not protect them against the decision of the censors.[10] The motion-picture producers, recognizing the danger of arbitrary and oppressive action by local police authorities and other official censors, organized a voluntary system of private censorship which they hoped would be a salutary check on public censorship, but the demand for further protection against indecent films persisted. This in turn stimulated a demand for further protection against the abuse of power by official censors. Meanwhile, sound had been added to the original silent picture, and the capacity of the new medium of communication to instruct had gained even more than its capacity to entertain. In 1952 the Supreme Court reversed itself and decided that the Fourteenth Amendment does apply to motion pictures.[11] In the particular case then before the Court, involving the condemnation of a controversial film called *The Miracle* on the ground that it was "sacrilegious," the law under which the censors were operating was declared unconstitutional under the due process clause of the Fourteenth Amendment on the ground that it provided no adequate standard for the guidance of the censors. Thus the principle of censorship was recognized as still applicable to the motion-picture industry.

The struggle to bring the motion-picture industry within the scope of the law governing freedom of speech and of the press has been complicated by that to reach a similar goal for the radio and television industries. Like the theater, these media of communication may be used primarily for public entertainment. But under modern conditions they have become important agencies of civic education, and freedom for persons of various opinions to make use of them forms an essential component of a general freedom of communication. Freedom to broadcast, however, is limited by the available channels for the transmission of electronic signals. Of course freedom of the press is restricted by the growing cost of newspaper plants and the exercise of an informal censorship by the owners of the plants. But the technical obstacles which stand in the way of free communication by electronic signals are more formidable than the financial obstacles resulting from the mounting cost of broadcasting installations. The use of available channels must be rationed by some reasonable method, and the most acceptable method has been to entrust the task to a federal administrative agency.

The regulation of broadcasting by the Federal Communications Commission involves the power to influence the programs of the broadcasters. The federal law under which the commission operates expressly repudiates the exercise of a censorship. The main weapon of the commissioners is cancellation of the license of the owners of a broadcasting station. This weapon is too potent for use on any but extraordinary occasions, and the influence of the commission has to be exerted mainly by admonition and advice. The Congress has strengthened its arm in special cases by issuing instructions in the form of amendments to the law. Thus, for instance, the law requires broadcasters to give equal time to all the candidates for the same office in a political campaign. However, the claims of candidates of major and minor parties, respectively, to the attention of the public are so unequal that the law serves the public interest in the freedom of discussion very imperfectly. The protection of the constitutional right of the people to a general freedom of communication requires different measures in the case of broadcasting from those which have been relied on in the cases of public speaking and printing. The Federal Communications Commission has been slow to find effective measures, and the regulation of broadcasting in the public interest has been far from satisfactory. It is clear that if the constitutional system is to be in the future the vital part of the American way of life that it has been up to now, it must continue to develop by adaptation to the changing conditions of this changing world. The sovereign people must be able to form their opinions and express their will in the most convenient way available under the ever-progressing art of communication.

It is evident that the principle of popular sovereignty is an ideal toward which we progress rather than the actual condition of the American people. The reality is the acceptance of the law as the most authentic expression of the will of the people at any particular time and of the constitutional system as the supreme law of the land. The first problem of American government, therefore, is to make the supreme law prevail in practice over lesser bodies of law, and law of all kinds over the wills of individuals and groups, pending changes in the law by constitutional methods. The maintenance of an actual reign of law must be the primary political concern of the sovereign people and of their agents in public offices of every kind. From this point of view the voters themselves are a kind of public officers, and the electorate is charged with the first responsibility for the observance and preservation of the fundamental freedoms. Hence the importance of the system of civic education. But every branch of government is theoretically responsible for the right interpretation of the fundamental law. The practical supremacy of the judges in the business of constitutional interpretation results from two solid facts. One is the fact that they speak last in the ordinary process of lawmaking and interpretation; the other, that there is no appeal from the Supreme Court except by the difficult process of constitutional amendment.

The Supreme Court has been less successful in maintaining a reign of law during war than in times of peace. The acts of Congress tend to reflect the fears and hatreds created or exaggerated by war, and the behavior of the chief executive tends to reflect the need for swifter and more vigorous action than is ordinarily required in times of peace. After each of our greatest wars the Supreme Court has seized the first opportunity to reassert the supremacy of law over the arbitrary and oppressive actions of overanxious military authorities and overzealous civilians, taken under the spur of what they conceived to be compelling necessity, but it has been ineffective in preventing such action during the course of hostilities. Special efforts were made by Chief Justice Stone during World War II to maintain the supremacy of the Constitution and to observe the proprieties of due process of law, but these did not prevent the gross injustices of the West Coast Japanese "relocation" proceedings. It was not until after the war that the Court finally rebuked the military authorities in Hawaii for the arbitrary arrest and imprisonment of civilians without due process of law.[12]

American judges like to quote the eloquent words in which, long after the Civil War, Justice Miller of the Supreme Court laid down the law to the superintendent of the Arlington National Cemetery across the Potomac from Washington.[13] The land on which the cemetery lies had been a part of the estate of General Robert E. Lee and had been seized during the war by federal officers for nonpayment of taxes, without regard to the provisions of the law which had been enacted to govern such seizures. Justice Miller, speaking for a majority of the Court, declared: "No man in this country is so high as to be above the law. No officer of the law may set that law at defiance with impunity. All the officers of the government, from the highest to the lowest, are creatures of the law, and are bound to obey it. It is the only supreme power in our system of government." But after World War II the Supreme Court refused to take jurisdiction over the special tribunals established in Manila and Tokyo by General MacArthur for the trial and punishment of vanquished Japanese generals and civilian war leaders. Most of the justices took the view that, since the General was the agent of all the Allies in the Far East, his acts were political in the eyes of the American courts and not to be judged like those of a general acting solely in the service of the United States.[14]

The Supreme Court was more successful in imposing the rule of law on President Truman than on General MacArthur. In April 1952, the President, acting in his capacity of Commander in Chief and being responsible for military operations in Korea nominally under the direction of the United Nations, seized all the American steel plants in order to maintain the production of munitions. His immediate problem was to avert a threatened strike, but he intended to use possession of the plants to establish a system of wage and price controls believed to be necessary to prevent dangerous inflation and to secure the efficient conduct of the war. Acts of Congress in the statute books established procedures for the seizure of plants in connection with the settlement of wage disputes and also in connection with the maintenance of munitions production. The President, however, preferred in this case to employ a different procedure, not authorized by any act of Congress. The plants were actually seized under the direction of the Secretary of Commerce, but the decision to make the seizure was the President's.

This action raised the same constitutional issue that had been presented to the Supreme Court in the Arlington National Cemetery Case. The decision was the same and was reached as in the earlier case by a divided Court.[15] Chief Justice Vinson, speaking for the dissenting justices, noted that under the Constitution the executive power—the whole of it—is vested in the President and argued that this was a proper occasion for exercising a part of such massive authority. Justice Black wrote the opinion for the Court, and with the aid of concurring opinions by Justices Frankfurter and Jackson, showed that the only power which could authorize the seizure of steel plants under the Constitution was legislative, not executive, and that the legislation authorizing the seizure of industrial plants under various circumstances by prescribed processes excluded the employment of other methods. "The Founders of this Nation," Justice Black concluded, "entrusted the law-making power to the Congress alone in both good and bad times."

Justice Jackson stated the essence of the principle of a reign of law in pithy language. "The essence of our free Government," he declared, "is 'leave to live by no man's leave, underneath the law'—to be governed by those impersonal forces which we call law. Our Government is fashioned to fulfill this concept so far as humanly possible. . . . With all its defects, delays and inconveniences, men have discovered no technique for long preserving free government except that the Executive be under the law, and that the law be made by parliamentary deliberations." The Supreme Court demonstrated in this case that it would do its part to maintain a reign of law, but of course in the long run the Congress too must do its part by duly enacting necessary and proper legislation for meeting all foreseeable emergencies.

The Congress may also fail to do its part in maintaining the rule of law by enacting improper measures which do not square with the Constitution. The Supreme Court showed recently by two controversial decisions that it could deal effectively with such measures. These were the closely contested Expatriation Cases.[16] The Congress had passed two laws designed to discourage draft-dodging by American citizens, one of which sought to deprive draft-dodgers of their citizenship, the other to prevent their return to the country if they should leave it to escape the draft. Two acknowledged draft-dodgers, one of whom sought to get a passport in order to return to the United States, the other to prevent deportation after his return, brought suit against the Secretary of State and the Attorney General, respectively, in order to establish their right as American citizens to live in the country for which they had refused to fight. The Supreme Court declared that the two culprits derived their right to citizenship directly from the Constitution and that it could not be taken from them without due process of law. The Congress certainly had power to provide for their punishment, but not by depriving them of their citizenship without at least a trial by jury. The draft-dodging acts were therefore unconstitutional and would have to be sacrificed in the interest of the supremacy of the higher law of the Constitution, a more important matter than the prompt punishment of draft-dodgers by administrative officers, desirable as proper punishment might be.

In these cases the Supreme Court reversed a trend which seemed to have subordinated the due process of law—that is, the right to trial by jury—to a natural demand for summary proceedings against draft-dodgers. Four of the justices would have decided the cases differently, believing that the Congress had power to prescribe the procedure under which citizenship might be taken away. If Justice Frankfurter, who had recently retired from the Court, had been present, the dissenting judges would presumably have been in the majority, since he had taken their side of the argument in previous similar cases. But Justice Goldberg, Justice Frankfurter's successor, who wrote the opinion for the new majority of the Court, was convinced that American citizens cannot be deprived of their citizenship as punishment for any crime without the benefit of all the procedural rights designed for the protection of persons charged with crime. It is disturbing to find that constitutional rights sometimes seem to depend upon accidental circumstances rather than the clear dictates of reason, but this is part of the price that must be paid for the blessings of a living Constitution in a changing world.

Nevertheless it is now clear that there are no persons outside the law under the American constitutional system. The image of the American people is broad enough to include in the body politic those who do wrong as well as those who do right. The principle of universal citizenship for all those born in the United States, or duly naturalized, is firmly established, and the effective protection of the equal rights of all citizens will follow as rapidly and completely as circumstances permit. The nature of the American community is determined in the last analysis by the self-consciousness of the sovereign people. The full expression of popular sovereignty, however, depends not only on the force of public opinion but also on the maintenance of the supremacy of the law.

CHANGING VIEWS OF THE PRINCIPLES OF 1776

The modern welfare state is a development well within the purposes of government as understood by the framers of the Constitution. The language of the Preamble is broad enough to cover the systematic promotion of the general welfare by any means capable of commanding the support of public opinion, provided that the necessary measures are adopted and put into effect by due process of law. Though the Supreme Court, while under the domination of judges appointed by conservative Presidents of both parties, read a strong infusion of laissez-faire doctrines into the spirit of the Constitution, these doctrines were eventually read out again by the New Deal judges. The dissenting opinions of their doctrinal predecessors, Holmes, Brandeis, Stone, and Cardozo, became the sources of constitutional maxims which supplied a firm legal foundation for the new twentieth-century constitutional spirit. There is one important feature of the modern welfare state, however, developed under the New Deal, for which suitable constitutional maxims cannot be found in the opinions of the Great Dissenters.

The separation of church and state formed no part of the original American constitutional system. Neither the Declaration of Independence nor the first state constitutions mention it. The Massachusetts Declaration of Rights, the most systematic and comprehensive of the original bills of rights, made the proper care of religion one of the first duties of a free commonwealth. But in Virginia, Jefferson's Statute of Religious Freedom was enacted into law not long before the Convention of 1787 met at Philadelphia, and the framers of the Constitution could not ignore the rising tide of opinion in favor of excluding the care of religion from the constitutional functions of government. The federal Constitution provided that no religious test should ever be required as a qualification for any office under the United States, and the First Amendment added the injunction that the Congress should make no law respecting an establishment of religion or prohibiting the free exercise thereof.

The Fourteenth Amendment, so the Supreme Court was bound to declare when a suitable case should come before it, extended these principles to the states. The last state church, that of Massachusetts, had been disestablished thirty-five years before the adoption of the Fourteenth Amendment, and a century passed before the relations between church and state became a live problem of constitutional law. Then attack against the existing system of church disestablishment and religious freedom came from two opposite quarters. One came from a Protestant sect of extreme conscientious sensitivity and missionary zeal calling themselves Jehovah's Witnesses, and the second from Roman Catholics and other religious bodies deeply concerned with religious education. Jehovah's Witnesses alone were responsible for fifty-five cases in the Supreme Court up to the year 1958, of which they won forty-four.[17] These cases gave the Supreme Court the difficult task of finding a clear and generally acceptable definition of the free exercise of religion. Litigation arising out of various controversial relationships between parochial and public schools revealed equal or greater difficulties standing in the way of determining what is an establishment of religion.

The Flag Salute Cases, decided in the early years of World War II when effective provision for the common defense was uppermost in the minds of most Americans, put the Supreme Court to a severe test of its capacity to find an acceptable interpretation of the First Amendment.[18] Some Jehovah's Witnesses living in Pennsylvania objected to their children saluting the flag at the opening exercises in the local public schools, and the school authorities objected to their attending school unless they would join in the salute to the flag. The Witnesses were conscientious objectors to idolatry in any form, and the school authorities were determined to promote by all lawful means the development of sound patriotic sentiments among their pupils. For the Court, Justice Frankfurter argued fervently for the superior validity of the public interest in patriotic civic education over that in protecting such odd religious scruples as those of the Witnesses. Justice Stone, the lone dissenter, who possessed what seemed at the time odd constitutional scruples of his own, contended earnestly for the primary importance of the religious freedom guaranteed by the First and Fourteenth Amendments.

Three years later, when a similar case came up from West Virginia, Justice Stone, then Chief Justice, was joined by five of his colleagues in reversing the earlier decision.[19] Justice Jackson, in an eloquent opinion for the new majority of the Court, restated the arguments for giving the freedom of religion a preferred position among the constitutional rights of the American people. "If there is any fixed star in our constitutional constellation," he declared, "it is that no official, high or petty, can prescribe what shall be orthodox in politics, nationalism, religion, or other matters of opinion or force citizens to confess by word or act their faith therein." Nevertheless Justice Frankfurter and two of his colleagues still thought that it was a not unreasonable act of a state legislature to promote good citizenship by requiring all school children to salute the flag. Justice Jackson pointed out a real difficulty in deciding such cases when he wrote: "The case is made difficult not because the principles of its decision are obscure but because the flag involved is our own."

A few years after the Flag Salute Cases, three cases involving the application of the principle of the separation of church and state came before the Supreme Court and put its capacity to decide to another severe test.[20] These cases related to (1) the use of public school buses to carry pupils to parochial schools at public expense; (2) the admission of clergymen to public schools during regular school hours in order to give instruction in religion and morality to the pupils; and (3) the release of pupils from public schools for instruction in parochial schools during regular school hours. In the first and third of these cases state legislation authorizing the challenged practices was declared to be compatible with the separation of church and state; in the second case a state law was declared unconstitutional on the ground that it was legislation respecting an establishment of religion. Chief Justice Vinson, who possessed a strong sense of duty to maintain the solidarity of his Court, voted with the majority in each of these cases, but only one of his judicial associates agreed with him in all three decisions. The other judges held contrary opinions in one or more of the cases, disclosing a deplorable degree of uncertainty in the Court concerning the exact location of the "wall of separation" between church and state.

More recently the use of official prayers and reading from the Bible at the opening of public schools each morning has been challenged on the ground that legislation authorizing such practices is incompatible with the free exercise of religion or otherwise breaches the principle of separation of church and state. With only one dissent the Supreme Court decided in 1962 that a prayer composed by state officials should not be included in the opening exercises of public schools in New York and that legislation authorizing such a practice was unconstitutional.[21] Though this decision was widely criticized by advocates of religious instruction in the public schools, it could not have been otherwise without conflicting with the final decision in the Flag Salute Cases. In an opinion for the Court, Justice Black put the essence of the decision in emphatic words: "Each separate government in this country should stay out of the business of writing or sanctioning official prayers and leave that purely religious function to the people themselves and to those the people choose to look to for religious guidance."

The prescribed recital of the Lord's Prayer and reading from the Holy Scriptures at the opening of public schools threatened to cause the Supreme Court further difficulties in drawing a line between the rights of religious minorities and the constitutional power of political majorities to promote the general welfare as they deem proper. By the middle of the twentieth century all sectarian religious bodies in the United States had become minorities. Some advocates of freedom of religion claimed for these minorities a preferred position under the First Amendment over agnostic and atheistic minorities; others contended that agnostics and atheists were entitled under the Constitution to the same rights as other persons. In 1963 two cases were decided by the Supreme Court involving these conflicting contentions.[22] One was brought by a Unitarian who objected to a Pennsylvania statute requiring the reading of the Bible and recitation of the Lord's Prayer at the opening exercises in the public schools; the other was brought by a Maryland atheist who objected to similar exercises in the public schools of Baltimore.

The Supreme Court used these cases to confirm the constitutional principle that the care of religion shall be excluded from the purposes of government. The opinion for the Court was written by Justice Clark. "In the relationship between men and religion," he declared, "the state is firmly committed to a position of neutrality." In four separate concurring opinions Justices Brennan, Douglas, Goldberg, and Harlan made clear their repudiation of the charge that these decisions reflected an unfriendly attitude toward religion by the members of the Court. They explicitly approved the study of the Bible in public schools in courses on the history of religion and the practice of morality. But they were firm in the conviction that there can be no mandatory religious exercises in public schools under the Constitution of the United States. The people of the United States may be predominantly a religious people, but their representatives cannot use their lawmaking power to establish any particular form of religion or to give a preferred position to religious exercises of any kind.

That governments derive their just powers from the consent of the governed is another principle of 1776 which has given the Supreme Court difficult problems of interpretation in recent years. It is not enough that the right to vote should be so defined as to exclude discrimination on account of race, color, or sex. Elections must be so conducted that the people find the results acceptable. There is a multitude of practical problems connected with the registration of voters, nominations, campaigns, and elections which require careful planning and eternal vigilance. The outstanding problem before the Supreme Court, however, has been that of fixing suitable election districts for purposes of representation.

The original basis of representation was the most convenient unit of local government, normally the town or county. Until early in the present century the town or county continued to form an acceptable basis of representation in most states. Unequal rates of growth in different towns and counties, particularly the extraordinarily rapid growth of cities, make these natural units of representation increasingly unacceptable to people interested in the political equality of the individual citizen. An urbanized nation calls for the establishment of electoral districts designed to equalize the influence of equal numbers of voters, regardless of their location, in the choice of representatives. The great inequalities that have developed between the representation of rural and urban voters have caused state legislatures under the domination of rural representatives to make inequitable redistributions of legislative seats between town and country or even to refuse altogether to readjust an unfair system of representation by establishing suitable election districts. In some states no reapportionment of representatives or redistricting of any kind was made over long periods of years despite specific requirements in the state constitutions for periodic revision of the basis of representation.

These objectionable practices raised the question of their constitutionality under the federal Constitution. There is the guarantee of a republican form of government to every state in the Constitution of 1787 and the further guarantee to every person under the Fourteenth Amendment of the equal protection of the laws. Is a state government republican in form when the vote of a rural resident possesses many times the weight in legislative election of that of a city dweller? Do urban residents enjoy the equal protection of the laws when the laws are made by a legislature unfairly controlled by rural representatives? Can the Supreme Court give effective protection to the right of the people to have their consent to the exercise of governmental power properly ascertained?

The Supreme Court's first answer to these questions was unsatisfactory.[23] In a case brought by a public-spirited university professor to test the constitutionality of an outdated system of congressional districts in Illinois, in the decision of which only seven members of the Court participated, three judges were of the opinion that the Court possessed both the power and the duty to bring about an equitable redistricting of the state and three other judges were of the contrary opinion. The former believed that the Court should do something to secure to the people the equal protection of the laws, whereas the latter contended that the case raised a political question which the Court should leave to the political branches of the state government. The seventh judge agreed with the first three in principle and with the last three in practice, for reasons which no other judge could understand. It was a matter of "equitable discretion," this judge averred, to decline to take jurisdiction over a case of this kind.

A more satisfactory answer has come from the Supreme Court in two recent cases.[24] In the Tennessee Reapportionment Case an outdated legislative reapportionment was declared unconstitutional on the ground stated by the minority of the Court in the earlier Illinois case. A spirited dissent by the judge who had spoken for the majority in the Illinois case emphasized the troubles the Court would make for itself if it took over from the politicians the responsibility for righting all the wrongs perpetrated by state legislatures in dealing with the basis of representation. Nevertheless, a year later the Court declared unconstitutional a Georgia statute sanctioning a county unit system of representation in the state legislature, under which a vote in one small rural county had been worth ninety-nine times as much as a vote in the city of Atlanta. These decisions, though not providing any clear rule for the guidance of politicians in laying out election districts, stimulated a rush in many states to establish more equitable systems of representation.[25]

The Supreme Court seems to have assumed a responsibility for fair reapportionment and redistricting practices in the states as formidable as that assumed for fair school districts and admission practices in state school systems. The refusal in recent years to avoid this responsibility by means of an ill-defined distinction between political and justiciable questions reveals a growing recognition that changes in the American way of life and in the thinking of the sovereign people call for corresponding changes in the judicial interpretation of the Constitution. That this ever-growing body of fundamental law means what the judges say it means has become a more respected maxim of the constitutional system than it was when Charles E. Hughes, not at the time a member of the Supreme Court, first emphasized its importance. The Court still stands as the most impressive symbol of the reign of law in this country, but the sovereign people know that judges must occasionally behave more like politicians than guardians of traditional interpretations of an eighteenth-century document. The sovereign people may rightly assume also that, like good politicians, the judges of the highest courts will be mindful of their duty in a democratic republic to listen respectfully to the voice of public opinion.

The revolutionary principle which has caused the Supreme Court the most trouble in recent years is the right of revolution itself. This, the climactic principle of 1776, is not mentioned in the Constitution of 1787, though it is clearly implied in the proceedings of the Philadelphia Convention. Recognizing the need for changes in the fundamental law by some method more convenient than fighting, the framers introduced into the Constitution two procedures for its amendment, both easier than that provided for amending the Articles of Confederation but difficult enough to insure due deliberation before action. Better than constitutional changes, however, for dealing with governments which have lost the confidence of the people, is a ready and easy way of changing the men who are in power. This the people have learned to accomplish through the regular operation of the unplanned bipartisan system of party government.

The efficient operation of the bipartisan system requires certain essential good habits on the part of both voters and politicians. The bulk of the voters must ordinarily be willing to choose between the candidates of two major parties, which are capable of dividing the electorate into two fairly equal parts and of commanding the support of the bulk of their partisans during successive elections regardless of unpredictable changes in the paramount issues and the lack of important differences concerning fundamental principles. It is a system which gives the voters a direct control over the choice of men for public office, by choosing one of two major-party candidates, but only an indirect and uncertain control over the choice of policies and of measures for carrying them into effect, through the influence of public opinion. The bulk of the voters must also be willing to tolerate minor parties, capable of bringing up new issues and preparing the public for the consideration of new measures without resort to violence despite long-continued failure at the polls. The men in power must be willing to accept electoral defeats and turn over their offices to their successful opponents with sufficient grace to enable the party system to serve as an acceptable substitute for the natural but inconvenient right of revolution.

The greatest problem in the operation of the party system has been that of tolerating minor parties with unpopular programs of policies and measures. The programs of minor parties are necessarily unpopular; if this were not so, their policies and measures would be taken up by one or both of the major parties. Their programs may not deserve to be popular, in which case the parties will languish and sooner or later disappear. They may even be subversive and tend toward an eventual resort to violence. But unless their leaders and members are protected in their constitutional rights to freedom of speech, the press, and association, the formation of sound public opinion will be threatened at its source and the bipartisan system will not function as effectively as it should. Unless a minor party may look forward to such a growth as will enable it under favorable circumstances to force a realignment of the major parties or to become a major party itself, there will not be the kind of government for which the American Whigs fought in 1776.

This problem in recent years has taken the form of a struggle over the rights and duties of Communists. The Communist party leaders have claimed for themselves the same freedoms of communication as other citizens enjoy and for their party the same freedoms to nominate candidates and participate in elections as other parties. Anti-Communists have objected to Communist political activities on the ground that they constituted a standing threat to the peace and to the security of the constitutional system too dangerous to be tolerated in a free country where error ordinarily possesses the same rights as truth, or that they were a dangerous abuse of the acknowledged right of Americans to discuss on its merits the theory of revolution as a philosophical abstraction or its application to a historical event. It ought to be clear that direct incitement to violence should be prevented or punished by due process of law and that philosophical discussions should be protected and even encouraged in a free country where truth is expected to be able to defend itself against error in a fair contest held under the constitutional rules. But it is not so clear how dangerous to the peace partisan political activities may become if pursued with fanatical zeal.

The investigation of this problem occupied the Supreme Court in three important cases involving the existence and activities of the Communist party. In the first of these cases, decided in 1951, eleven of the highest officers of the party—the national politburo—were prosecuted under a federal sedition act adopted in 1940, commonly called the Smith Act, which prohibited conspiracies to overthrow the government of the United States by force and violence.[26] The particular charge against the members of the politburo was that of organizing the Communist party and planning to use it to accomplish the forcible overthrow of the government at some future time when such an attempt might seem more promising than in the 1940's. Four members of the Court joined in an opinion by Chief Justice Vinson that the Smith Act was a constitutional effort on the part of Congress to make the government more secure against seditious conspiracies, and that the Communist party leaders had created a clear and present danger of revolutionary activities which the act was designed to prevent. Justices Frankfurter and Jackson concurred in the result without committing themselves to the view that there was a clear and present danger of the success of the conspiracy. It was enough for them that the existence of the Communist party constituted a conspiracy which under the circumstances of modern politics Congress had power to make criminal, regardless of the prospects of immediate success. As Justice Jackson phrased the essence of his opinion, "the Constitution does not make conspiracy a civil right."

Dissenting opinions by Justices Black and Douglas offered a different view of the case. Justice Black emphasized certain facts, the importance of which he thought the majority of the Court had underestimated. The members of the politburo, he pointed out, were not charged with an attempt to overthrow the government; they were not charged with overt acts of any kind designed to lead to the overthrow of the government; they were not even charged with saying or writing something tending to bring about the overthrow of the government. They were charged merely with conspiring to organize a party which might at some future time advocate the forcible overthrow of the government. This, he believed, was "a virulent form of prior censorship of speech and press," which was prohibited by the First Amendment. Justice Douglas was fairly lyrical in his support of the same view. "The First Amendment" he wrote, "makes confidence in the common sense of our people and in their maturity of judgment the great postulate of our democracy. . . . The political censor has no place in our public debates."

Six years later the cases of some Communist party leaders of the second rank came before the Supreme Court.[27] These were the party leaders in the State of California who had been prosecuted under the Smith Act after the conviction of the national leaders. The Court, with only one member dissenting, reversed their convictions, setting some of the defendants free and ordering new trials for the others. The opinion for the Court, written by Justice Harlan, contended that the federal judges in California had misinterpreted the Smith Act and has misunderstood the significance of the Supreme Court's decision in the earlier case. This opinion, however, failed to make clear how the Smith Act, as reinterpreted, would be applied in the future. It seemed likely that there would be no more prosecutions of Communists for conspiracy on the sole ground of membership in the party. If a party member could not be prosecuted for some personal act, his partisanship alone would apparently not be regarded thereafter as an unlawful activity.

The drive against the Communist party was continued under the Internal Security Act of 1950, commonly known as the McCarran Act. This novel piece of legislation shifted the line of attack against communism from attempted suppression to repression by publicity. Organizations, acknowledging various degrees of infestation by Communists, were required to register with a Subversive Activities Control Board and to furnish specified kinds of information about themselves. Since registration might be followed by prosecution, this requirement raised the question whether the registrant was not being compelled to incriminate himself contrary to due process of law. The act was also challenged on the ground that it violated basic freedoms protected by the First Amendment.

The Communist party managed by various dilatory tactics to postpone a decision on the main issue for more than a decade. Since the Supreme Court was closely divided in its opinion of the law, it may have facilitated the delay, but in 1961 it finally decided by a vote of five to four that members of the Communist party would have to register.[28] The majority of the Court held that the Congress, in the exercise of its power to legislate for the common defense, could require a party with important foreign relations to identify itself, since the public interest in the freedoms of the First Amendment would have to yield to the greater interest in the security of the nation. Several of the dissenting judges took a dim view of the future of the nation if fundamental freedoms were not to be preserved, while the Chief Justice thought that further delay was justified in deciding an issue of such great importance, since the judges possessed imperfect knowledge of the circumstances under which the balancing of public interests had been made by the Congress. A decision concerning the obligation of the party officers to register—the most important issue in the case—was postponed until a later time.

It must be confessed that the judicial interpretation of the McCarran Act, like that of the Smith Act, leaves a great deal to the imagination. The Supreme Court has been closely divided and uncertain of itself. Fresh appointments to the Court could easily upset the balance between its libertarian members and those only slightly more numerous who would defer in these difficult cases to the judgment of the Congress. Public opinion is beginning to reflect the sober second thoughts of informed citizens concerning the importance in a democratic republic of tolerating unpopular minor parties, even when their leaders seem to be, as Justice Douglas expressed it, "miserable merchants of unwanted ideas." Misguided minor party politicians who would appeal to their natural right of revolution should not be aided and abetted by denying to their followers their constitutional rights to the free communication of ideas. It seems unlikely that the Supreme Court, as presently composed, will sanction the punishment of Communist party officials for refusing to be conscribed as agents of the party for the purpose of its registration under a law designed to discourage membership in the party. How, then, is party registration to be accomplished, if no person will volunteer to incur the risks of acting as the party's agent?

CHANGING VIEWS OF THE PRINCIPLES OF 1787

The principle of the separation of powers, as applied in the system of checks and balances, is the heart of the constitutional system. Many decisions of the Supreme Court involving the interpretation of the Constitution go more or less directly to its heart. Controversies have arisen concerning the extent of the lawmaking powers of the Congress and of the powers of the President in fulfilling his obligation to see that the laws are faithfully executed, concerning the delegation of policy-making powers by the Congress to administrative officers vested with wide discretionary authority, and concerning the power of the Supreme Court itself to review the decisions of politicians and administrative officials in various kinds of offices. In all these areas of judicial action the Supreme Court has been struggling with new views of the meaning of the Constitution, growing out of the new conditions and problems of a changing world. A convenient and useful illustration of the way the checks and balances system is developing is afforded by the trend of recent decisions relating to the power of legislative committees to investigate situations which might call for legislative action.

There has been a long line of cases dealing with the power of congressional committees to examine witnesses at hearings designed presumably to aid in the collection of information which might be helpful to the Congress in exercising its legislative powers. Chief Justice Warren, speaking for six of the seven members of the Court participating in a recent case, has made an effective statement of an important limitation on the legislative power to investigate.[29] A union labor leader named Watkins was examined by a subcommittee of the House Committee on Un-American Activities concerning his relations with the Communist party during World War II. He denied that he had ever been a member of the party but admitted having been in contact with party leaders. He refused, however, to discuss the relations with Communists of former associates of his, who to his best knowledge and belief had long since separated themselves from the Communist movement. He justified this refusal by claiming a constitutional right not to be forced to become an informer against old friends. He was cited to the House for his refusal to answer the subcommittee's questions and eventually convicted of contempt of Congress.

The Supreme Court reversed Watkins' conviction on the ground that neither Congress nor the committee had defined "un-American activities" with sufficient precision to enable the witness to know whether the questions he refused to answer were "pertinent to the subject under inquiry." His conviction, therefore, was void under the due process clause of the Fifth Amendment on account of the vagueness of the proceedings. Chief Justice Warren seized the opportunity to make a solid contribution to the education of the American people concerning the rights of witnesses before congressional committees. The constitutional rights of witnesses, he declared, should be respected by such committees as they would be in a court of justice. They "cannot be compelled to give evidence against themselves" and ' there is no Congressional power to expose for the sake of exposure."

Yet only two years later the Supreme Court refused by a narrow majority of five to four to give similar protection to a college teacher named Barenblatt who had been investigated by this same committee.[30] In this case the offending witness had refused to say whether he himself was, or ever had been, a member of the Communist party. He relied entirely on the decision in the Watkins Case for his defense. But the majority of the Court found that the questions which Barenblatt refused to answer were pertinent to the inquiry, since the committee was avowedly trying to find out to what extent the Communist party had infiltrated college and university faculties. The Court concluded that the public interest in protecting Barenblatt's rights under the First Amendment was overbalanced by its interest in the national security.

The minority of the Supreme Court were unreconciled to this decision. They could see no purpose in the investigation except exposure of the witness's association with Communists, if any, for the sake of exposure. Such exposure, by subjecting the witness to public ignominy and unpredictable injury, was in their opinion a kind of punishment without due process of law. The committee, by inviting such punishment, was usurping a judicial power, they concluded, which the Congress had no right to confer upon it. Two members of the Court, Justices Frankfurter and Harlan, seemed to the minority to have switched their votes between the decisions in the Watkins and Barenblatt cases from a libertarian to an authoritarian view of the rights of witnesses in legislative investigations. It was evident that a single switch in the opposite direction would reverse the judicial interpretation of the Constitution a second time.

The opportunity for the reinterpretation of the Constitution came four years later.[31] The president of the Miami branch of the National Association for the Advancement of Colored People had refused to produce a list of the members of his branch in response to a demand by a Florida legislative committee investigating Communist infiltration into the NAACP. His conviction in the Florida state courts for contempt was reversed by the Supreme Court of the United States by a new majority of five to four. The newly appointed Justice Goldberg joined the four judges who had dissented in the Barenblatt Case and wrote the opinion for the Court. It was an opinion which brought the trend of the Court's decisions back into line with the earlier decision in the Watkins Case.

Justice Goldberg made short work of the balance of interests argument employed by the Court majority in the Barenblatt Case. "Groups," he declared, "which themselves are neither engaged in subversive or other illegal or improper activities nor demonstrated to have any substantial connections with such activities are to be protected in their rights of free and private association." He was careful to explain that this decision did not impair the legislative right to investigate subversive activities by Communists or anyone else. But, he added, "the constitutionally protected free trade in ideas and beliefs may not be substantially infringed" without more evidence of wrongdoing than had been offered in this case. The legislative power to investigate, it is now clear, is limited by all the requirements of due process of law, which are the more necessary, Justice Goldberg pointed out, "when the challenged privacy is that of persons espousing beliefs already unpopular with their neighbors."

The present majority of the Supreme Court is manifestly determined to interpret the principle of the separation of powers in such a way as to maintain an effective system of checks and balances. In the long series of cases of witnesses before legislative investigating committees, it finally appeared that inquiries could not be pursued into the private affairs of presumably innocent persons without trespassing on the province of the judiciary. The Supreme Court has demonstrated its purpose to preserve the judicial power intact. Of course Supreme Court judges, like other public officers, may abuse their constitutional powers. If their self-control should be insufficient, fresh appointments to the Court should eventually produce a remedy. But the public interest clearly demands that the judges not shrink from the full performance of their duty to take care that the Constitution be rightly interpreted and that all public officers, by no means excluding themselves, keep within their constitutional bounds.

The cases of witnesses before legislative investigating committees also throw a revealing light upon the present condition of the second of the constitutional principles of 1787, that of federalism. In 1787, as has been shown, there was little disposition to look to the Supreme Court of the United States for the protection of the rights of the people of the states against infringement by their own state governments. On the contrary, there was a presumption in the federal Convention that the state courts, acting under the impact of the state declarations of rights, would protect the people against trespasses on their liberties not only by the state governments but also by the federal government. The general sense of a need for all possible protection of the people's rights led to the adoption of the first ten amendments to the Constitution, but these were designed to impose constitutional limitations upon the power of the federal government and were not intended to disturb the position of the states in the constitutional system. That situation was changed by the Fourteenth Amendment, and the way was cleared for an indefinite development of the authority of the Union at the expense of that of the states.

The litigation growing out of the anti-Communist drives in recent years illustrates how far the shift of power from the states to the Union has gone. For instance, the prosecutions under the Smith and McCarran Acts led eventually to a declaration by the Supreme Court that the federal government had preempted the field and relieved the states of further responsibility for hunting down and punishing offenders against the sedition laws.[32] The proceedings against uncooperative witnesses before legislative committees led eventually to the conclusion that the federal courts would determine the conditions under which state committee investigations might be conducted. In the recent case in which the rights of witnesses were finally determined by the Supreme Court, it was a state legislative committee, not a congressional committee, that provided the occasion for the judicial statement of the law.[33] The rights of citizens of the states to a general freedom of communication and association seem to have been effectively merged into the corresponding rights of citizens of the United States.

It is too soon to say, however, as some melancholy observers have noted, that the role of the states has become hopelessly inferior to what it was designed to be and that they have no future in the evolving constitutional system. To be sure, they are hard pressed between the mighty national government above and the demanding metropolitan authorities below. Nevertheless, they are spending more money than ever before and rendering greater services to their respective peoples. The preservation of suitable functions for the states offers substantial advantages to a nation possessing such diversified local interests and facing such multifarious obligations as those of the United States. In view of the increasing activity and usefulness of the state governments within the areas of their efficient service, it is untimely to speak of the wasting away of the states or the end of the federal system.

The third of the constitutional principles of 1787, the principle of pluralism, is best illustrated in recent years by the operation of the party system. The Republican party is now more than a hundred years old; the Democratic party goes back to the age of Jackson. Each of them is a unity for the purpose of nominating and electing Presidents. Both of them, however, are egregious diversities when faced by victory at the polls with the necessity of using the power to govern. Candidates for the presidency and for the Congress who can cooperate effectively in partisan electoral campaigns find frustrating obstacles to efficient cooperation thereafter in translating party policies into legislative action. The unequal growth of population in rural and urban areas and in different sections of the country has profoundly affected the relative strength of different local and special interests within the parties and greatly strains the traditional bonds tying the factions within the parties together. Yet the party organizations maintain their functional utility in national elections, thereby promoting the democratic character of the general government in a pluralistic nation. Thus the party system continues to be a major component of the constitutional system.

The essential characteristics of a living constitution are well exemplified by recent developments in the operation of the party system. Although, as has been shown, there was originally among the framers of the Constitution general hostility to factionalism in politics and considerable uncertainty regarding the theoretical nature and practical utility of partisanship, the two-party system was eventually accepted as an indispensable and beneficial feature of the constitutional system. Nevertheless, the political party was universally regarded as a strictly private and voluntary association of politicians and voters. The selection of party candidates for public office was considered to be no proper part of the electoral process that was subject to regulation by law. Party nominations were excluded from the legal regulation of elections.

Unforeseen circumstances compelled a change in the general practice of ignoring the problems of party government in the development of the constitutional system. The introduction of the official or so-called Australian ballot in lieu of ballots prepared by party managers for their own private convenience called for regulation of the conditions on which the names of the party candidates could be printed and distributed by state and local election officers. The introduction of direct nominations of party candidates by the voters in lieu of nominations at delegate conventions called for further control of primary elections in the public interest. But still the view prevailed that primary elections were not elections in the constitutional sense of the term. Governmental regulation of the organization and activities of parties seemed in direct conflict with the free enterprise system in politics.

In recent years it has proved impossible to maintain this traditional view of the place of partisan primaries in the constitutional system. The practice in parts of the South of restricting the primaries of the Democratic party to white voters raised the question whether such a practice was compatible with a constitutional system in which Negroes were supposed to possess the same rights as other men. It was easy for the federal courts to decide that, where the exclusion of Negroes from white primaries was authorized by state laws, there was a clear denial of the equal protection of the laws. But the question became more difficult when the exclusion of Negroes was the act of a party convention, representing a voluntary association of party members. In some of the Southern states the election laws were amended expressly to make clear that party authorities were not acting as agents of the state in regulating the conditions of party membership and participation in primary elections.

The Supreme Court was of two minds concerning the proper answer to this question. In the first case before the Court where an answer to this question became necessary, the judges agreed unanimously that the party was not an organ of the state and that the primary managers were not state officials in such a sense that their actions at primary elections were state actions.[34] They were bound, therefore, to follow the orders of the party convention and exclude Negroes from the party primaries. The fact that the principal primary election officials were the regular county clerks did not affect the decision of the Court, because in its opinion these officials were acting as agents of a political party which possessed the power to determine its own membership and select its own agents as long as not restrained by any law of the state. Since the Democratic white primaries in fact determined in advance the result of the official general elections, this decision seemed to sanction the denial of an effective vote to Negroes on account of their race, regardless of the Fourteenth and Fifteenth Amendments to the Constitution.

A few years later another case, raising the same question, came before the Supreme Court.[35] Eight of the nine judges thereupon reversed their opinions, holding that the right to vote in such a primary, like the right to vote in a general election, is a right secured by the Constitution. "When primaries become a part of the machinery for choosing officials, state and national," the Court declared, "as they have here, the same tests to determine the character of discrimination or abridgment should be applied to the primary as to the general election." Thus the Court recognized the existence of a changing political situation and changed its view of the practical application of an unchanging constitutional principle. The lone dissenter, who had written the opinion for the Court in the earlier case, protested bitterly, but without avail, that such abrupt overruling of the earlier decision "tends to bring adjudications of this tribunal into the same class as a restricted railroad ticket, good for this day and train only." However, the decision has stood without further change for twenty years. Its contribution to the Court's assumed task of infusing a new spirit into the old Constitution is now unchallenged.

The role of the national party in the constitutional system has been subjected to its severest test by the recent claim of a right by presidential electors, elected on a majority party ticket, to refuse to be bound by the nominations of the national convention and to cast their ballots for candidates of their own choice. Under the Constitution presidential electors are apparently entitled to vote for candidates of their own choice. The question is, what are their obligations to the political party which has nominated them for the office of elector? If there is a moral obligation to support the regular party candidate for President, can this obligation be legally enforced? If it cannot be enforced, what becomes of the two-party system regarded as an indispensable component of the constitutional system?

After the definitive establishment of the two-party system in the age of Jackson, the tradition of a moral obligation on the part of presidential electors to support the candidates of their party rapidly developed and was universally respected for many years. In 1876, when contested electoral votes seemed likely to be awarded to the Republican candidate on what seemed to most Democrats and some Republicans to be dubious grounds, thus giving him a majority of a single vote, a Republican elector, James Russell Lowell of Massachusetts, was urged to vote for the Democratic candidate in order to avert threatened resistance by outraged Democrats to the seating of the Republican candidate. Despite the danger of a renewal of civil war, Lowell refused to transfer his vote from the Republican to the Democratic candidate. He was morally bound, he declared, to support the candidate of the party which had chosen him to be an elector, and he could not repudiate this obligation, even to prevent civil war, without committing a gross breach of trust. But at more than one recent presidential election, electors nominated as Democrats have supported so-called Dixiecrat candidates. Their refusal to support the regular party candidate has not affected the result of an election, but it has raised the question whether the two-party system can operate in an acceptable manner if electors nominated by one of the major parties are free to vote for candidates of other parties. If they are free to bolt their party and thereby throw the election to the candidate of a different party, can the two-party system survive?

Time was when the Supreme Court would have refused to interfere with the freedom of presidential electors to vote as they pleased. It would have treated the question as political, to be decided by the political branches of government. Since the decision that the question of the validity of state districting laws is justiciable, there is the possibility that a similar view might prevail if a question were raised concerning the freedom of presidential electors to repudiate their party's choice of a presidential candidate. Has the two-party system, regarded as the indispensable means of making the constitutional system suitable for the people of a modern democracy, become an institution which the Supreme Court can try to protect? Or is the preservation of a democratic constitutional system dependent on the party loyalty of factious politicians? These questions could of course be disposed of by the adoption of a constitutional amendment establishing a system of direct presidential nominations and elections by the people. Under a living Constitution, which treats the two-party system as a preferred instrument of the democratic spirit, may these questions also be answered by the Supreme Court?

While the bipartisan system of party government continues to operate at least tolerably well, the principle of pluralism, like the other principles of 1787, will continue to serve as one of the effective means of protecting the people of the United States against the abuse of power by their representatives in the national government. The major party leaders know well that their leadership depends upon their showing due consideration for the various interests of the different factions of which the parties are composed. The major parties are normally more convenient combinations of factions representing special and local interests than other possible combinations of a more casual nature. If this were not so, there would be a growing popular demand for a realignment of parties. The ever-present possibility of such a party realignment is the best guaranty that the power to govern, which the bipartisan system tends to give to the leaders of one or the other of the major parties, will be used with studied moderation and with a rational regard for the public interest. The party system has developed in a different way from what was originally expected by James Madison and the other early advocates of a pluralistic political system. But the essential soundness of their concept of political pluralism seems to have been vindicated by the operation of the traditional bipartisan system.[36]

There can be no final interpretation of a living Constitution. It is not only the party system which occupies an uncertain position in the national constitutional system. The system of checks and balances still remains in uncertain equilibrium. The illogical but convenient arrangements for the distribution of function and power between the federal and state governments also illustrate the provisional character of that aspect of the Constitution that we call federalism. Nevertheless, despite the uncertainties inherent in a growing constitutional system, the American people can rely upon a settled practice for the adjudication of constitutional issues which has served more than tolerably well in the past and should continue to serve at least equally well in the future.

CHAPTER SEVEN

Frontiers

The frontier has always played a leading role in the development of the American constitutional system. Throughout the first century under the Constitution of 1787 the subjugation of the wilderness offered the greatest challenge to the people of the United States and the settlement of the West supplied the greatest problems to their political leaders. As the political scene shifted from a rural to a predominantly urban stage, there were bound to be corresponding changes in the political order. The old regional frontiers gave way to new frontiers in the cities. The American idea of a democratic republic met the challenge of new political ideas from abroad.

POLITICAL CONSEQUENCES OF THE NEW TECHNOLOGY

With the universal recognition that modern technology has brought revolutionary changes in man's relations to nature, there has come a slower and more faltering acknowledgment that there must also be revolutionary changes in man's relations with his fellow men. When Albert Einstein warned Franklin D. Roosevelt of the imminence of a revolutionary change in the art of war, and of the vital importance of anticipating the enemy in the mastery of the processes of atomic fission and fusion, he met with a ready and capable response to his warning. Einstein's subsequent warning to the peoples of the world that they must prepare for a corresponding revision of their relationship to one another found them less responsive. History tells us what the invention of gunpowder did to the feudal castles and walled cities of the Middle Ages and to the military and political systems founded on walls of masonry and knights in armor. The history of the impact of the most modern thermonuclear weapons on the contemporary world of so-called sovereign states is still in the making.

It is not only the atom bomb that is threatening the end of the traditional relations between the peoples of the world; motion pictures, radio and television, and other changes in the art of communication are affecting the struggle for power within the modern constitutional state no less profoundly. As printing combined with gunpowder to subvert the political order of the Middle Ages, so modern world-wide communications are combining with thermonuclear weapons and intercontinental delivery systems to bring about great changes in the distribution of power within the contemporary political order. It is the biggest and strongest states that profit most from the opportunity to make ultramodern weapons. It is the most conspicuous and ablest statesmen who profit most from the opportunity to utilize ultramodern means of communication.

Within the American constitutional system it is the executive power, and above all that of the chief executive and commander in chief, that has gained most from the new technology. The President has the readiest access both to the nation-wide networks and to the electronic push buttons. He decides when he will take to the airwaves to speak to his countrymen, and in the sudden moment of international crisis he will decide whether or not to push the buttons. The Founding Fathers never contemplated such a concentration of power as this. Their elaborate arrangements for the division and distribution of power among the separate branches of government and centers of authority provide no adequate means of checking the contemporary shifting of power and of maintaining the balance of the system.

The Congress, which might be expected to be the first to try to keep the balance in good working order, has resorted to a variety of expedients. The Twenty-second Amendment, submitted to the states in 1947 and ratified by the necessary three fourths of them in 1951, restricted the President to two terms of office. This "anti-FDR amendment," as it was sometimes called because it was designed to prevent a repetition of Roosevelt's achievement in getting himself re-elected for more than the traditional two terms, simply restored the presidency to its condition while the two-term tradition was operative. Obviously more than this was required to restore the political balance of power. In the nature of things the newly expanded authority of a constitutional President could not return of itself to its former dimensions. The Twenty-second Amendment might be a wise precaution for an uncertain future. Its immediate effect was negligible.

The wiser course for the Congress, instead of trying to reduce the power of the President in an age when the new technology inevitably increased that power, was to strengthen its own position by improving its methods of work. This it attempted to do by the adoption of the Legislative Reorganization Act of 1946. This carefully prepared measure reduced the number of congressional committees and increased their size, thereby enabling congressmen to give more attention to the work of their committees and make committee work more effective. It also provided more numerous and more competent technical and professional assistance for the committees and in a few cases established joint committees which were expected to gain greater prestige and perhaps also greater authority. But the Congress was unwilling to abolish the undemocratic and inefficient seniority system for selecting committee chairmen or to put necessary limits on their powers or on obstructive debate in the Senate. The Legislative Reorganization Act was a useful measure, but its reforms did not go far enough toward effective majority rule in the Congress.

The problem of strengthening the Congress by improving its methods of work is not an easy one. The majority party, which should be expected to take the lead in the enactment into law of the most important controversial measures, needs to control the working time of the two houses and their order of business. But it must not be permitted to deny to the minority party reasonable opportunity to present its views on controversial party measures by open and adequate debate. Moreover, there must also be due opportunity for other majorities, consisting of members of each of the two great parties, to get time for the consideration of other important measures which the majority party cannot or will not treat as party issues. Furthermore, there must be due opportunity for individual members, regardless of party, to get consideration for legitimate local and private business which does not interest a majority of any kind. Since the total volume of potential business is great, the more important measures must be privileged under the rules. Yet some time must be made available for the consideration of unprivileged business, provided that it is not too controversial for adoption by some sort of summary proceedings.

The two branches of Congress have met the pressure of business upon their time by developing two radically different methods of work. The House of Representatives, where because of the larger membership the volume of business is greater and the lack of time more pressing, has put the responsibility for getting business done in the leadership of the majority party, but it has dispersed the leadership so widely among the official party leaders and the chairmen of the standing committees that accountability to the party membership is seriously restricted. The Senate, on the other hand, has gone so far in the opposite direction, by assuring as much freedom of speech and action as possible to the individual senator, that effective party leadership is all but lost. The party leaders are compelled to conduct the business of the Senate by general consent, and objection by a senator to the leaders' plans for the conduct of business may bring proceedings to a halt. One senator, belonging to an intransigent minor party, could seriously obstruct the legislative process, and a resolute faction within either of the major parties can ordinarily prevent the enactment of any measure to which it is strongly opposed. In the House of Representatives, on the other hand, obstructionists can be easily brushed aside or even ignored. Each branch of the Congress pretends to possess a system of party government, but in neither is the system in its actual operation a happy combination of democracy and efficiency.

Many critics of the Congress believe that its methods of work could be greatly improved by improving the party system. Some wish to improve the party system by making it more responsive to presidential leadership. This kind of improvement, however, would not tend to create a better balance in the distribution of power between the executive and legislative branches of the government. Others would improve it by making the President more responsive to congressional leadership. This kind of improvement, however, would be contingent on the revival of methods of nominating candidates for the presidency which were tried and abandoned many years ago. More democratic methods of nominating candidates for the presidency than those now in use could be devised and might perhaps even be adopted. But the kind of method most likely to meet with popular acceptance, such as the direct nomination of candidates in nation-wide primaries, would not tend to restore the balance between the presidency and the Congress.

Nevertheless there are numerous minor improvements in congressional methods of work which taken together would strengthen the position of Congress. The abolition of the seniority system in both branches and the substitution of a more rational method of choosing committee chairmen would make for a more responsible and efficient legislative process by improving the relations between the official party leaders and their nominal followers. Members of Congress protest that the seniority system is justified by its convenience and that any system of election of committee chairmen by the majority party or appointment by the party leaders would cost more in terms of impaired party morale and solidarity than it would be worth in terms of improved legislative efficiency. Their protests, however, are unconvincing. Further experimentation with projects for the improvement of party government in the Congress would seem to promise some improvement also in the balance of the legislative system.

Other minor improvements in the legislative process are possible. But the legislative power is itself suffering impairment in this neotechnical age. The progressive development of the welfare state calls for more and more delegation of discretionary authority to administrative agencies. The lawmaking activities of the Congress are increasingly supplemented by the production of bylaws and other administrative regulations having the force of law, and the regulatory agencies take an ever greater share in the practical exercise of the federal lawmaking power. In the traditional area of the legislative process the Congress is fighting a losing battle against the possessors of the executive power.

A third recourse of the Congress in its search for a better balance between the executive and legislative branches of the national government is a more purposeful and systematic use of its power to investigate. The power to gather information concerning matters which may become the subjects of legislative action is a necessary and proper part of the legislative power. The vigorous use of the investigatory power has always been a prime mark of a vigilant and energetic Congress. But the temptation is strong to use this potentially great power for strictly partisan or merely personal instead of public purposes. Its partisan use is not improper in a partisan system of government, but the perversion of the investigatory power for the private ends of ambitious politicians can bring appalling abuses, as was convincingly demonstrated by the inquisitorial investigations of the Senate Committee on Government Operations under the spectacular and unscrupulous leadership of Senator Joseph R. McCarthy.

The Congress could and should make greater efforts to develop its power to investigate into a more efficient means of supervising and controlling the activities of the executive authorities. Existing legislative agencies, particularly the Comptroller General of the United States, can be helpful within the limits of their authority, but the Comptroller General can act only after the executive has acted, and the primary need is for more effective legislative action before the event. The Joint Committee on the Economic Report and the Joint Committee on Atomic Energy illustrate the good results that may be expected from intelligent efforts to improve the qualifications of the Congress for effective participation in the formulation of public policy respecting matters of increasing importance in a progressive welfare state in this neotechnical age. The further use of joint committees and the further development of their technical staffs could make a solid contribution to the strengthening of the position of the Congress in the constitutional system. It is too soon to conclude that the balance of the system has been irretrievably disturbed in the field of domestic affairs.

It is not only the Congress whose traditional place in the constitutional system has been threatened by the political consequences of the new technology; the Supreme Court also confronts the challenge of this neotechnical age. The executive power was never clearly defined by the framers of the Constitution. For their purposes it was enough to vest the whole of the power in the chief executive. Because of the deep silence of the Constitution concerning the nature and extent of this great but ill-defined power and its possible division and distribution among various kinds of executive authorities, endless conflicts arise between executive and judicial interpretations of the fundamental law.

The early years of the constitutional system were spent under the spell of the revolutionary distrust of kings. The framers came slowly and reluctantly to the conclusion that the executive power should be vested in a single person and that he should be permitted to seek re-election for more than a single term. Impressive titles were denied to him and special restraints were placed upon his powers of appointment and of management of the country's foreign relations. President Washington did what he could to exalt the authority of his office by introducing dignified rites and ceremonies for official occasions, but an ornate coach and two or three pairs of horses with footmen and outriders made less impression in an age of rudimentary communications than they might have made with the aid of ubiquitous television cameramen and radio newscasters. The practical problem in 1787 and for many years thereafter was to make the presidency as strong an office as it ought to be under a well-balanced constitutional system.

The constitutional history of the United States has been deeply marked with the conflicts between vigorous Presidents and resolute Chief Justices. Jefferson and Jackson contended with John Marshall, Lincoln with Roger B. Taney, and Franklin D. Roosevelt with Charles E. Hughes. Lesser Presidents, particularly Grover Cleveland and Theodore Roosevelt, contended with less certain Courts under lesser Chief Justices. Both the executive and the judicial power flowed and ebbed under the impact of varying personalities and changing circumstances. Yet certain trends have clearly emerged.

In the field of domestic affairs, though the actual power of chief executives has greatly increased, the practical capacity of the Supreme Court has proved equal to the responsibility vested in it. The last great trial of strength between the Court and the President was in the Steel Plants Seizure Case, where President Truman came off second best, even though the Chief Justice, whom he himself had appointed, was on his side.[1] The supremacy of the laws was impressively vindicated. Though none of the judges concurring in the decision stated the grounds for upholding the reign of law as effectively as they had been stated by Justice Miller in the earlier Arlington National Cemetery Case, the principle was made sufficiently clear. Presidents, like other public servants and like the people themselves, are governed by the law.

The authority of the Supreme Court is subject to occasional impairment by differences of opinion among the judges. Every close decision, where five judges favor one side of a case and four the other, and one judge seems to represent the margin of victory for the principle involved, is obviously more questionable than one in which the judges all agree. In all cases where dissenting judges assail the opinions of the majority with persuasive adverse arguments, the effect of the decision on the opinion of the general public is to some extent diminished. Such cases recall Lincoln's comment on the Taney Court's decision in the Dred Scott Case. It must be accepted as the law of the land as far as the particular case is concerned, but it cannot be allowed to stand unchallenged as a guide to the meaning of the fundamental law for all future time. Men who think it wrong will strive to change it by constitutional methods and occasionally, like Lincoln and his associates after the Dred Scott decision, they will succeed. It is clear that the rule of *stare decisis* is a sound rule in ordinary cases. But it is equally clear that an enlightened Supreme Court should not hesitate to overturn a questionable precedent when a majority of the judges are thoroughly convinced that a different decision is called for by better information or altered circumstances.

Lawyers, who look to the decisions of the Supreme Court for the most authentic authority in advising their clients, naturally prefer the certainty that follows from strict adherence to sound precedents. But the people themselves, who look to the Supreme Court as the most authoritative teacher of the principles of government under the constitutional system, want a Court which is equal to its responsibility as the head of the national system of political education. Excessive zeal for the judicial correction of petty errors in minor points of doctrine is to be deplored by all good citizens as well as by lawyers. But conscientious adherence to essential truth is the hallmark of the kind of Supreme Court that will best serve the public as chief educator of the sovereign people as well as chief dispenser of judicial power. In the long run such a Supreme Court will also contribute most to maintaining the balance of the constitutional system.

That the Supreme Court has exerted itself vigorously to play a constructive role in the development of the constitutional system in this neotechnical age is attested by the criticism which it has called down upon itself by several of its recent decisions. In 1962 the State Assembly of the Council of State Governments, a semiofficial agency with a self-appointed mission to preserve a suitable role for the states in the constitutional system, proposed a package of three amendments to the Constitution designed to curb the activities of the Supreme Court and diminish its political influence. The first of the three proposed amendments would revise the method of amending the Constitution so as to permit state legislatures to initiate amendments and secure their submission to the states for ratification without the approval of the Congress. The second would restrict the authority of the Court to deal with "political" questions by denying it jurisdiction over cases affecting the apportionment of representatives in state legislatures. The third would create a new "Court of the Union," consisting of the chief justices of the highest courts in the fifty states, with power to hear appeals from the Supreme Court in constitutional cases and correct such errors as in the opinion of this new super-supreme court might be committed by the Supreme Court.

The adoption of the first and third of these proposed amendments would destroy the balance of the federal system under the existing Constitution. That such destruction would cripple the power of the Supreme Court to maintain the balance of the national government is only one of the weighty objections to these proposals. Like other proposals by persons dissatisfied with particular Supreme Court decisions, proposals designed to impose constitutional limitations on the judicial power vested in the Supreme Court, these are likely to come to nothing. They serve to remind the Supreme Court that other organs of government under the Constitution besides itself must be presumed to be capable of governing according to their nature and that their actions should not be reviewed and set aside by the Supreme Court without clear and compelling reasons. That the Court will act effectively, when it is necessary to do so, is essential to the preservation of the constitutional system in good working order.

In the field of foreign affairs the Supreme Court has been less effective in maintaining the supremacy of law than in the field of domestic affairs. This has always been true, since the power of the chief executive is re-enforced in this field of action by his practical capacity as commander in chief to create situations in which it is difficult for a patriotic Congress and Court to refuse to support him. Moreover, his relations with foreign powers may be governed by executive agreements as well as by treaties, and the former are not contingent for their effectiveness upon the prior approval of the Congress. There is no need for the President to put his foreign policies in the form of treaties, which are a part of the law of the land, unless he needs to call upon the courts to assist in their enforcement. As long as he can enforce them by the military and other forces at his disposal, executive agreements with foreign powers afford the courts little opportunity to check what might seem to them to be abuses of the executive power. The President's control of policy in foreign affairs, therefore, is greater than in domestic affairs. Neither the Supreme Court nor the Congress can function as effectively in the former field as in the latter, and the system of checks and balances takes a different form.

Now the new technology has greatly increased the importance of the nation's foreign relations. Improvements in the means of communication and transportation have brought all the nations closer together. The development of thermonuclear weapons and intercontinental ballistic missiles has all but destroyed the defensive function of international boundaries. As recently as World War II, so-called sovereign states could still hope to protect their territory against attack from the air. But now attack with ultramodern weapons may come from outer space, against which obsolete doctrines of national sovereignty give no aid or comfort. The new responsibilities of the chief executive in the field of international politics call for new checks on the expansion of the executive power. Whether the balance of the constitutional system can be maintained under the changing conditions cannot be determined without investigating the nature and implications of the developing organization of peace.

POLITICAL CONSEQUENCES OF THE ORGANIZATION OF PEACE

The spirit of the new age in international politics appears most clearly in the Four Freedoms which President Roosevelt and Prime Minister Churchill formed into a fighting platform for the United Nations. The first of these freedoms—freedom of speech and communication—sprang from the American Declaration of Independence, and the second—freedom of religion—from the Virginia Statute of Religious Freedom, both cherished items in the American tradition of constitutional government. The third and fourth freedoms, however, were new. Freedom from want called for a collective effort to meet the most urgent needs of less developed peoples animated by a new and growing sense of world-wide community, and freedom from fear called for a collective effort to supply a suitable political organization for all peoples.

This was to be an organization in which the old revolutionary principles would have their proper place, but that place would be alongside new revolutionary principles struggling to be born.

The new revolutionary principles are authoritatively set forth in the second article of the first chapter of the United Nations Charter. By subscribing to the Charter the members of the United Nations renounced resort to aggressive war as an instrument of national policy and agreed to seek settlement of their disputes with one another by none but pacific methods. The adoption of these principles by the victors in World War II marked the beginning of a new era in the conduct of international relations. It meant an expanded role for politics in world affairs. The founders of the United Nations Organization did not expect the member states to cease to have serious disputes with each other, but they did expect a new world in which political controversies between such nations as themselves would be sustained with dignity until they could be adjusted by political means.

The revolution in world politics brought with it a corresponding revolution in world law. The old international law was the product of a system of independent states in which the leadership had been taken by the imperial and colonial powers. They made a body of international law responsive to their own views of their national interests. They enforced it by such measures as they deemed compatible with their interests and with their national honor. Logical consistency required that national statesmen and international lawyers recognize and respect the implied limitations on the scope of international law in a world of sovereign states.

The newly emerging international law rests upon the Charter of the United Nations. The Charter calls for a system of law administered by international agencies with global authority. The United Nations Organization is far from perfect, and the jurisdiction of its International Court of Justice leaves a great deal to be desired, but the new international law was intended to be veritable world law. The Statute of the International Court of Justice leaves no room for doubt on this point; it tolerates no rival legal system.

The first principle of the new system of world law is that the Organization is founded on the sovereign equality of the member states. But this principle is to be interpreted in the light of the structure of the Organization. Not all independent states hold an equal position before the law of the Charter. The Charter may be amended by a process which does not require the approval of all the member states, but all are bound by amendments, if adopted by the necessary majorities in accordance with the provisions of the Charter. The only states which cannot be bound by amendments to which they have not consented are the five permanent members of the Security Council, without whose consent proposed amendments cannot be adopted. These five member states enjoy a preferred position in the Organization. Other member states do not possess political equality with them, though they are equal to one another. Moreover, under the Charter, states which are not members of the United Nations are to act in accordance with its principles, so far as may be necessary for the maintenance of international peace and security, and the Organization is to insure that they do so act. The result seems to be the existence of three classes of so-called sovereign states under the law of the Charter.

The heart of the new system of world law is not the principle of sovereign equality but the maxim that all men are created equal. This self-evident truth, as it seemed to the signers of the American Declaration of Independence, leads now as then to a recognition that all men are endowed with some rights which are the same everywhere and which are secured by governments that derive their just powers from the consent of the governed. Consent may be expressed in different countries in different ways, since the self-determination of peoples may take various forms. It may even be tacit in countries with less developed constitutional systems. But if these principles of the Charter are interpreted in the light of the purposes of the Organization as expressed in Article I, they are clearly compatible with the corresponding principles of the American Revolution.

The last of the United Nations' principles is that of the right of member states to manage their own internal affairs without outside interference. This principle implies to Americans respect for the third of the American revolutionary principles. The right of revolution is not expressly reserved to the peoples of the member states, and it certainly may not be employed in such a way as to constitute a threat to the peace and security of other peoples. To this extent the third of the American revolutionary principles of government is limited by the terms of the United Nations Charter. This limitation, however, is not incompatible with the view that the foundations of the organization of peace under the Charter are consistent with American principles of political order.

The law of the United Nations Charter is a part of the law of the land in the United States. This follows from the provision of the Constitution which declares that all treaties made under the authority of the United States shall be the supreme law of the land, and that the judges in every state shall be bound thereby, anything in the Constitution or laws of any state to the contrary notwithstanding. Likewise any amendments to the Charter that may be duly adopted hereafter will become a part of the law of the land without further action by the American government. This is important, because there seems to be no constitutional limit to the world legislation that may be enacted by the process of negotiating multilateral international conventions which, when ratified by the United States, also become part of the nation's supreme law. The charters of the various specialized agencies of the United Nations became a part of the supreme law of the United States in this way, and the bylaws and administrative regulations having the force of law, which these agencies are producing in growing numbers, likewise would seem to be enforceable in the United States like other parts of the law of the land. Manifestly the reign of law in the United States can be greatly expanded by the process of international and world lawmaking.

Much of this new law is a timely response to the challenge of the new technology. The regulations of the World Health Organization, the Food and Agriculture Organization, the International Civil Aviation Organization, the International Telecommunications Union, the World Meteorological Organization, and the International Atomic Energy Agency clearly serve the interests, needs, or convenience of the United States as well as the rest of the world. The usefulness to the United States of other parts of the new law may be debatable. There has been controversy over some of the regulations proposed by the International Labor Organization and other projects proposed by the United Nations Educational, Scientific, and Cultural Organization. In fact the United States has refused to ratify many of the controversial measures, not actually enacted into law but proposed in the form of multilateral conventions, particularly those proposed by the International Labor Organization. It has also refused to ratify some important multilateral conventions proposed by the United Nations Organization itself, notably the antigenocide convention. Despite such refusals the expanding role of world law is plainly becoming an important factor in the development of the American constitutional system.

The most active critics of world lawmaking by the new world organizations have been those who feared the impact of the new legislation on the position of the states in the American federal system. They recalled how the national government had gained power, not granted by the Constitution, to preserve migratory wildfowl by negotiating a treaty with Canada for the protection of the birds.[2] None but unreasonable sportsmen objected to this alteration in the federal system. The objectors to more stringent factory laws and other legislation regulating the employment of labor were more influential. There were also growing fears that new world laws, if their incorporation into the law of the land were not checked, would interfere seriously with interracial relations in the United States. Those who preferred that these relations be regulated by the individual states in their own ways, rather than in a uniform manner by the United States, naturally were opposed to the practice of regulating them by world laws incorporated into the national system of legislation. The possible further extension of such a practice seemed to threaten the foundations of the federal system.

This was the kind of criticism which led to the proposed Bricker amendment to the Constitution. This proposal was discussed in the Congress through several years in the early 1950's and on one occasion came within a single vote of passing the Senate. It provided that treaties should not have the force of law, insofar as they contained provisions which could not have been enacted into law by the Congress under the existing Constitution. That the adoption of such an amendment would protect the federal system against erosion by such measures as the Migratory Wildfowl Treaty is clear. But objections to the limitation of the treaty-making power by an amendment of such uncertain scope and future effect eventually brought the effort to procure its adoption to an end.

The extension of the reign of law within the United States by the incorporation into the law of the land of new world law through the treaty-making power affects the constitutional system in other ways. Since treaties are made by the President, by and with the advice and consent of the Senate, this method of bringing law into existence excludes the House of Representatives from its normal participation in the lawmaking process. Since the Senate requires a two-thirds vote for the approval of treaties, this method of lawmaking also excludes the majority party from playing its normal role in the same process. The former consequence of the organization of peace under the United Nations Charter adds something to the other circumstances, which tend to exalt the Senate at the expense of the House of Representatives. The latter tends to complicate the operation of the party system, since the majority party rarely possesses a two-thirds majority in the Senate.

The major political parties have never been able to play the same role in the management of foreign affairs as in domestic politics. The maxim that party politics should stop at the water's edge is supported by sound patriotic sentiment. It is supported also by the consideration that a major party cannot safely make a partisan issue out of a promise to pursue a controversial policy in the field of foreign affairs, which may require a treaty for its successful implementation, since it cannot ordinarily hope to gain a two-thirds majority in the Senate by victory in a national election. Instead of majority rule, the method of consensus must be employed by an administration which seeks to play an active part in world politics. It is not necessary that it should hold the confidence of majorities of both parties, but it must be able to win sufficient support from the opposition party to give its supporters within its own party the means of ratifying treaties. Under ordinary conditions it is difficult enough, as every President discovers sooner or later, to make the two-party system work smoothly in domestic politics. Party government becomes excessively difficult, as Woodrow Wilson discovered after World War I, when an administration tries to extend it into the field of world politics.

The most politic administrations have sought to strengthen their position in world politics, wherever possible, by avoiding resort to the treaty-making power. The record of the annexation of foreign territory illustrates the resourcefulness of the party leaders in dealing with controversial international measures. Neither Texas nor Hawaii could be annexed by the normal process of treaty ratification. Both could be and were annexed by joint resolutions of the Congress. It is probable that much more might be accomplished by energetic and politic Presidents than has yet been attempted, through resort to the consent of both branches of the Congress expressed by ordinary majority votes, in lieu of invoking the treaty-making power.

Firm but prudent Presidents can also do much to carry out their policies in controversial areas by utilizing the power to make executive agreements with the heads of foreign states. It was by virtue of such agreements that the Nuremburg trials of so-called war criminals were conducted at the close of World War II. The trial and punishment of Japanese politicians and military commanders in Manila and Tokyo were similarly accomplished, though not without causing mental anguish to some American citizens and judges with exceptionally tender consciences. The volume of such executive agreements has increased greatly in recent years, and in some cases they have been recognized in the United States courts as superior in legal effect to the laws of individual states. In cases involving the confiscated assets of Russian insurance companies after the recognition of the Soviet Union by President Roosevelt, the claims of the United States government were preferred by the Supreme Court to those of the State of New York, which had been first to recognize the existence of a problem and to adopt a policy for dealing with it.[3] By its action the Supreme Court indicated a purpose to bring the operation of executive agreements within the rule of law, when it possessed jurisdiction over them. In time of peace, if not in time of war, the Court seemed capable of making good its proper authority under a constitutional system dedicated to the maintenance of the supremacy of law.

The organization of peace in this neotechnical age doubtless increases the opportunities of the President of the United States to play an influential role in world politics. At the same time it should increase also the influence of law in the governmental processes of the United States. The world organization is based on principles which are harmonious with corresponding principles of the American constitutional system. The reception of world law into the supreme law of the land should tend to counterbalance to a significant degree the revolutionary effects of modern technology on the constitutional system. As the President of the United States becomes a more powerful figure abroad as well as at home, he should become also an outstanding symbol not only of respect for the principle of popular sovereignty but also of submission to the supremacy of law in the relations between men and between nations.

President Kennedy promptly addressed himself to the realization of this vision. Speaking before the General Assembly of the United Nations, September 25, 1961, he declared that "we far prefer world law, in the age of self-determination, to world war, in the age of mass extermination." He went on to elaborate this declaration in carefully measured words. "To destroy arms," he said, "is not enough. We must create even as we destroy—creating worldwide law and law enforcement as we outlaw worldwide war and weapons. . . . The American delegation will suggest a series of steps to improve the United Nations' machinery for the peaceful settlement of disputes, for on-the-spot factfinding, mediation, and adjudication, for extending the rule of international law. For peace is not solely a matter of military or technical problems; it is primarily a problem of politics and people."

THE SPIRIT OF THE CONSTITUTIONAL SYSTEM

January 1, 1963, was the one-hundredth anniversary of the issuance of the Emancipation Proclamation. President Lincoln's epochal act may be regarded from the viewpoint of its immediate effects as a political and military stratagem. The preliminary announcement in September 1862 that the proclamation would be issued, if violent resistance to the laws of the land continued, helped win the congressional elections of that year, and the actual declaration that slaves held within the lines of the resisting forces would be freed contributed to the eventual military victory. The more distant effects of the Emancipation Proclamation are less obvious, but at least it put a new spirit into the constitutional system.

There has been much controversy concerning the spirit of the Constitution and its place in the practical operation of a system of constitutional government. One of the original arguments against the adoption of the Constitution was that the authority of the Supreme Court would be superior to that of the Congress in the interpretation and practical application of the Constitution, and that the power of the Court to construe the laws according to the spirit of the Constitution would enable it to mold them into whatever shape it might think proper. Addressing himself to this argument in the eighty-first number of *The Federalist,* Alexander Hamilton remarked that "there is not a syllable in the plan under consideration [that is, the proposed Constitution] which *directly* empowers the national courts to construe the laws according to the spirit of the Constitution, or which gives them any greater latitude in this respect than may be claimed by the courts of every State." He admitted, however, "that the Constitution ought to be the standard of construction for the laws, and that wherever there is an evident opposition, the laws ought to give place to the Constitution." Hamilton, it may fairly be inferred from these and other remarks in this number of *The Federalist,* was not dismayed at the thought that judges, both federal and state, might be guided in constitutional cases by what they believed to be the spirit of the Constitution, and doubtless he cherished the hope that this part of the business of the courts under the constitutional system would give additional protection to the interests of those classes of the people which he believed to be most in need of protection against the abuse of power by legislative majorities under the influence of what he termed "those ill humors, which the arts of designing men . . . sometimes disseminate among the people themselves."[4]

Whether or not the spirit of the Constitution should be a guide in its interpretation is a question which the Supreme Court, speaking for itself, was long reluctant to answer. In general the judges professed a purpose to stick to the letter of the fundamental law, leaving the interpretation of its spirit to the political branches of the government. In the close case of *United States v. Macintosh,* decided in 1931, a Yale professor of theology, who had been a chaplain in the Canadian Army during World War I and had made an excellent record for bravery under fire, wished to become a naturalized citizen of the United States. However, he declined to take the oath of allegiance without a mental reservation that, though not opposed to fighting for his country in a just war, he could not take part in a war which his conscience might tell him was unjust. Chief Justice Hughes and several of his associates were of the opinion that the spirit of the Constitution implied respect for such conscientious scruples on the part of the Congress which had made the law governing the admission of aliens to citizenship, though it had not expressly said so in the text of the Naturalization Act. But a majority of the Court were unwilling to give the act such a construction without a clear indication that this was in fact the intention of the Congress, and citizenship was denied to Macintosh.

Chief Justice Hughes was greatly chagrined by the Court's refusal to breathe what he believed to be a proper spirit into the Constitution. In a vigorous dissent he declared that such a construction as the majority had put on the Naturalization Act was "directly opposed to the spirit of our institutions. . . . Apart from the terms of the oath it is said that the respondent [Macintosh] has failed to meet the requirement of 'attachment to the principles of the Constitution.' Here again is a general phrase which should be construed, not in opposition to, but in accordance with, the theory and practice of our government in relation to freedom of conscience." Fifteen years later this view of the spirit of the Constitution was adopted by a new majority of a rejuvenated Court in the definitive case of *Girouard v. United States*. Justice Douglas, speaking for the new majority, declared that "the victory for freedom of thought recorded in our Bill of Rights recognizes that in the domain of conscience there is a moral power higher than the State." Thus at last, for the reasons first clearly stated by Chief Justice Hughes, the opinion of the dissenting judges in the Macintosh Case became the law of the land.[5]

Whatever may have been the expectations of the framers concerning the role of the judges in constitutional cases—Jefferson's, as we have seen, were different from Hamilton's in certain respects—there can be no doubt of the perennial importance in the constitutional system of the views which successive generations of judges have held concerning the spirit of the Constitution. At first there was a general disposition to assign to the Constitution an aristocratic spirit. Adams and Jefferson agreed in distinguishing between the natural aristocracy of talent, which regarded public office as a public trust, and the artificial aristocracy of inherited position and wealth, which in their opinion was apt to put its special interests ahead of the general public interest. That the Supreme Court under the Federalist judges did tend to read an aristocratic spirit into the constitutional system is clear from the record of their actions on the bench. That this spirit was Hamiltonian rather than Jeffersonian is also clear.

The basic fact in the history of the American people during the nineteenth century is the subjugation of the wilderness and the settlement of the West. The frontier did not finally disappear until near the end of the century, and its influence tended to dominate national politics, as has been noted, from the age of Jackson on through the age of Lincoln and the Antislavery Republicans. It also tended to dominate the interpretation of the spirit of the Constitution. Jacksonian judges under Chief Justice Taney began the process of reading a democratic spirit into the fundamental law. Under the impact of the Emancipation Proclamation, Lincolnian judges broadened and deepened this democratic spirit. The last special champion of this particular spirit was the elder John Marshall Harlan, who bequeathed to later times the seminal maxim, the Constitution is color-blind.

In the present century the Supreme Court has read into the Constitution, and then read out of it again, the spirit of the free-enterprise system. No person, the Fifth and Fourteenth Amendments declare, shall be deprived of liberty without due process of law. Now liberty, as many a judge has observed, is a word of many meanings and may include much or little according to the mood of the moment. It came to include for a while a nearly unlimited freedom of contract, which lawmakers were held incompetent to abridge by measures which might seem to a majority of the judges to be unreasonable. John Stuart Mill's treatise *On Liberty* and Herbert Spencer's *Principles of Sociology* supplied an acceptable justification for the expansion of the due process clause into a constitutional guarantee of the free-enterprise system in American industry.

The failure of the government-sponsored Reconstruction Finance Corporation in the Great Depression of the early 1930's to conserve the crumbling foundations of nineteenth-century capitalism marked the beginning of the end for the dominance of the free-enterprise spirit in the Constitution. The new concept of the welfare state began with the establishment of the Federal Deposit Insurance Corporation by the New Deal administration. In the heart of the free-enterprise system, the realm of business finance, the freedom of individual bankers to pursue their own interests in their own way had to yield to the superior public interest in the development of a system of banking capable of supplying greater protection for the savings of the people. Justice Cardozo's opinions in the Social Security Cases marked the definitive triumph of the new spirit in the interpretation of the Constitution. The Supreme Court which read the new spirit into the Constitution proved capable with the advent of fresh judges of determining acceptably how much of the new spirit would be appropriate for the constitutional system of the new welfare state.

The process of infusing the Constitution with the new spirit took time. The final seal of approval on the welfare state came in 1963 with the decision of the last in a long series of right-to-counsel cases involving the duty of the trial courts under the developing concept of due process of law to see that indigent persons charged with crime are provided with competent lawyers for their defense.[6] The right of alleged criminals to their day in court had been recognized long before the Revolution as an essential possession of a free people and was expressly protected in the Constitution of 1787. Their right to have competent counsel by their side during their trial was recognized more slowly, and the duty of the courts to supply such counsel at public expense, if necessary, was stoutly contested by tradition-bound judges. But judges who recognized such a duty became a majority of the Supreme Court when Justice Goldberg succeeded Justice Frankfurter in 1962, and they lost no time in making their view of the obligations of a welfare state prevail over earlier views concerning the responsibilities of a national government to its people.

It cannot be supposed that the process of change in the spirit of the Constitution ends with the triumph of the welfare-state spirit. The welfare state itself is presumably only a phase of the evolutionary process in the development of the American people. Changing conditions in the American way of life will continue to call for corresponding changes in the thinking of the people, which will be reflected in the policies of the government and in the spirit of the Constitution. The earlier spirits of the Constitution have not vanished without trace. The free-enterprise spirit, the democratic spirit, the aristocratic spirit—all continue to contribute to the existing tone of the constitutional system. Their respective influences will long be felt in the interpretation of a living Constitution designed, as John Marshall declared, for the ages to come. But the dominant spirit in the immediate future will be the welfare-state spirit.

It might have been supposed that the one-hundredth anniversary of the Emancipation Proclamation would be widely celebrated in the United States by all good people interested in the spirit of the Constitution. Such, however, was not the case. It was not even widely celebrated by that portion of the people presumably most interested in a broad interpretation of the democratic spirit—the American Negroes. Neither Emancipation Proclamation Day nor Lincoln's birthday received marked special attention by Afro-American citizens in 1963. On the contrary, that was the year selected for massive demonstrations of dissatisfaction with the condition of the Negro race generally in the American way of life and particularly in the constitutional system.

The framers of the Fourteenth Amendment expected that the first and fifth sections of that amendment would produce quick and substantial progress toward equality of opportunity for all Americans regardless of race or color. The power conferred upon the Congress by the fifth section to enforce the constitutional guarantees of the first section by appropriate legislation seemed adequate to secure the objects intended, the protection of the freedmen against unjust discrimination by state action in the former slave states and assurance of the full enjoyment everywhere of the privileges and immunities of American citizenship. But the early civil rights bills, enacted by the Congress, were declared by the Supreme Court to be inappropriate legislation insofar as they went beyond the narrow limits of measures designed merely to prevent open discrimination against Negroes by state law.[7] The Supreme Court refused also to set aside state laws making formal distinctions between the races, which could become the basis of informal discrimination against the colored race, provided that discrimination was not expressly authorized by these laws.[8] Eventually the Supreme Court even struck down those portions of the congressional civil rights laws, protecting the equal rights of Negroes to make use of facilities for interstate travel, which were clearly within the scope of the federal lawmaking power. This was done on the ground that the judges could not presume that the Congress would have passed acts of such limited application if the lawmakers had foreseen that the Court would not sanction the main body of the federal civil rights legislation.[9] These decisions enabled the Southern states to establish separate public school systems for the races and to extend their policy of racial segregation to railroads and steamship lines serving interstate as well as local travelers. They made possible a kind of second-class citizenship for Negroes which was clearly in conflict with the spirit, if not the letter, of the Fourteenth Amendment.

To prevent this result was one of the reasons for the adoption of the Fifteenth Amendment. Congressional lawmakers hoped that Negroes who possessed the right to vote would be able to protect themselves against the enactment of unfriendly legislation by state lawmakers. These hopes proved vain for more than three quarters of a century. In the Southern states, legislatures intent on keeping the freedmen in a condition of second-class citizenship found ways of excluding them from effective participation in elections. In the North and West the voters showed by their reaction to congressional efforts to enforce the Fifteenth Amendment, notably at the congressional election of 1890, their repugnance to federal intervention in Southern elections for the purpose of protecting the right of the freedmen to vote. Problems which could not be solved satisfactorily under the existing circumstances were by tacit consent left to the healing processes of time.

Eventually the indefinite postponement of effective enforcement of the provisions of the Fourteenth and Fifteenth Amendments relating to the civil and political rights of Negroes produced vigorous protests from the Negroes themselves. It proved impossible to continue to confine them to second-class educational and employment opportunities. Enforced participation in a war to make the world safe for democracy generated a demand for untrammeled participation in the practice of democracy at home. Enforced participation in a second World War, for the purpose of enabling all peoples everywhere to enjoy the four major freedoms, fostered more resolute determination to gain a greater share in their enjoyment for Americans of African extraction. Belated efforts to secure the blessings of liberty to the Negroes on the plea that, armed with the ballot, they could defend their claims to a proper share in such blessings, culminated in the civil rights crisis of 1963.

The case for the wider application of the new spirit in the constitutional system recalls Justice Jackson's plea for proper respect for the rights of indigent Americans suffering from the impact of the Great Depression.[10] The language of this eloquent plea for respect for the rights of one oppressed class of Americans can be shaped to fit the case of another oppressed class of Americans. If I doubted whether the citizenship of Afro-Americans were enough to open the gates to first-class membership in the American Commonwealth, the valiant justice might have declared, my doubt would disappear on consideration of the obligations of such citizenship. The Afro-American owes a duty to render military service, and this Court has said that this duty is the result of his citizenship.[11] A contention that a citizen's duty to render military service is suspended by the color of his skin, Justice Jackson might have continued, would meet with little favor. Black or white, a person's citizenship under the Constitution pledges his strength to the defense of the United States, and his right to enjoy the blessings of liberty in the land he must defend is something that must be respected under the same instrument. Unless this Court, he might have concluded, is willing to say that citizenship of the United States means at least this much to the citizen, then our heritage of constitutional privileges and immunities is only a promise to the ear to be broken to the hope, a teasing illusion like a munificent bequest in a pauper's will.

The time came when Afro-Americans were no longer content to regard the promises of the Fourteenth and Fifteenth Amendments as no more than teasing illusions. They refused to consider a mandate of the sovereign people as an empty promise. They rushed to the registration offices in unprecedented numbers in often vain efforts to make good their claim to an equal right to vote. They sat in silent protest in places presumably open to the public, where they insisted they were entitled to the same treatment as other Americans. They thronged the streets to demonstrate their determination to be first-class citizens.

The time has also come for the Supreme Court to face its full responsibilities as the best available interpreter of the letter of the Constitution and a potentially highly useful interpreter of its spirit. It should furnish the American people with an authentic description of the privileges and immunities of citizenship and to that end make the most of the opportunities which will be afforded by cases growing out of the arrests of citizens for demonstrating in the streets their attachment to the purposes and principles of the Constitution. The equal protection of the laws clause of the Fourteenth Amendment is not broad enough to prevent all the various unlawful abridgments of the rights of citizens. The due process clause cannot conveniently be employed to secure all the promised blessings of liberty to all Americans. It is the privileges and immunities of citizenship clause of the Fourteenth Amendment that was originally intended to be, and should presently become, the main bulwark of the rights of Americans.

The desirability of making a more constructive use than in the previous seventy years of the privileges and immunities of citizenship clause of the Fourteenth Amendment was argued by members of the Supreme Court in the leading free speech case of the C.I.O. against Mayor Hague of Jersey City. Justice Roberts contended persuasively that the right to assemble peaceably for the purpose of discussing national legislation such as the National Labor Relations Act is a privilege inherent in national citizenship and should be so declared by the Court. Justice Black and Chief Justice

Hughes were of the same opinion and also would have liked to see such a broad interpretation of the Fourteenth Amendment announced by the Court. But Justice (later Chief Justice) Stone objected strongly to the adoption of novel doctrines of constitutional interpretation when the case could be conveniently and rightly decided under the due process clause, and no majority could be found for the broader view of the rights of national citizenship. This favorable opportunity to put greater vitality into the privileges and immunities of citizenship clause of the Fourteenth Amendment was unhappily lost.

Justice Jackson referred to this memorable debate between distinguished members of the Supreme Court in his later opinion in the "Okie" Case. "I do not ignore or belittle the difficulties," he declared, "of what has been characterized by this Court as an 'almost forgotten' clause. But the difficulty of the task does not excuse us from giving these general and abstract words whatever of specific content and concreteness they will bear as we mark out their application, case by case. That is the method of the common law, and it has been the method of this Court with other no less general statements in our fundamental law. This Court has not been timorous about giving concrete meaning to such obscure and vagrant phrases as 'due process,' 'general welfare,' 'equal protection,' or even 'commerce among the several States.' But it has always hesitated to give any real meaning to the privileges and immunities clause, lest it improvidently give too much." If the Supreme Court would act upon Justice Jackson's good advice, it could give this almost forgotten clause a greater amplitude than it might have received when he was protesting against its long neglect.

The method of constitutional development by judicial interpretation in controversial cases, recommended by Justice Jackson, is well suited for an age of profound and rapid change. The present neotechnical age is one of the most dynamic in history and calls for changes in the constitutional system as well as in other aspects of the American way of life. There is no more appropriate means of making the necessary adjustments between the age that is passing away and the age that is coming into being than to put a new spirit into the Constitution. This cannot be accomplished as well by a single revolutionary political act of sweeping content as by a gradual adaptation of traditional rules of law to the changing conditions by the judicial process. In a time like the present the Supreme Court doubtless does act as a lawmaking and not merely as a law-administering body. But it is a lawmaking body capable of greater deliberation than ordinary representative legislatures. It is or should be more capable of balancing the needs of the foreseeable future against the more exigent claims of an insistent present.

The Supreme Court, moreover, has a broader function in the constitutional system than that of breathing a new spirit, suitable to the coming age, into the Constitution by the technical administration of justice. It must not only decide the cases that are brought before it; it must also justify the decisions by reasoning that can enlighten and inspire the people of the country. When Chief Justice Earl Warren sought to justify the decision of the Court in the School Desegregation Cases by observing that "separate facilities are inherently unequal," he was not only explaining to the parties in these cases the grounds for reversing the earlier rule that separate but equal schools for the two races were consistent with the Fourteenth Amendment, but was also giving to the American people a better understanding of one of the basic principles of the Constitution. The successful teacher knows that his answers must be persuasive as well as authoritative. This educational function of the Supreme Court is in the long run no less important than the Court's strictly judicial functions, since in the long run, in a democratic country, the law of the Constitution cannot be other than what a sovereign people wish it to be.

The system of political education is the true foundation of any constitutional system. This basic principle of political science, first announced by Aristotle in the age of the classical Greek commonwealths,[12] must be learned anew by every generation that lives in an age of change. In a democratic age it is not only the professional teachers who play an important role in the educational system, the servants of the people in public offices of various kinds, particularly the judges, must take their parts in the process of political education. Our great Chief Justices have clearly understood the transcendant importance of this creative role and have manifestly composed their published opinions in the great leading cases with one eye on the parties to the case and the other steadily directed toward the sovereign people of the United States. Thus popular sovereignty and the reign of law may be maintained in fruitful partnership and the essential character of the constitutional system preserved. It is a system to which, in the strictest sense of the words, the spirit gives life.

The spirit of the constitutional system is, of course, something more than the spirit of the written Constitution. The constitutional system includes the Declaration of Independence as well as the Constitution of 1787. Moreover, the unplanned party system is an indispensable component of the constitutional system, and politicians as well as judges have made an essential contribution to the American way of political life. A constitutional system is not a theoretical scheme written on paper but a body of people, including politicians and judges, engaged in certain kinds of actions in ways which constitute what is called political behavior and which are recognizable as characteristic of the membership of the body. The American constitutional system has always been a high-spirited system, in which different blends of spirit have been dominant in the successive stages of its development. The successive stages can be most conveniently distinguished by the relations between the most influential judges and the political parties from which the judges have been chosen.

The Federalist Supreme Court was inspired by the same political philosophy that animated the authors of the Virginia Plan for a more perfect Union. The Federalist judges naturally strove to infuse the new constitutional system with the aristocratic nationalistic spirit which had so greatly influenced, without wholly dominating, the framing of the Constitution. The supreme expression of this spirit was Marshall's opinion for the Court in the great case of *Marbury v. Madison.* Marshall asserted not only the supremacy of the Constitution over ordinary laws but also that of the Court over the other branches of the national government. The subsequent impeachment of Justice Chase came near enough to success to make Marshall more cautious in challenging the authority of the President and the Congress. Under his leadership, however, the Jeffersonian Republican Court was no less zealous than the Federalist Court in vindicating the authority of the national government over the people of the more perfect Union. On the whole the prevailing spirit was Hamiltonian rather than Jeffersonian.

At the end of his judicial career, as at the beginning, Chief Justice Marshall came into sharp conflict with the President of the United States. He fared no better in his attempt to dictate to Andrew Jackson than in his attempt to dictate to Thomas Jefferson. The Jacksonian Court under Chief Justice Taney began by showing a marked deference to the political branches of the government. The spirit of the Court seemed to harmonize with the spirit of the age. But the age of Jackson proved to have a split personality, and the Dred Scott decision repeated the error of *Marbury v. Madison.* Taney, originally a Federalist, ended his judicial career by reverting to type in a fruitless challenge to the authority of Abraham Lincoln. Meanwhile the democratic nationalist spirit of the early Jacksonians merged into the new democratic nationalist spirit of the Antislavery Republicans.

The Antislavery Republican Court under Chief Justices Chase and Waite had a more difficult task than its predecessors and lacked the advantage of equally masterful leadership. Judges of the stature of Miller and Field and of Bradley and Harlan were well qualified to protect and preserve the national and democratic spirit of Antislavery Republicanism, but the assimilation into the constitutional system of radical precedents established by resolute wielders of the war power in an age of unprecedented domestic violence severely taxed the statesmanship of the Court. As has been shown, the Reconstruction amendments to the Constitution did not secure to the freedmen the full enjoyment of the rights of citizens, but they did compel the Court to face the changing needs of an emerging industrial age before the implications of an industrial-age spirit could be justly appreciated. Under Chief Justice Fuller, originally a Democratic selection for the Court, there was a protracted transition from the spirit of the Radical Republican to that of the Conservative Republican period. The triumph of the free-enterprise spirit under the Conservative Republican Court was qualified by the intrusion of the first harbingers of a new spirit, more suitable for a welfare state, under Chief Justices White, Taft, and Hughes.

Under Chief Justices Stone and Vinson the New Deal and the Fair Deal registered their necessary and proper effects on the now complex traditional spirit of the constitutional system. The welfare-state spirit was well expressed by Justice Cardozo in his opinions for the Court in the Social Security Cases.[13] These acts were found to be valid as exercises in the congressional spending power. "The governmental power of the purse," declared this learned and liberal-minded judge, "is a great one." The definition of the general welfare in particular cases and the choice of methods of promoting it lie within the sound discretion of the Congress.

Under the Republican Chief Justice Warren, a rejuvenated Democratic Court is bringing into operation a new blend of the various constitutional spirits which have contended for the mastery of the constitutional system. Under the bold leadership of a Chief Justice gifted with rare sensitivity to the changing temper of the times, the Court is striking a new balance between the rival forces of tradition and reason. A new insistence on the equal rights of all citizens, regardless of race or color, is supported by a new interest in the essential nature of the basic rights that flow from American citizenship. The first provision of the Fourteenth Amendment, which long seemed destined to studied neglect by the Supreme Court, at last is coming into its own as the cornerstone of the American system of ordered liberty. The dissenting opinion of Chief Justice Hughes in the Macintosh Case, the concurring opinion of Justice Jackson in the "Okie" Case, and the dissenting opinions of Justices Black and Douglas in the Politburo Case—all of which reflect Chief Justice Hughes' cherished vision of a higher freedom under the Constitution—are demonstrating their sterling worth as rational guides to the spirit of the constitutional system on its newest frontier.

In the development of the constitutional system the great judges have done constructive work in dissenting opinions as well as when they spoke for a majority of the Court. They have been able to function in this way because the system is a developing system based on a living Constitution. They have responded to a sense of duty not only to maintain a reign of law but also to inspire a sovereign people. These judges have been aware that they headed both the judicial branch of the national government and the national system of political education. They have been aware too that they should strive to be both great judges and great teachers. They have known that they were not only the custodians of a great inheritance from the past but also the guardians of the frontiers of the future. They have known too that a people can be a truly sovereign people only when they are capable of maintaining their basic rights and fundamental freedoms as if forced to gain them by their own efforts each day anew.

In the long run the American system of political education is the foundation of the American constitutional system. The American political way of life rests upon the faith that a real sovereignty of the people may coexist with an actual reign of law. Since 1776 the American people have learned that by taking thought they can make such progress toward their political goal as to justify that traditional and rational faith.

FOOTNOTES

CHAPTER ONE

1. A copy of the Declaration of Independence engrossed on parchment, signed on August 2, 1776, and later by fifty-six members of the Continental Congress, is on public view in the National Archives at Washington. The best account of the various texts of the Declaration and of its actual drafting is that edited by Julian P. Boyd, *The Declaration of Independence*, rev. ed. (Princeton: Princeton University Press, 1945). For instructive commentaries on the sources of the political ideas in the Declaration and on their subsequent interpretation, see Carl L. Becker, *The Declaration of Independence: A Study in the History of Political Ideas* (New York: Harcourt, Brace & Company, 1922), and Edward Dumbauld, *The Declaration of Independence and What It Means Today* (Norman, Okla.: University of Oklahoma Press, 1950).

2. For a systematic and comprehensive discussion of the development of the American Whig political philosophy, see Ralph Barton Perry, *Puritanism and Democracy* (New York: Vanguard Press, Inc., 1944).

3. John Locke, *Two Treatises of Civil Government* (London: 1690). There have been many later editions, both in England and in the United States, of this influential work by the American Whigs' favorite political philosopher. An excellent recent edition is that by Peter Laslett (Cambridge, Eng.: Cambridge University Press, 1960).

4. The first edition of Sir William Blackstone's *Commentaries on the Laws of England* was published in four volumes at Oxford, 1765-1769. The first American edition, also in four volumes, was published at Philadelphia in 1771-1772.

CHAPTER TWO

1. A witty and wise investigation of the meaning of this expression is Howard Mumford Jones' *The Pursuit of Happiness* (Cambridge, Mass.: Harvard University Press, 1953).

2. The first edition of Jean Jacques Rousseau's *Le Contrat Social* was published in Amsterdam in 1762. There have been numerous subsequent editions, in many different languages, of this most popular and controversial of all political treatises.

3. The first edition of Thomas Hobbes' *The Leviathan* was published in London in 1651. A recent scholarly edition is that edited by Thomas I. Cooke (New York: The Macmillan Co., 1947).

4. The most complete account of the business transacted by the Continental Congress is Edmund C. Burnett's *The Continental Congress* (New York: The Macmillan Co., 1941). The best interpretation of its spirit is Lynn Montross' *The Reluctant Rebels: The Story of the Continental Congress, 1774-1789* (New York: Harper & Brothers, 1950).

CHAPTER THREE

1. For the definitive account of Washington's attitudes at this stage of his career, see Douglas Southall Freeman, *George Washington: A Biography*, 6 vols. (New York: Charles Scribner's Sons, 1948-1954); see especially Vol. V (1952), ch. 27, "Peace Is Almost an Anti-Climax," and Vol. VI (1954), ch. 3, "Influence Is No Government."

2. For the important contribution of James Madison to the development of the Virginia Plan, see Irving Brant, *The Life of James Madi-*

son, 6 vols. (Indianapolis: The Bobbs-Merrill Co., Inc., 1941-1961), Vol. II, *James Madison the Nationalist, 1780-1787* (1948); see especially ch. xxvi, "Prologue to the Constitution."

3. See Publius, *The Federalist,* No. 51. Publius was the pen name of the three collaborators—Alexander Hamilton, James Madison, and John Jay—who together wrote eighty-five papers in support of the ratification of the federal Constitution; they appeared in New York newspapers during the interval between the adjournment of the Constitutional Convention in September 1787 and the meeting of the New York ratifying convention the following summer. Madison was the author of No. 51. The collected papers were published in two volumes at New York in 1788 and quickly became the foremost American treatise on the science of government. There have been many subsequent editions. The most recent, and scholarly, editions are those edited by Benjamin F. Wright (*The Federalist,* Cambridge, Mass.: Harvard University Press, 1961) and Jacob E. Cooke (*The Federalist,* Middletown, Conn.: Wesleyan University Press, 1961). The Wright edition contains an introduction which is a valuable commentary on the philosophy of government expounded in *The Federalist.*

4. There are several excellent accounts of the framing of the federal Constitution. The most thorough is that by Charles Warren, *The Making of the Constitution* (Boston: Little, Brown & Co., 1928; rev. ed., 1937); the liveliest is that by Carl Van Doren, *The Great Rehearsal: The Story of the Making and Ratifying of the Constitution of the United States* (New York: Viking Press, 1948). For other references, see Arthur N. Holcombe, *Our More Perfect Union* (Cambridge, Mass.: Harvard University Press, 1950).

5. For further discussion of this topic, see Arthur N. Holcombe, "The Role of Washington in the Framing of the Constitution," *The Huntington Library Quarterly.* XIX (August 1956), 317-334.

6. For the text of the Virginia Plan, see the *Debates in the Federal Convention of 1787 As Reported by James Madison, May 29, 1787.* There was no official record of the debates in the Federal Convention. Madison kept a private record, based on his personal shorthand notes, taken day by day and completed after the end of the Convention. This record of the debates was not made public until after his death, when the Madison papers were purchased by Congress and published in 1840. The *Debates* were reprinted in 1845 as Volume V in the second edition of Jonathan Elliot's *The Debates in the Several State Conventions on the Adoption of the Federal Constitution, Together with the Journal of the Federal Convention,* etc. (1st ed., 4 vols., Washington: published by the editor by authority of the Congress, 1836). The best edition of Madison's *Debates* is that edited by Gaillard Hunt and James Brown Scott (Washington: Carnegie Endowment for International Peace, 1920). This version of the text was reprinted in a volume entitled *Documents Illustrative of the Formation of the Union of the American States* and was published by direction of the Congress under the editorial supervision of the Legislative Reference Division of the Library of Congress, Sixty-ninth Congress, First Session, House Document No. 398 (Washington: Government Printing Office, 1927). This document also contains notes on the debates, discovered up to that time, kept by other delegates, of which those by Judge Yates of New York are the most important. The most complete collected edition of the various sets of notes on the debates in the Convention is that edited by Max Farrand, *Records of the Federal Convention,* 3 vols. (New Haven: Yale University Press, 1911; rev. ed., 4 vols., 1937). The text of the New Jersey Plan appears in Madison's *Debates,* June 15, 1787.

7. *Debates,* June 19, 1787.

8. *Debates,* August 6, 1787.

9. *Debates,* September 12, 1787.

10. *Debates,* June 25, August 10, 1787.

11. *Debates,* July 5, 13, 1787.

12. *Debates,* August 7, 10, 1787.

CHAPTER FOUR

1. *Debates,* June 8, July 17, 1787.

2. *Debates,* June 18, 1787.

3. *Debates,* June 27, 1787.

4. *Debates,* June 16, 1787.

5. *Debates,* June 2, 3, 7, 1787.

6. *Debates,* June 21, 29, 1787.

7. *Debates,* June 20, 1787.

8. *Debates,* July 6, 1787.

9. Montesquieu's *L'Esprit des Lois,* published in Geneva in 1748, was known to the framers chiefly through Blackstone's references to it in his *Commentaries.* See also *The Federalist,* No. 47.

10. *The Federalist,* No. 51.

11. *Debates,* June 18, 1787.

12. See the Congressional or Farrand edition of the Convention debates.

13. *Debates,* July 3, 1787.

14. See C. M. Walsh, *The Political Science of John Adams* (New York: G. P. Putnam's Sons, 1915).

15. *Debates,* August 7, 10, 1787.

16. *Debates,* August 15, 1787.

17. *The Federalist,* No. 51; see also No. 10.

CHAPTER FIVE

1. See Holcombe, *Our More Perfect Union,* ch. IV, "The Unplanned Institution of Organized Partisanship."

2. *Ibid.,* ch. V, "The Natural Limits to Partisan Power." This analysis does not lead to a general theory of political parties in modern democracies, but it does throw light on the special case of the two-party system in the national politics of the United States. For further light on the general theory of parties, see Madison's much discussed tenth number of *The Federalist.*

3. *Texas v. White,* 7 Wall. 700 (1868).

4. The Civil Rights Cases, 109 U.S. 3 (1883).

5. *Crandall v. Nevada,* 6 Wall. 35 (1868).

6. *Edwards v. California,* 314 U.S. 160 (1941).

7. For further discussion of this important question, see *Hague v. C.I.O.,* 307 U.S. 496 (1939). In this leading free speech case, besides the official opinion for the Court, the concurring opinions of Justice Stone and Chief Justice Hughes should be particularly noted.

8. *Plessy v. Ferguson,* 163 U.S. 537 (1896).

9. This subject is best treated in Robert G. McCloskey, *The American Supreme Court* (Chicago: University of Chicago Press, 1960). See especially Ch. V, "Constitutional Evolution in the Gilded Age: 1865-1900." The latest decision expanding the procedural rights of persons under the due process clause is *Gideon v. Wainwright,* 372 U.S. 335 (1963), guaranteeing to indigent defendants in criminal cases a right to counsel.

10. *Holden v. Hardy,* 169 U.S. 366 (1898).

11. *Lochner v. New York,* 198 U.S. 45 (1905).

12. *Stettler v. O'Hara,* 243 U.S. 629 (1917).

13. *Adkins v. Children's Hospital,* 261 U.S. 525 (1923).

14. *Morehead v. Tipaldo,* 298 U.S. 587 (1936).

15. *West Coast Hotel Company v. Parrish,* 360 U.S. 379 (1937).

16. Robert H. Jackson, *The Struggle for Judicial Supremacy* (New York: Alfred A. Knopf, Inc., 1941).

17. Arthur M. Schlesinger, *The Age of Roosevelt,* Vol. I, *The Crisis of the Old Order, 1919-1933* (Boston: Houghton Mifflin Co., 1957).

18. The Income Tax Cases, 157 U.S. 429; 158 U.S. 601 (1895).

19. U.S. Bureau of the Census, *Congressional District Data Book* (Districts of the 88th Congress) supplement to *Statistical Abstract of the United States* (Washington: Government Printing Office, 1963). See also periodical reports in *Congressional Quarterly Almanac,* published by Congressional Quarterly, Inc., Washington, D.C.

20. U.S. Department of Commerce, *1960 Census of Housing,* Vol. II, *Metropolitan Housing* (Washington: Government Printing Office, 1963).

21. See Holcombe, *Our More Perfect Union,* ch. XII, "To Perfect the More Perfect Union," especially pp. 415-424.

CHAPTER SIX

1. For the complete and interesting correspondence on this subject between Roger Sherman and John Adams, see C. F. Adams, *The Works of John Adams,* 10 vols. (Boston: Little, Brown & Co., 1850-1856), Vol. VI, pp. 427-442.

2. *The Federalist,* No. 10; see also No. 39. Both these numbers were written by James Madison.

3. *Luther v. Borden,* 7 How. 1 (1849).

4. *Pacific States Telephone and Telegraph Company v. Oregon,* 223 U.S. 118 (1912).

5. *Plessy v. Ferguson,* 163 U.S. 537 (1896).

6. *Brown v. Board of Education,* 347 U.S. 483 (1954).

7. *Brown v. Board of Education,* 349 U.S. 294 (1955).

8. *Mary Hamilton v. Alabama,* 84 Sup. Ct. Rep. 982 (1964). In this case Miss Hamilton, who had been brought into court on charges growing out of an antisegregation demonstration, refused regardless of her color to answer questions put to her by a public prosecutor who persisted in addressing her by her first name instead of by her last name like white persons in that court. She was adjudged to be in contempt of court. The Supreme Court, in reversing her conviction, declared the Alabama court's action to be "a manifest violation of the State's duty to deny no one the equal protection of the laws." See also *Johnson v. Virginia,* 373 U.S. 61 (1963).

9. *Schenck v. United States,* 249 U.S. 47 (1919).

10. *Mutual Film Corporation v. Industrial Commission of Ohio,* 236 U.S. 230 (1915).

11. *Burstyn v. Wilson,* 343 U.S. 495 (1952).

12. *Duncan v. Kahanamoku,* 327 U.S. 304 (1946).

13. *United States v. Lee,* 106 U.S. 196 (1882).

14. *Hirota v. MacArthur,* 335 U.S. 876 (1948).

15. *Youngstown Sheet and Tube Company v. Sawyer,* 343 U.S. 579 (1952).

16. *Kennedy v. Mendoza-Martinez; Rusk v. Cort,* 372 U.S. 144 (1963).

17. Glendon A. Schubert, *Constistitutional Politics: The Political Behavior of Supreme Court Justices and the Constitutional Policies That They Make* (New York: Holt, Rinehart and Winston, Inc., 1960), p. 78.

18. *Minersville School District v. Gobitis,* 310 U.S. 586 (1940).

19. *West Virginia State Board of Education v. Barnett,* 319 U.S. 624 (1943).

20. *Everson v. Board of Education,* 330 U.S. 1 (1947); *McCollum v. Board of Education,* 333 U.S. 203 (1948); *Zorach v. Clauson,* 343 U.S. 306 (1952).

21. *Engel v. Vitale,* 370 U.S. 421 (1962).

22. *School District v. Schempp; Murray v. Board of School Commissioners,* 374 U.S. 203 (1963).

23. *Colegrove v. Green,* 328 U.S. 549 (1946).

24. *Baker v. Carr,* 369 U.S. 186 (1962); *Gray v. Sanders,* 372 U.S. 368 (1963).

25. A year later, in the case of *Wesberry v. Sanders,* decided February 17, 1964, the Supreme Court supplemented these decisions by supplying a rule for establishing constitutional election districts. This case also arose in Georgia, but unlike the previous case it applied to congressional districts. The earlier decision in the Illinois Congressional Districts Case was expressly overruled, and the Georgia legislature was instructed to lay out congressional districts in such a way that "as nearly as practicable one man's vote in a congressional election is to be worth as much as another's." This, the Court declared, was the plain meaning of Article I, Section 2 of the Constitution, which provides that representatives in Congress be chosen "by the people of the several states."

26. *Dennis v. United States,* 341 U.S. 494 (1951).

27. *Yates v. United States,* 354 U.S. 298 (1957).

28. *Communist Party of the United States of America v. Subversive Activities Control Board,* 367 U.S. 1 (1961).

29. *Watkins v. United States,* 354 U.S. 178 (1957).

30. *Barenblatt v. United States,* 360 U.S. 109 (1959).

31. *Gibson v. Florida Legislative Investigation Committee,* 372 U.S. 539 (1963).

32. *Pennsylvania v. Nelson,* 350 U.S. 497 (1956).

33. See the Gibson Case above.

34. *Grovey v. Townsend,* 295 U.S. 45 (1935).

35. *Smith v. Allwright,* 321 U.S. 649 (1944).

36. See Holcombe, *Our More Perfect Union,* ch. XII, pp. 400-407.

CHAPTER SEVEN

1. *Youngstown Sheet and Tube Company v. Sawyer,* 343 U.S. 579 (1952).

2. *Missouri v. Holland,* 252 U.S. 416 (1920).

3. *United States v. Pink,* 315 U.S. 203 (1942).

4. *The Federalist,* Nos. 78 and 81.

5. *United States v. Macintosh,* 283 U.S. 605 (1931); *Girouard v. United States,* 382 U.S. 1 (1946).

6. *Gideon v. Wainwright,* 372 U.S. 335 (1963).

7. The Civil Rights Cases, 109 U.S. 3 (1883).

8. *Plessy v. Ferguson,* 163 U.S. 537 (1896).

9. *Butts v. Merchants and Miners Transportation Company,* 230 U.S. 126 (1913).

10. *Edwards v. California,* 314 U.S. 160 (1941).

11. See Chief Justice White's opinion for the Court in the Selective Service Act Cases, 245 U.S. 366 (1918).

12. See Aristotle's *Politics,* Book V, ch. 10 (§1310a). See also Book VIII, ch. 1 (§1337a).

13. The Social Security Cases, 301 U.S. 508; 301 U.S. 619 (1937).

14. For a discussion of the Politburo Case (*Dennis v. United States*), see text, pp. 133-135.

BIBLIOGRAPHICAL ESSAY

The data of the science of government are the acts of men. In a developing constitutional system, the men whose acts are most important are those who articulate the purposes of the body of people concerned and who define the principles on which the body politic is organized. In the great political experiment known as the American constitutional system, the most significant data are those relating to the drafting of the Declaration of Independence and the Constitution of the United States and to their subsequent interpretation.

That which contributes most to the permanence of a constitution, as Aristotle observed long ago, is the adaptation of education to the constitutional form of government. American constitution-makers, however, have given little attention to formal political education. In general the political education of the American people is an unplanned by-product of the American way of life. Something is achieved toward a popular understanding of the American way of political life by formal instruction in public schools. More is achieved through the activity of political leaders who by precept and especially by example have taught the essentials of American democratic republicanism.

The outstanding teachers have been the leading members of the drafting committees in the Continental Congress of 1776 and in the Federal Convention of 1787, together with the most influential Supreme Court judges at successive stages in the further development of the constitutional system. The references in this brief essay have been chosen from a vast mass of material dealing with the public and private lives of these famous men who have put the essentials of the system in durable form. This material is useful not only because it throws light on their political behavior and thinking, but also because it gives a better understanding of the relations between the actions of public men and the circumstances of their lives as well as of the conditions of the people for whom they acted. Some of the material is autobiographical, but most of it is the work of modern writers who have had improved opportunities to study the contributions of the Founding Fathers and their successors.

The roots of the American constitutional system reach far back into the origins of the English constitution. The medieval jurists who sponsored the maxim *Non sub homine sed sub Deo et lege* were in their way the first of the Founding Fathers. Men who possessed the courage and intelligence to tell English kings that they were not above the law, but like other men were subject to God and the law, hold an important place in American constitutional history. So do the outstanding colonial governors, such as Governor Bradford of Plymouth, who led the Pilgrims in their struggle to live under the Mayflower Compact, and Governor Winthrop of the Massachusetts Bay Colony, who transformed the charter of an English trading company into the constitution of an American commonwealth. Our concern, however, is not with history but with the principles and practices which compose the substance of our constitutional system.

The records of the proceedings in the Continental Congress in 1776 (see chapter II, note 4) and of the debates in the federal Convention of 1787 (see chapter III, note 6) show what the Founding Fathers did, and much of what they said, in giving form to the constitutional system, but they do not show enough about the purposes and principles of the outstanding leaders. The most active and influential members of the committee which drafted the Declaration of Independence were Benjamin Franklin, John Adams, and Thomas Jefferson, about each of whom we now possess incomparable stocks of information. Complete collections of their writings, both public and private, have been or are being published together with fresh and intimate accounts of their lives. Similar scholarly work has been done on the lives of some of the leaders in the Convention of 1787 and in the Supreme Court.

How free a freedom-loving man could be in the freest of the English colonies in North America before the Revolution is best revealed in Benjamin Franklin's *Autobiography*. The definitive edition of Franklin's writings is in course of publication by the Yale University Press under the general title *The Papers of Benjamin Franklin*. Volume 7, published in 1963, brings the collection only to 1758. The *Autobiography* can be found in many separate editions and in the earlier collections of Franklin's works edited by John Bigelow (12 vols., New York: G. P. Putnam's Sons, 1904) and by A. H. Smythe (10 vols., New York: The Macmillan Co., 1907). For the reader interested primarily in Franklin's political ideas and career, the best of his many biographies is still Carl Van Doren's *Benjamin Franklin* (New York: Viking Press, 1938). Franklin was not a political theorist but a practical politician, and his acquaintance with the British government at Westminster was too close to permit him, like some other American Revolutionists, to substitute admiration of the supposed principles of the British constitution for a systematic philosophy of government. He was America's first great national democrat and became the outstanding symbol of a way of political thinking which greatly influenced the behavior of the average man in early American politics.

John Adams was not only the most vigorous champion of the Declaration of Independence on the floor of the Continental Congress but also the most systematic and persistent theorist of constitutional government in his time. The definitive edition of his writings is in course of publication by the Harvard University Press under the general title *The Adams Papers*. The *Diary and Autobiography of John Adams* (Cambridge, Mass.: Harvard University Press) are contained in four volumes published in 1961. Page Smith has written an excellent life of Adams utilizing material recently made available (2 vols., Garden City, N.Y.: Doubleday & Company, Inc., 1962). The outstanding monument to Adams' political thinking is the Declaration of Rights and Frame of Government, composing the Constitution of Massachusetts adopted in 1780. Adams' aristocratic republicanism, though not without influence in the framing of the federal Constitution, was never clearly understood by his countrymen. The best comprehensive study of Adams' political ideas is Correa M. Walsh's *The Political Science of John Adams* (New York: G. P. Putnam's Sons, 1915).

Thomas Jefferson, the actual draftsman of the Declaration of Independence, was the most influential writer on American government and politics in the years of the Founding Fathers. Though he never composed a systematic and comprehensive treatise on the science of government, his political ideas were set forth with extraordinary effectiveness in numerous state papers and in the extensive private correspondence that he carried on throughout his life. A definitive edition of his writings, public and private, edited by Julian Boyd, is in course of publication by the Princeton University Press under the general title *Papers of Thomas Jefferson*. Since 1950, sixteen volumes have appeared and the total seems likely to be near fifty. Among the earlier editions of Jefferson's writings, the most nearly satisfactory is Paul Leicester Ford's (10 vols., New York : G. P. Putnam's Sons, 1892-1899). A judicious selection from Jefferson's writings of special interest to students of his political ideas is Edward Dumbauld's *Jefferson's Political Writings: Representative Selections* (New York: Liberal Arts Press, 1956).

Jefferson's political ideas in the earlier stages of his career were most clearly stated in his *Notes on Virginia,* published shortly after the end of his term as governor. Appended to the *Notes* was a memorandum on the Virginia state constitution, which he considered seriously defective. This memorandum had little effect on constitutional reform in Virginia (the original constitution was not revised until more than a half-century after its adoption), but Jefferson's views on constitution-making were well known by the framers of the Virginia Plan for a national constitution and through that plan exerted a germinal influence on the federal Constitution of 1787. In the later stages of Jefferson's career his political ideas were set forth more adequately in his private letters than in his public papers. His correspondence in his old age with John Adams is of special interest and has been separately published (Paul Wilstach, ed., *Correspondence of John Adams and Thomas Jefferson,* Indianapolis: The Bobbs-Merrill Co., Inc., 1925). Also of special interest is Gilbert Chinard, ed., *The Correspondence of Jefferson and DuPont de Nemours* (Baltimore: The Johns Hopkins Press, 1931). The best life of Jefferson is now Dumas Malone's *Jefferson and His Time* (Boston: Little, Brown & Co., 1948-), of which three volumes had appeared by 1962, bringing the narrative to Jefferson's election to the presidency. For the student of the science of government, the most satisfactory one-volume life is Gilbert Chinard's *Thomas Jefferson: The Apostle of Americanism,* 2nd rev. ed. (Boston: Little, Brown & Co., 1948). On the relations between Jefferson's political thinking and the conditions of his time, the most stimulating book continues to be Charles A. Beard's *Economic Origins of Jeffersonian Democracy* (New York: The Macmillan Co., 1915). Beard's earlier study, *An Economic Interpretation of the Constitution of the United States* (New York: The Macmillan Co., 1913), is less satisfactory and must be read with caution (see particularly Beard's new introduction to the second edition, published in 1935). An interesting appraisal of Jefferson's influence on the later development of the constitutional system is C. M. Wiltse's *The Jeffersonian Tradition in American Democracy* (Chapel Hill: University of North Carolina Press, 1935).

Any realistic account of the political thinking of the framers of the Constitution of 1787 must begin with the president of the federal Convention. Because Washington maintained a strict compliance with the injunction of secrecy imposed by the Convention on its members, there is nothing to be found in his businesslike diary or in his private letters on the political conversations which went on behind the scenes at Philadelphia in the hot summer of 1787; and since he took no active part in the debates on the Convention floor, some writers have supposed that his influence in the actual making of the Constitution must have been small. This notion is certainly a mistake. The role of the strong silent man in a deliberative assembly may baffle historians and biographers, as it apparently did Washington's greatest biographer, Douglas Southall Freeman, but that role need not be without an important influence on the proceedings. The latest biographer of Washington's close friend and host in Philadelphia during the Convention, Robert Morris (Eleanor M. Young, *Forgotten Patriot, Robert Morris,* New York: The Macmillan Co., 1950), who like Washington had very little to say during the proceedings on the floor, ventures to claim more for her hero than Freeman does for Washington. "If all the facts were known," this author concludes, "it would be found that Robert Morris was a factor of more consequence than casually appears." My reasons for thinking that this conjecture is even more applicable to Washington are set forth in an essay, "The Role of Washington in the Framing of the Constitution," *Huntington Library Quarterly,* XIX (August 1956). Nevertheless, Freeman's account of Washington's activities at the Philadelphia Convention illuminates the business of constitution-making (see the sixth volume of his magisterial life of Washington, *Patriot and President,* New York: Charles Scribner's Sons, 1954).

The framer whose activities in the summer of 1787 at Philadelphia have been rated most highly is James Madison. His latest and best biographer, Irving Brant, devotes the second of six outstanding volumes on Madison's life mainly to this topic under the title *James Madison: Father of the Constitution* (Indianapolis: The Bobbs-Merrill Co., Inc., 1950). Instead of using this dubious figure of speech, I would prefer to describe young Congressman Madison in this stage of his eminent career as the most helpful of Washington's junior partners in the political business of constitution-making. Madison was much more than an eighteenth-century "brain-truster" but hardly the "father" of even the Virginia Plan, which was obviously the product of difficult compromises within the Virginia delegation. He was indeed the most active and influential of a group of brilliant young politicians who, under Washington's leadership, bore the burden of the constructive work in the committees and on the floor on behalf of the Nationalist cause, as Brant's excellent account makes sufficiently clear.

Three of these able young men, Madison, Gouverneur Morris, and Rufus King, served on the important Committee on Postponed Matters and Unfinished Business, which near the close of the Convention worked out the final set of compromises which gave the Constitution its definitive structure and tone and enabled the Convention to bring its deliberations to a successful conclusion. These same three young men, together with Alexander Hamilton, served under the highly respected Dr. Johnson of Connecticut on the Committee of Style and Arrangement, which put the text of the Constitution in its final form. The standard biographies of all these framers throw light on the making of the Constitution. Of special interest to the student of the science of government is Charles R. King's *The Life and Correspondence of Rufus King,* 6 vols. (New York: G. P. Putnam's Sons, 1894-1900). Alexander Hamilton's collected papers, though numerous and well edited, are less useful to the reader interested primarily in the actual framing of the Constitution. Hamilton was one of Washington's principal political aides as well as a one-time favorite military aide, but his services were more important in the operations leading up to the Convention and in the struggle for ratification than in the proceedings at Philadelphia. The final form of the Constitution, as Hamilton frankly confessed on the floor of the Convention, was far from what he would have liked best.

There is a notable scarcity of useful biographical material relating to the activities of most of the leading framers. The injunction of secrecy was sedulously respected. Of the five members of the Commitee of Detail, which prepared the first draft of the Constitution, there are helpful biographies of only three and no extensive collections of personal papers. Richard Barry's *Mr. Rutledge of South Carolina* (New York: Duell, Sloan & Pierce, Inc., 1942) is an interesting account of the activities of the committee chairman, whom the author contends was the true father of the Constitution. C. P. Smith's *James Wilson, Founding Father* (Chapel Hill: University of North Carolina Press, 1956) is a scholarly appraisal of the services of Madison's associate in the defense of the Nationalist cause in the Convention. W. G. Brown's *Oliver Ellsworth* (New York: The Macmillan Co., 1905) emphasizes the achievements of that one of the principal framers who was perhaps best satisfied with the finished work of the Convention. There is much room for the play of the imagination, and hence for disagreement, in interpreting such evidence as exists concerning the actual framing of the Constitution.

Next to the lives of the framers, the lives of the great Chief Justices throw the most light on the development of the constitutional system. Outstanding is Albert J. Beveridge's *The Life of John Marshall*, 4 vols. (Boston: Little, Brown & Co., 1916-1919), which is an epic though excessively eulogistic study of the last of the Virginia Nationalists. Carl B. Swisher has supplied a searching and judicious study of *Roger B. Taney* (New York: The Macmillan Co., 1935). Modern times also have their strong-minded Chief Justices. Merlo J. Pusey's *Charles Evans Hughes*, 2 vols. (New York: The Macmillan Co., 1951) should be compared with Alpheus T. Mason's *Harlan Fiske Stone: Pillar of the Law* (New York: Viking Press, 1956).

Among the associate justices there are several whose biographies are noteworthy. Donald G. Morgan's *Justice William Johnson: The First Dissenter* (Columbia: University of South Carolina Press, 1954) deals effectively with the transition from a Jeffersonian Republican to a Jacksonian Democratic Court. Francis P. Weisenburger's *The Life of John McLean* (Columbus: Ohio State University Press, 1937) throws light on the relations between law and politics in the age of Jackson. Charles Fairman's *Mr. Justice Miller and the Supreme Court, 1862-1890* (Cambridge, Mass.: Harvard University Press, 1939) is a valuable contribution to an understanding of constitutional development after the Civil War. It should be compared with Carl B. Swisher's scholarly study of Miller's formidable rival on the Court, *Stephen J. Field: Craftsman of the Law* (Washington: Brookings Institution, 1930). Alpheus T. Mason's *Brandeis—A Free Man's Life* (New York: Viking Press, 1946) should be compared with Joel F. Paschal's *Mr. Justice Sutherland: A Man Against the State* (Princeton: Princeton University Press, 1951). More light on the causes of the great court-packing battle in 1937 is shed by studies of the "great dissenter" Oliver Wendell Holmes. Max Lerner's *The Mind and Faith of Justice Holmes* (Boston: Little, Brown & Co., 1948) is a useful selection of Holmes' writings, both on and off the Court, and furnishes an excellent introduction to the study of the judicial transition from the free-enterprise system to the modern welfare state. Mark De Wolfe Howe's *Justice Oliver Wendell Holmes* (Cambridge, Mass.: Harvard University Press, 1957-), of which two volumes have appeared, bringing the story as far as Holmes' appointment to the Massachusetts Supreme Court in 1882, promises to rival Beveridge's life of Marshall as a study in judicial statesmanship.

DECLARATION OF INDEPENDENCE

In Congress, July 4, 1776
The unanimous Declaration of the thirteen united States of America

When in the Course of human events, it becomes necessary for one people to dissolve the political bands which have connected them with another, and to assume among the Powers of the earth, the separate and equal station to which the Laws of Nature and of Nature's God entitle them, a decent respect to the opinions of mankind requires that they should declare the causes which impel them to the separation.

We hold these truths to be self-evident, that all men are created equal, that they are endowed by their Creator with certain unalienable Rights, that among these are Life, Liberty and the pursuit of Happiness. That to secure these rights, Governments are instituted among Men, deriving their just powers from the consent of the governed, That whenever any Form of Government becomes destructive of these ends, it is the Right of the People to alter or to abolish it, and to institute new Government, laying its foundation on such principles and organizing its powers in such form, as to them shall seem most likely to effect their Safety and Happiness. Prudence, indeed, will dictate that Governments long established should not be changed for light and transient causes; and accordingly all experience hath shown, that mankind are more disposed to suffer, while evils are sufferable, than to right themselves by abolishing the forms to which they are accustomed. But when a long train of abuses and usurpations, pursuing invariably the same Object evinces a design to reduce them under absolute Despotism, it is their right, it is their duty, to throw off such Government, and to provide new Guards for their future security.—Such has been the patient sufferance of these Colonies; and such is now the necessity which constrains them to alter their former Systems of Government. The history of the present King of Great Britain is a history of repeated injuries and usurpations, all having in direct object the establishment of an absolute Tyranny over these States. To prove this, let Facts be submitted to a candid world.

* * *

We, therefore, the Representatives of the united States of America, in General Congress, Assembled, appealing to the Supreme Judge of the world for the rectitude of our intentions, do, in the Name, and by authority of the good People of these Colonies, solemnly publish and declare, That these United Colonies are, and of Right ought to be Free and Independent States; that they are Absolved from all Allegiance to the British Crown, and that all political connection between them and the State of Great Britain, is and ought to be totally dissolved; and that as Free and Independent States, they have full power to levy War, conclude Peace, contract Alliances, establish Commerce, and to do all other Acts and Things which Independent States may of right do. And for the support of this Declaration, with a firm reliance on the Protection of Divine Providence, we mutually pledge to each other our Lives, our Fortunes and our sacred Honor.

ARTICLES OF CONFEDERATION

To all to whom these Presents shall come, we the undersigned Delegates of the States affixed to our Names send greeting.

Whereas the Delegates of the United States of America in Congress assembled did on the fifteenth day of November in the Year of our Lord One Thousand Seven Hundred and Seventy-seven, and in the Second Year of the Independence of America agree to certain articles of Confederation and perpetual Union between the States of Newhampshire, Massachusetts-bay, Rhodeisland and Providence Plantations, Connecticut, New York, New Jersey, Pennsylvania, Delaware, Maryland, Virginia, North-Carolina, South-Carolina and Georgia in the Words following, viz.

"Articles of Confederation and perpetual Union between the States of Newhampshire, Massachusetts-bay, Rhodeisland and Providence Plantations, Connecticut, New-York, New-Jersey, Pennsylvania, Delaware, Maryland, Virginia, North-Carolina, South-Carolina and Georgia.

ARTICLE I. The stile of this confederacy shall be "The United States of America."

ARTICLE II. Each State retains its sovereignty, freedom and independence, and every power, jurisdiction and right, which is not by this confederation expressly delegated to the United States, in Congress assembled.

ARTICLE III. The said States hereby severally enter into a firm league of friendship with each other, for their common defence, the security of their liberties, and their mutual and general welfare, binding themselves to assist each other, against all force offered to, or attacks made upon them, or any of them, on account of religion, sovereignty, trade, or any other pretence whatever.

ARTICLE IV. The better to secure and perpetuate mutual friendship and intercourse among the people of the different States in the Union, the free inhabitants of each of these States, paupers, vagabonds and fugitives from justice excepted, shall be entitled to all privileges and immunities of free citizens in the several States; and the people of each State shall have free ingress and regress to and from any other State, and shall enjoy therein all the privileges of trade and commerce, subject to the same duties, impositions and restrictions as the inhabitants thereof respectively, provided that such restrictions shall not extend so far as to prevent the removal of property imported into any State, to any other State of which the owner is an inhabitant; provided also that no imposition, duties or restriction shall be laid by any State, on the property of the United States, or either of them.

If any person guilty of, or charged with treason, felony, or other high misdemeanor in any State, shall flee from justice, and be found in any of the United States, he shall upon demand of the Governor or Executive power, of the State from which he fled, be delivered up and removed to the State having jurisdiction of his offence.

Full faith and credit shall be given in each of these States to the records, acts and judicial proceedings of the courts and magistrates of every other State.

ARTICLE V. For the more convenient management of the general interests of the United States, delegates shall be annually appointed in such manner as the legislature of each State shall direct, to meet in Congress on the first Monday in November, in every year, with a power reserved to each State, to recall its delegates, or any of them, at any time within the year, and to send others in their stead, for the remainder of the year.

No State shall be represented in Congress by less than two, nor by more than seven members; and no person shall be capable of being a delegate for more than three years in any term of six years; nor shall any person, being a delegate, be capable of holding any office under the United States, for which he, or another for his benefit receives any salary, fees or emolument of any kind.

Each State shall maintain its own delegates in a meeting of the States, and while they act as members of the committee of the States.

In determining questions in the United States, in Congress assembled, each State shall have one vote.

Freedom of speech and debate in Congress shall not be impeached or questioned in any court, or place out of Congress, and the members of Congress shall be protected in their persons from arrests and imprisonments, during the time of their going to and from, and attendance on Congress, except for treason, felony, or breach of the peace.

★ ★ ★

ARTICLE XIII. Every State shall abide by the determinations of the United States in Congress assembled, on all questions which by this confederation are submitted to them. And the articles of this confederation shall be inviolably observed by every State, and the Union shall be perpetual; nor shall any alteration at any time hereafter be made in any of them; unless such alteration be agreed to in a Congress of the United States, and be afterwards confirmed by the Legislatures of every State.

And whereas it has pleased the Great Governor of the world to incline the hearts of the Legislatures we respectively represent in Congress, to approve of, and to authorize us to ratify the said articles of confederation and perpetual union. Know ye that we the undersigned delegates, by virtue of the power and authority to us given for that purpose, do by these presents, in the name and in behalf of our respective constituents, fully and entirely ratify and confirm each and every of the said articles of confederation and perpetual union, and all and singular the matters and things therein contained: and we do further solemnly plight and engage the faith of our respective constituents, that they shall abide by the determinations of the United States in Congress assembled, on all questions, which by the said confederation are submitted to them. And that the articles thereof shall be inviolably observed by the States we respectively represent, and that the Union shall be perpetual.

In witness whereof we have hereunto set our hands in Congress. Done at Philadelphia in the State of Pennsylvania the ninth day of July in the year of our Lord one thousand seven hundred and seventy-eight, and in the third year of the independence of America.

THE CONSTITUTION OF THE UNITED STATES OF AMERICA

We the People of the United States, in Order to form a more perfect Union, establish Justice, insure domestic Tranquility, provide for the common defence, promote the general Welfare, and secure the Blessings of Liberty to ourselves and our Posterity, do ordain and establish this Constitution for the United States of America.

ARTICLE I.

Section 1.

All legislative Powers herein granted shall be vested in a Congress of the United States, which shall consist of a Senate and House of Representatives.

Section 2.

The House of Representatives shall be composed of Members chosen every second Year by the People of the several States, and the Electors in each State shall have the Qualifications requisite for Electors of the most numerous Branch of the State Legislature.

No Person shall be a Representative who shall not have attained to the Age of twenty five Years, and been seven Years a Citizen of the United States, and who shall not, when elected, be an Inhabitant of that State in which he shall be chosen.

Representatives and direct Taxes shall be apportioned among the several States which may be included within this Union, according to their respective Numbers, which shall be determined by adding to the whole Number of free Persons, including those bound to Service for a Term of Years, and excluding Indians not taxed, three fifths of all other Persons.[1] The actual Enumeration shall be made within three Years after the first Meeting of the Congress of the United States, and within every subsequent Term of ten Years, in such Manner as they shall by Law direct. The Number of Representatives shall not exceed one for every thirty Thousand, but each State shall have at Least one Representative; and until such enumeration shall be made, the State of New Hampshire shall be entitled to chuse three, Massachusetts eight, Rhode-Island and Providence Plantations one, Connecticut five, New-York six, New Jersey four, Pennsylvania eight, Delaware one, Maryland six, Virginia ten, North Carolina five, South Carolina five, and Georgia three.

When vacancies happen in the Representation from any State, the Executive Authority thereof shall issue Writs of Election to fill such Vacancies.

The House of Representatives shall chuse their Speaker and other Officers; and shall have the sole Power of Impeachment.

Section 3.

The Senate of the United States shall be composed of two Senators from each State, chosen by the Legislature thereof, for six Years; and each Senator shall have one Vote.

Immediately after they shall be assembled in Consequence of the first Election, they shall be divided as equally as may be into three Classes. The Seats of the Senators of the first Class shall be vacated at the Expiration of the second Year, of the second Class at the Expiration of the fourth Year, and of the third Class at the Expiration of the sixth Year, so that one third may be chosen every second Year; and if Vacancies happen by Resignation, or otherwise, during the Recess of the Legislature of any State, the Executive thereof

---

1. "Other Persons" being Negro slaves. Modified by Amendment XIV, Section 2.

may make temporary Appointments until the next Meeting of the Legislature, which shall then fill such Vacancies.[2]

No Person shall be a Senator who shall not have attained to the Age of thirty Years, and been nine Years a Citizen of the United States, and who shall not, when elected, be an Inhabitant of that State for which he shall be chosen.

The Vice President of the United States shall be President of the Senate, but shall have no Vote, unless they be equally divided.

The Senate shall chuse their other Officers, and also a President pro tempore, in the Absence of the Vice President, or when he shall exercise the Office of President of the United States.

The Senate shall have the sole Power to try all Impeachments. When sitting for that Purpose, they shall be on Oath or Affirmation. When the President of the United States is tried the Chief Justice shall preside: And no Person shall be convicted without the Concurrence of two thirds of the Members present.

Judgment in Cases of Impeachment shall not extend further than to removal from Office, and disqualification to hold and enjoy any Office of honor, Trust or Profit under the United States: but the Party convicted shall nevertheless be liable and subject to Indictment, Trial, Judgment and Punishment, according to Law.

Section 4.

The Times, Places and Manner of holding Elections for Senators and Representatives, shall be prescribed in each State by the Legislature thereof; but the Congress may at any time by Law make or alter such Regulations, except as to the Places of chusing Senators.

The Congress shall assemble at least once in every Year, and such Meeting shall be on the first Monday in December, unless they shall by Law appoint a different Day.[3]

Section 5.

Each House shall be the Judge of the Elections, Returns and Qualifications of its own Members, and a Majority of each shall constitute a Quorum to do Business; but a smaller Number may adjourn from day to day, and may be authorized to compel the Attendance of absent Members, in such Manner, and under such Penalties as each House may provide.

Each House may determine the Rules of its Proceedings, punish its Members for disorderly Behaviour, and, with the Concurrence of two thirds, expel a Member.

Each House shall keep a Journal of its Proceedings, and from time to time publish the same, excepting such Parts as may in their Judgment require Secrecy; and the Yeas and Nays of the Members of either House on any question shall, at the Desire of one fifth of those Present, be entered on the Journal.

Neither House, during the Session of Congress, shall, without the Consent of the other, adjourn for more than three days, nor to any other Place than that in which the two Houses shall be sitting.

Section 6.

The Senators and Representatives shall receive a Compensation for their Services, to be ascertained by Law, and paid out of the Treasury of the United States. They shall in all Cases, except Treason, Felony and Breach of the Peace, be privileged from Arrest during their Attendance at the Session of their respective Houses, and in going to and returning from the same; and for any Speech or Debate in either House, they shall not be questioned in any other Place.

No Senator or Representative shall, during the Time for which he was

2. Provisions changed by Amendment XVII.

3. Provision changed by Amendment XX, Section 2.

elected, be appointed to any civil Office under the Authority of the United States, which shall have been created, or the Emoluments whereof shall have been encreased during such time; and no Person holding any Office under the United States, shall be a Member of either House during his Continuance in Office.

Section 7.

All Bills for raising Revenue shall originate in the House of Representatives; but the Senate may propose or concur with Amendments as on other Bills.

Every Bill which shall have passed the House of Representatives and the Senate, shall, before it become a Law, be presented to the President of the United States; If he approve he shall sign it, but if not he shall return it, with his Objections to that House in which it shall have originated, who shall enter the Objections at large on their Journal, and proceed to reconsider it. If after such Reconsideration two thirds of that House shall agree to pass the Bill, it shall be sent, together with the Objections, to the other House, by which it shall likewise be reconsidered, and if approved by two thirds of that House, it shall become a Law. But in all such Cases the Votes of both Houses shall be determined by yeas and Nays, and the Names of the Persons voting for and against the Bill shall be entered on the Journal of each House respectively. If any Bill shall not be returned by the President within ten Days (Sundays excepted) after it shall have been presented to him, the Same shall be a Law, in like Manner as if he had signed it, unless the Congress by their Adjournment prevent its Return, in which Case it shall not be a Law.

Every Order, Resolution, or Vote to which the Concurrence of the Senate and House of Representatives may be necessary (except on a question of Adjournment) shall be presented to the President of the United States; and before the Same shall take Effect, shall be approved by him, or being disapproved by him, shall be repassed by two thirds of the Senate and House of Representatives, according to the Rules and Limitations prescribed in the Case of a Bill.

Section 8.

The Congress shall have Power To lay and collect Taxes, Duties, Imposts and Excises, to pay the Debts and provide for the common Defence and general Welfare of the United States; but all Duties, Imposts and Excises shall be uniform throughout the United States;

To borrow Money on the credit of the United States;

To regulate Commerce with foreign Nations, and among the several States, and with the Indian Tribes;

To establish an uniform Rule of Naturalization, and uniform Laws on the subject of Bankruptcies throughout the United States;

To coin Money, regulate the Value thereof, and of foreign Coin, and fix the Standard of Weights and Measures;

To provide for the Punishment of counterfeiting the Securities and current Coin of the United States;

To establish Post Offices and post Roads;

To promote the Progress of Science and useful Arts, by securing for limited Times to Authors and Inventors the exclusive Right to their respective Writings and Discoveries;

To constitute Tribunals inferior to the supreme Court;

To define and punish Piracies and Felonies committed on the high Seas, and Offences against the Law of Nations;

To declare War, grant Letters of Marque and Reprisal, and make Rules concerning Captures on Land and Water;

To raise and support Armies, but no Appropriation of Money to that Use shall be for a longer Term than two Years;

To provide and maintain a Navy;

To make Rules for the Government and Regulation of the land and naval Forces;

To provide for calling forth the Militia to execute the Laws of the Union, suppress Insurrections and repel Invasions;

To provide for organizing, arming, and disciplining, the Militia, and for governing such Part of them as may be employed in the Service of the United States, reserving to the States respectively, the Appointment of the Officers, and the Authority of training the Militia according to the discipline prescribed by Congress;

To exercise exclusive Legislation in all Cases whatsoever, over such District (not exceeding ten Miles square) as may, by Cession of particular States, and the Acceptance of Congress, become the Seat of the Government of the United States, and to exercise like Authority over all Places purchased by the Consent of the Legislature of the State in which the Same shall be, for the Erection of Forts, Magazines, Arsenals, dock-Yards, and other needful Buildings;—And

To make all Laws which shall be necessary and proper for carrying into Execution the foregoing Powers, and all other Powers vested by this Constitution in the Government of the United States, or in any Department or Officer thereof.

Section 9.

The Migration or Importation of such Persons as any of the States now existing shall think proper to admit, shall not be prohibited by the Congress prior to the Year one thousand eight hundred and eight, but a Tax or duty may be imposed on such Importation, not exceeding ten dollars for each Person.

The Privilege of the Writ of Habeas Corpus shall not be suspended, unless when in Cases of Rebellion or Invasion the public Safety may require it.

No Bill of Attainder or ex post facto Law shall be passed.

No Capitation, or other direct, Tax shall be laid, unless in Proportion to the Census or Enumeration herein before directed to be taken.

No Tax or Duty shall be laid on Articles exported from any State.

No Preference shall be given by any Regulation of Commerce or Revenue to the Ports of one State over those of another: nor shall Vessels bound to, or from, one State, be obliged to enter, clear, or pay Duties in another.

No Money shall be drawn from the Treasury, but in Consequence of Appropriations made by Law; and a regular Statement and Account of the Receipts and Expenditures of all public Money shall be published from time to time.

No Title of Nobility shall be granted by the United States: And no Person holding any Office of Profit or Trust under them, shall, without the Consent of the Congress, accept of any present, Emolument, Office, or Title, of any kind whatever, from any King, Prince, or foreign State.

Section 10.

No State shall enter into any Treaty, Alliance, or Confederation; grant Letters of Marque and Reprisal; coin Money; emit Bills of Credit; make any Thing but gold and silver Coin a Tender in Payment of Debts; pass any Bill of Attainder, ex post facto Law, or Law impairing the Obligation of Contracts, or grant any Title of Nobility.

No State shall, without the Consent of the Congress, lay any Imposts or Duties on Imports or Exports, except what may be absolutely necessary for executing its inspection Laws: and the net Produce of all Duties and Imposts, laid by any State on Imports or Exports, shall be for the Use of the Treasury of the United States; and all such Laws shall be subject to the Revision and Controul of the Congress.

No State shall, without the Consent of Congress, lay any Duty of Tonnage, keep Troops, or Ships of War in time of Peace, enter into any Agreement or Compact with another State, or with a foreign Power, or engage in War, unless actually invaded, or in such imminent Danger as will not admit of delay.

ARTICLE II.

Section 1.

The executive Power shall be vested

in a President of the United States of America. He shall hold his Office during the Term of four Years, and, together with the Vice President, chosen for the same Term, be elected, as follows:

Each State shall appoint, in such Manner as the Legislature thereof may direct, a Number of Electors, equal to the whole Number of Senators and Representatives to which the State may be entitled in the Congress: but no Senator or Representative, or Person holding an Office of Trust or Profit under the United States, shall be appointed an Elector.

The Electors shall meet in their respective States, and vote by Ballot for two Persons, of whom one at least shall not be an Inhabitant of the same State with themselves. And they shall make a List of all the Persons voted for, and of the Number of Votes for each; which List they shall sign and certify, and transmit sealed to the Seat of the Government of the United States, directed to the President of the Senate. The President of the Senate shall, in the Presence of the Senate and House of Representatives, open all the Certificates, and the Votes shall then be counted. The Person having the greatest Number of Votes shall be the President, if such Number be a Majority of the whole Number of Electors appointed; and if there be more than one who have such Majority, and have an equal Number of Votes, then the House of Representatives shall immediately chuse by Ballot one of them for President; and if no Person have a Majority, then from the five highest on the List the said House shall in like Manner chuse the President. But in chusing the President, the Votes shall be taken by States, the Representation from each State having one Vote; A quorum for this Purpose shall consist of a Member or Members from two thirds of the States, and a Majority of all the States shall be necessary to a Choice. In every Case, after the Choice of the President, the Person having the greatest Number of Votes of the Electors shall be the Vice President. But if there should remain two or more who have equal Votes, the Senate shall chuse from them by Ballot the Vice President.[4]

The Congress may determine the Time of chusing the Electors, and the Day on which they shall give their Votes; which Day shall be the same throughout the United States.

No Person except a natural born Citizen, or a Citizen of the United States, at the time of the Adoption of this Constitution, shall be eligible to the Office of President; neither shall any Person be eligible to that Office who shall not have attained to the Age of thirty five Years, and been fourteen Years a Resident within the United States.

In Case of the Removal of the President from Office, or of his Death, Resignation, or Inability to discharge the Powers and Duties of the said Office, the Same shall devolve on the Vice President, and the Congress may by Law provide for the Case of Removal, Death, Resignation or Inability, both of the President and Vice President, declaring what Officer shall then act as President, and such Officer shall act accordingly, until the Disability be removed, or a President shall be elected.

The President shall, at stated Times, receive for his Services, a Compensation, which shall neither be encreased nor diminished during the Period for which he shall have been elected, and he shall not receive within that Period any other Emolument from the United States, or any of them.

Before he enter on the Execution of his Office, he shall take the following Oath or Affirmation:—"I do solemnly swear (or affirm) that I will faithfully execute the Office of President of the United States, and will to the best of my Ability, preserve, protect and defend the Constitution of the United States."

Section 2.

The President shall be Commander in Chief of the Army and Navy of the United States, and of the Militia of the

---

4. Provisions superseded by Amendment XII.

several States, when called into the actual Service of the United States; he may require the Opinion, in writing, of the principal Officer in each of the executive Departments, upon any Subject relating to the Duties of their respective Offices, and he shall have Power to grant Reprieves and Pardons for Offences against the United States, except in Cases of Impeachment.

He shall have Power, by and with the Advice and Consent of the Senate, to make Treaties, provided two thirds of the Senators present concur; and he shall nominate, and by and with the Advice and Consent of the Senate, shall appoint Ambassadors, other public Ministers and Consuls, Judges of the supreme Court, and all other Officers of the United States, whose Appointments are not herein otherwise provided for, and which shall be established by Law: but the Congress may by Law vest the Appointment of such inferior Officers, as they think proper in the President alone, in the Courts of Law, or in the Heads of Departments.

The President shall have Power to fill up all Vacancies that may happen during the Recess of the Senate, by granting Commissions which shall expire at the End of their next Session.

Section 3

He shall from time to time give to the Congress Information of the State of the Union, and recommend to their Consideration such Measures as he shall judge necessary and expedient; he may, on extraordinary Occasions, convene both Houses, or either of them, and in Case of Disagreement between them, with Respect to the Time of Adjournment, he may adjourn them to such Time as he shall think proper; he shall receive Ambassadors and other public Ministers; he shall take Care that the Laws be faithfully executed, and shall Commission all the Officers of the United States.

Section 4.

The President, Vice President and all civil Officers of the United States, shall be removed from Office on Impeachment for, and Conviction of, Treason, Bribery, or other high Crimes and Misdemeanors.

ARTICLE III.

Section 1.

The judicial Power of the United States, shall be vested in one supreme Court, and in such inferior Courts as the Congress may from time to time ordain and establish. The Judges, both of the supreme and inferior Courts, shall hold their Offices during good Behaviour, and shall, at stated Times, receive for their Services, a Compensation, which shall not be diminished during their Continuance in Office.

Section 2.

The judicial Power shall extend to all Cases, in Law and Equity, arising under this Constitution, the Laws of the United States, and Treaties made, or which shall be made, under their Authority;—to all Cases affecting Ambassadors, other public Ministers and Consuls;—to all Cases of admiralty and maritime Jurisdiction;—to Controversies to which the United States shall be a Party;—to Controversies between two or more States;—between a State and Citizens of another State;—between Citizens of different States,—between Citizens of the same State claiming Lands under Grants of different States, and between a State, or the Citizens thereof, and foreign States, Citizens or Subjects.[5]

In all Cases affecting Ambassadors, other public Ministers and Consuls, and those in which a State shall be Party, the supreme Court shall have original Jurisdiction. In all the other Cases before mentioned, the supreme Court shall have appellate Jurisdiction, both as to Law and Fact, with such Exceptions, and under such Regulations as the Congress shall make.

The Trial of all Crimes, except in Cases of Impeachment, shall be by

---

5. Clause changed by Amendment XI.

Jury; and such Trial shall be held in the State where the said Crimes shall have been committed, but when not committed within any State, the Trial shall be at such Place or Places as the Congress may by Law have directed.

Section 3.

Treason against the United States, shall consist only in levying War against them, or in adhering to their Enemies, giving them Aid and Comfort. No person shall be convicted of Treason unless on the Testimony of two Witnesses to the same overt Act, or on Confession in open Court.

The Congress shall have Power to declare the Punishment of Treason, but no Attainder of Treason shall work Corruption of Blood, or Forfeiture except during the Life of the Person attainted.

ARTICLE IV.

Section 1.

Full Faith and Credit shall be given in each State to the public Acts, Records, and judicial Proceedings of every other State. And the Congress may by general Laws prescribe the Manner in which such Acts, Records and Proceedings shall be proved, and the Effect thereof.

Section 2.

The Citizens of each State shall be entitled to all Privileges and Immunities of Citizens in the several States.

A Person charged in any State with Treason, Felony, or other Crime, who shall flee from Justice, and be found in another State, shall on Demand of the executive Authority of the State from which he fled, be delivered up, to be removed to the State having Jurisdiction of the Crime.

No Person held to Service or Labour in one State, under the Laws thereof, escaping into another, shall, in Consequence of any Law or Regulation therein, be discharged from such Service or Labour, but shall be delivered up on Claim of the Party to whom such Service or Labour may be due.

Section 3.

New States may be admitted by the Congress into this Union; but no new State shall be formed or erected within the Jurisdiction of any other State; nor any State be formed by the Junction of two or more States, or Parts of States, without the Consent of the Legislatures of the States concerned as well as of the Congress.

The Congress shall have Power to dispose of and make all needful Rules and Regulations respecting the Territory or other Property belonging to the United States; and nothing in this Constitution shall be so construed as to Prejudice any Claims of the United States, or of any particular State.

Section 4.

The United States shall guarantee to every State in this Union a Republican Form of Government, and shall protect each of them against Invasion; and on Application of the Legislature, or of the Executive (when the Legislature cannot be convened) against domestic Violence.

ARTICLE V.

The Congress, whenever two thirds of both Houses shall deem it necessary, shall propose Amendments to this Constitution, or, on the Application of the Legislatures of two thirds of the several States, shall call a Convention for proposing Amendments, which, in either Case, shall be valid to all Intents and Purposes, as Part of this Constitution, when ratified by the Legislatures of three fourths of the several States, or by Conventions in three fourths thereof, as the one or the other Mode of Ratification may be proposed by the Congress; Provided that no Amendment which may be made prior to the Year One thousand eight hundred and eight shall in any Manner affect the first and fourth Clauses in the Ninth Section of the first Article; and that no State, without its Consent, shall be deprived of its equal Suffrage in the Senate.

ARTICLE VI.

All Debts contracted and Engagements entered into, before the Adoption of this Constitution, shall be as valid against the United States under this Constitution, as under the Confederation.

This Constitution, and the Laws of the United States which shall be made in Pursuance thereof; and all Treaties made, or which shall be made, under the Authority of the United States, shall be the supreme Law of the Land; and the Judges in every State shall be bound thereby, any Thing in the Constitution or Laws of any State to the Contrary notwithstanding.

The Senators and Representatives before mentioned, and the Members of the several State Legislatures, and all executive and judicial Officers, both of the United States and of the several States, shall be bound by Oath or Affirmation, to support this Constitution; but no religious Test shall ever be required as a Qualification to any Office or public Trust under the United States.

ARTICLE VII.

The Ratification of the Conventions of nine States, shall be sufficient for the Establishment of this Constitution between the States so ratifying the Same.

done in Convention by the Unanimous Consent of the States present the Seventeenth Day of September in the Year of our Lord one thousand seven hundred and Eighty seven and of the Independence of the United States of America the Twelfth[6] IN WITNESS whereof We have hereunto subscribed our Names,

G° WASHINGTON—Presidt
and deputy from Virginia

New Hampshire: JOHN LANGDON, NICHOLAS GILMAN

Massachusetts: NATHANIEL GORHAM, RUFUS KING

Connecticut: WM SAML JOHNSON, ROGER SHERMAN

New York: ALEXANDER HAMILTON

New Jersey: WIL: LIVINGSTON, DAVID BREARLEY., WM PATERSON., JONA: DAYTON

Pensylvania: B FRANKLIN, THOMAS MIFFLIN, ROBT MORRIS, GEO. CLYMER, THOS FITZSIMONS, JARED INGERSOLL, JAMES WILSON, GOUV MORRIS

Delaware: GEO: READ, GUNNING BEDFORD jun, JOHN DICKINSON, RICHARD BASSETT, JACO: BROOM

Maryland: JAMES MCHENRY, DAN OF ST THOS JENIFER, DANL CARROLL

Virginia: JOHN BLAIR—, JAMES MADISON JR.

North Carolina: WM BLOUNT, RICHD DOBBS SPAIGHT., HU WILLIAMSON

South Carolina: J. RUTLEDGE, CHARLES COTESWORTH PINCKNEY, CHARLES PINCKNEY, PIERCE BUTLER.

Georgia: WILLIAM FEW, ABR BALDWIN

6. The Constitution was submitted on September 17, 1787, by the Constitutional Convention, was ratified by the conventions of several states at various dates up to May 29, 1790, and became effective on March 4, 1789.

AMENDMENTS TO THE CONSTITUTION

[AMENDMENT I]

Congress shall make no law respecting an establishment of religion, or prohibiting the free exercise thereof; or abridging the freedom of speech, or of the press; or the right of the people peaceably to assemble, and to petition the Government for a redress of grievances.

[AMENDMENT II]

A well regulated Militia being necessary to the security of a free State, the right of the people to keep and bear Arms, shall not be infringed.

[AMENDMENT III]

No Soldier shall, in time of peace be quartered in any house, without the consent of the Owner, nor in time of war, but in a manner to be prescribed by law.

[AMENDMENT IV]

The right of the people to be secure in their persons, houses, papers, and effects, against unreasonable searches and seizures, shall not be violated, and no Warrants shall issue, but upon probable cause, supported by Oath or affirmation, and particularly describing the place to be searched, and the persons or things to be seized.

[AMENDMENT V]

No person shall be held to answer for a capital, or otherwise infamous crime, unless on a presentment or indictment of a Grand Jury, except in cases arising in the land or naval forces, or in the Militia, when in actual service in time of War or public danger; nor shall any person be subject for the same offense to be twice put in jeopardy of life or limb; nor shall be compelled in any criminal case to be a witness against himself, nor be deprived of life, liberty, or property, without due process of law; nor shall private property be taken for public use, without just compensation.

[AMENDMENT VI]

In all criminal prosecutions, the accused shall enjoy the right to a speedy and public trial, by an impartial jury of the State and district wherein the crime shall have been committed, which district shall have been previously ascertained by law, and to be informed of the nature and cause of the accusation; to be confronted with the witnesses against him; to have compulsory process for obtaining witnesses in his favor, and to have the Assistance of Counsel for his defence.

[AMENDMENT VII]

In Suits at common law, where the value in controversy shall exceed twenty dollars, the right of trial by jury shall be preserved, and no fact tried by a jury, shall be otherwise reexamined in any Court of the United States, than according to the rules of the common law.

[AMENDMENT VIII]

Excessive bail shall not be required, nor excessive fines imposed, nor cruel and unusual punishments inflicted.

[AMENDMENT IX]

The enumeration in the Constitution, of certain rights, shall not be construed to deny or disparage others retained by the people.

[AMENDMENT X]

The powers not delegated to the United States by the Constitution, nor prohibited by it to the States, are reserved to the States respectively, or to the people.[7]

[AMENDMENT XI]

The Judicial power of the United States shall not be construed to extend to any suit in law or equity, commenced or prosecuted against one of the United States by Citizens of another State, or by Citizens or Subjects of any Foreign State.[8]

[AMENDMENT XII]

The Electors shall meet in their respective states, and vote by ballot for President and Vice-President, one of whom, at least, shall not be an inhabitant of the same state with themselves; they shall name in their ballots the person voted for as President, and in distinct ballots the person voted for as Vice-President, and they shall make distinct lists of all persons voted for as President, and of all persons voted for as Vice-President, and of the number of votes for each, which lists they shall

---

7. The first ten amendments were all proposed by Congress on September 25, 1789, and were ratified and adoption certified on December 15, 1791.

8. Proposed by Congress on March 4, 1794, and declared ratified on January 8, 1798.

sign and certify, and transmit sealed to the seat of the government of the United States, directed to the President of the Senate;—The President of the Senate shall, in the presence of the Senate and House of Representatives, open all the certificates and the votes shall then be counted;—The person having the greatest number of votes for President, shall be the President, if such number be a majority of the whole number of Electors appointed; and if no person have such majority, then from the persons having the highest numbers not exceeding three on the list of those voted for as President, the House of Representatives shall choose immediately, by ballot, the President. But in choosing the President, the votes shall be taken by states, the representation from each state having one vote; a quorum for this purpose shall consist of a member or members from two-thirds of the states, and a majority of all the states shall be necessary to a choice. And if the House of Representatives shall not choose a President whenever the right of choice shall devolve upon them, before the fourth day of March next following, then the Vice-President shall act as President, as in the case of the death or other constitutional disability of the President.—The person having the greatest number of votes as Vice-President, shall be the Vice-President, if such number be a majority of the whole number of Electors appointed, and if no person have a majority, then from the two highest numbers on the list, the Senate shall choose the Vice-President; a quorum for the purpose shall consist of two-thirds of the whole number of Senators, and a majority of the whole number shall be necessary to a choice. But no person constitutionally ineligible to the office of President shall be eligible to that of Vice-President of the United States.[9]

9. Proposed by Congress on December 9, 1803; declared ratified on September 25, 1804; supplemented by Amendments XX and XXIII.

[AMENDMENT XIII]

Section 1.

Neither slavery nor involuntary servitude, except as a punishment for crime whereof the party shall have been duly convicted, shall exist within the United States, or any place subject to their jurisdiction.

Section 2.

Congress shall have power to enforce this article by appropriate legislation.[10]

[AMENDMENT XIV]

Section 1.

All persons born or naturalized in the United States, and subject to the jurisdiction thereof, are citizens of the United States and of the State wherein they reside. No State shall make or enforce any law which shall abridge the privileges or immunities of citizens of the United States; nor shall any State deprive any person of life, liberty, or property, without due process of law; nor deny to any person within its jurisdiction the equal protection of the laws.

Section 2.

Representatives shall be apportioned among the several States according to their respective numbers, counting the whole number of persons in each State, excluding Indians not taxed. But when the right to vote at any election for the choice of electors for President and Vice-President of the United States, Representatives in Congress, the Executive and Judicial officers of a State, or the members of the Legislature thereof, is denied to any of the male inhabitants of such State, being twenty-one years of age, and citizens of the United States, or in any way abridged, except for participation in rebellion, or other crime, the basis of representation therein shall be reduced in the proportion which the number of such male citizens shall bear to the whole number of male

10. Proposed by Congress on January 31, 1865; declared ratified on December 18, 1865.

citizens twenty-one years of age in such State.

Section 3.

No person shall be a Senator or Representative in Congress, or elector of President and Vice President, or hold any office, civil or military, under the United States, or under any State, who, having previously taken an oath, as a member of Congress, or as an officer of the United States, or as a member of any State legislature, or as an executive or judicial officer of any State, to support the Constitution of the United States, shall have engaged in insurrection or rebellion against the same, or given aid or comfort to the enemies thereof. But Congress may by a vote of two-thirds of each House, remove such disability.

Section 4.

The validity of the public debt of the United States, authorized by law, including debts incurred for payment of pensions and bounties for services in suppressing insurrection or rebellion, shall not be questioned. But neither the United States nor any State shall assume or pay any debt or obligation incurred in aid of insurrection or rebellion against the United States, or any claim for the loss or emancipation of any slave; but all such debts, obligations and claims shall be held illegal and void.

Section 5.

The Congress shall have power to enforce, by appropriate legislation, the provisions of this article.[11]

[Amendment XV]

Section 1.

The right of citizens of the United States to vote shall not be denied or abridged by the United States or by any State on account of race, color, or previous condition of servitude.

Section 2.

The Congress shall have power to enforce this article by appropriate legislation.[12]

[Amendment XVI]

The Congress shall have power to lay and collect taxes on incomes, from whatever source derived, without apportionment among the several States, and without regard to any census or enumeration.[13]

[Amendment XVII]

The Senate of the United States shall be composed of two Senators from each State, elected by the people thereof, for six years; and each Senator shall have one vote. The electors in each State shall have the qualifications requisite for electors of the most numerous branch of the State legislatures.

When vacancies happen in the representation of any State in the Senate, the executive authority of such State shall issue writs of election to fill such vacancies: *Provided,* That the legislature of any State may empower the executive thereof to make temporary appointments until the people fill the vacancies by election as the legislature may direct.

This amendment shall not be so construed as to affect the election or term of any Senator chosen before it becomes valid as part of the Constitution.[14]

[Amendment XVIII]

Section 1.

After one year from the ratification of this article the manufacture, sale, or transportation of intoxicating liquors within, the importation thereof into, or the exportation thereof from the United States and all territory subject to the

---

11. Proposed by Congress on June 13, 1866; declared ratified on July 28, 1868.

12. Proposed by Congress on February 26, 1869; declared ratified on March 30, 1870.

13. Proposed by Congress on July 12, 1909; declared ratified on February 25, 1913.

14. Proposed by Congress on May 13, 1912; declared ratified on May 31, 1913.

jurisdiction thereof for beverage purposes is hereby prohibited.

Section 2.

The Congress and the several States shall have concurrent power to enforce this article by appropriate legislation.

Section 3.

This article shall be inoperative unless it shall have been ratified as an amendment to the Constitution by the legislatures of the several States, as provided in the Constitution, within seven years from the date of the submission hereof to the States by the Congress.[15]

[AMENDMENT XIX]

The right of citizens of the United States to vote shall not be denied or abridged by the United States or by any State on account of sex.

Congress shall have power to enforce this article by appropriate legislation.[16]

[AMENDMENT XX]

Section 1.

The terms of the President and Vice President shall end at noon on the 20th day of January, and the terms of Senators and Representatives at noon on the 3d day of January, of the years in which such terms would have ended if this article had not been ratified; and the terms of their successors shall then begin.

Section 2.

The Congress shall assemble at least once in every year, and such meeting shall begin at noon on the 3d day of January, unless they shall by law appoint a different day.

Section 3.

If, at the time fixed for the beginning of the term of the President, the President elect shall have died, the Vice President elect shall become President. If a President shall not have been chosen before the time fixed for the beginning of his term, or if the President elect shall have failed to qualify, then the Vice President elect shall act as President until a President shall have qualified; and the Congress may by law provide for the case wherein neither a President elect nor a Vice President elect shall have qualified, declaring who shall then act as President, or the manner in which one who is to act shall be selected, and such person shall act accordingly until a President or Vice President shall have qualified.

Section 4.

The Congress may by law provide for the case of the death of any of the persons from whom the House of Representatives may choose a President whenever the right of choice shall have devolved upon them, and for the case of the death of any of the persons from whom the Senate may choose a Vice President whenever the right of choice shall have devolved upon them.

Section 5.

Sections 1 and 2 shall take effect on the 15th day of October following the ratification of this article.

Section 6.

This article shall be inoperative unless it shall have been ratified as an amendment to the Constitution by the legislatures of three-fourths of the several States within seven years from the date of its submission.[17]

[AMENDMENT XXI]

Section 1.

The eighteenth article of amendment to the Constitution of the United States is hereby repealed.

---

15. Proposed by Congress on December 18, 1917; declared ratified on January 29, 1919; repealed by Amendment XXI.

16. Proposed by Congress on June 4, 1919; declared ratified on August 26, 1920.

17. Proposed by Congress on March 2, 1932; declared ratified on February 6, 1933.

Section 2.
The transportation or importation into any States, Territory, or possession of the United States for delivery or use therein of intoxicating liquors, in violation of the laws thereof, is hereby prohibited.

Section 3.
This article shall be inoperative unless it shall have been ratified as an amendment to the Constitution by conventions in the several States, as provided in the Constitution, within seven years from the date of the submission hereof to the States by the Congress.[18]

[AMENDMENT XXII]

Section 1.
No person shall be elected to the office of the President more than twice, and no person who has held the office of President, or acted as President, for more than two years of a term to which some other person was elected President shall be elected to the office of the President more than once. But this Article shall not apply to any person holding the office of President when this Article was proposed by the Congress, and shall not prevent any person who may be holding the office of President, or acting as President, during the term within which this Article becomes operative from holding the office of President or acting as President during the remainder of such term.

Section 2.
This article shall be inoperative unless it shall have been ratified as an amendment to the Constitution by the legislatures of three-fourths of the several States within seven years from the date of its submission to the States by the Congress.[19]

[AMENDMENT XXIII]

Section 1.
The District constituting the seat of Government of the United States shall appoint in such manner as the Congress shall direct:

A number of electors of President and Vice President equal to the whole number of Senators and Representatives in Congress to which the District would be entitled if it were a State, but in no event more than the least populous State; they shall be in addition to those appointed by the States, but they shall be considered, for the purposes of the election of President and Vice President, to be electors appointed by a State; and they shall meet in the District and perform such duties as provided by the twelfth article of amendment.

Section 2.
The Congress shall have power to enforce this article by appropriate legislation.[20]

[AMENDMENT XXIV]

"*Section 1.* The right of citizens of the United States to vote in any primary or other election for President or Vice President, for electors for President or Vice President, or for Senator or Representative in Congress, shall not be denied or abridged by the United States or any State by reason of failure to pay any poll tax or other tax.

"*Section 2.* The Congress shall have power to enforce this article by appropriate legislation."[21]

---

18. Proposed by Congress on February 20, 1933; declared ratified on December 5, 1933.

19. Proposed by Congress on March 24, 1947; declared ratified on March 1, 1951.

20. Proposed by Congress on June 16, 1960; declared ratified on April 3, 1961.

21. Proposed by Congress on August 27, 1962; declared ratified on January 23, 1964.

INDEX

A

Adams, John, 11, 32, 74, 88, 93, 115, 116, 122, 159
Albany Conference of 1754, 10
Amendments to U. S. Constitution: *1st,* 51, 119, 120, 121, 122, 128, 134, 135, 137; *5th,* 51, 52, 101, 160; *9th,* 52–53, *10th,* 52–53; *11th,* 87; *12th,* 82, 88–89; *13th,* 97; *14th,* 97–102, 103–104, 109, 117, 118, 119, 120, 121, 122, 123, 128, 131, 138, 140, 160, 161–162, 163, 164, 165, 167; *15th,* 104, 136, 140, 162, 163; *16th,* 108–109, 110; *20th,* 89; *22nd,* 146
American Revolution. *See* Revolution, American.
"American System," 93, 105
Anglicanism. *See* Church of England.
Annapolis Convention of 1786, 40–41, 68
Antifederalists, 67, 78
Apportionment, 104, 131, 132, 151
Arlington National Cemetery Case, 125, 150
Articles of Association of 1774, 10
Articles of Confederation, 11, 34–41, 44, 45, 48, 49, 53, 55–57, 63, 65–68, 96, 132
Articles of Union, 46, 53, 65, 68

B

Bible, 2, 5, 129, 130
Bill of Rights, 50–53, 78, 81, 159
Bill of Rights of 1689, 5
Black, Hugo L., 125, 126, 129, 134, 163, 167
Blackstone, William, 6, 23, 26–27, 28, 52, 101
Brandeis, Louis D., 102, 103, 127
Brennan, William J., Jr., 130.
Bricker amendment, 155
Bryan, William Jennings, 105, 106
Business, 100, 101, 105–106, 109, 110

C

Calhoun, John C., 90, 91, 92, 94, 104
Calvinism, 3, 6–7, 8
Cardozo, Benjamin N., 103, 127, 160, 167
Checks and balances, 29–31, 71–81, 82, 116, 117, 136, 138, 142, 152
Church of England, 3–4, 6, 9, 23
Civil rights, 22, 100, 117, 120, 161, 162
Civil War, 65, 96, 104–106, 109
Clay, Henry, 90–94, 104, 105
"Clear and present danger," 122, 134
Cleveland, Grover, 106, 150
Commentaries on the Laws of England, 6, 23, 52
Commerce, 82–83, 99, 103
Committee of Detail, 45–47, 48, 65, 73, 77, 82, 83
Committee of Style and Arrangement, 47, 56
Committee of the Whole, 44–45, 65–68, 76
Committee on Postponed Matters and Unfinished Business, 47, 78, 84
Communist party, 122, 133–138
Compromise of 1850, 96
Compromise, Missouri, 96
Confederate States of America, 53, 65
Confederationists, 67, 70, 76, 78, 79, 81, 84
Congress, 46, 50, 51, 63–66, 68, 72, 77–83, 88–90, 95–99, 103–108, 116, 123–126, 128, 134–137, 139, 146–149, 151, 152, 155, 156, 158, 159, 161
Connecticut Compromise, 45, 70, 71
Constitutional Convention. *See* Convention of 1787.
Continental Army, 11, 34, 35, 39
Continental Congress, 9–13, 15, 20, 23, 34, 35, 38–41, 44, 45
Convention of 1787, 20, 31, 35, 36, 38, 41–62, 67, 97, 98, 127, 132
Conventions, political, 94–95
Council of Appointment, 31
Council of Revision, 31–32
Court of the Union, 151

D

Debates in the Federal Convention of 1787, 49, 57, 58, 72
Declaration of Independence, 1, 9–14, 19, 20, 24, 27, 33, 34, 55, 59, 127, 154, 165
Democratic party, 90–94, 104–113, 139–141, 167
Depression, Great, 108, 109, 111, 160, 162
Dickinson, John, 47, 67–68, 77, 78
District of Columbia, 102, 105
Dixiecrats, 111, 141
Dorr's Rebellion, 115–116
Douglas, William O., 99, 130, 134, 135, 159, 167
Dred Scott decision, 98, 109, 117, 150, 166

E

Education, 105, 117, 119
Elections, 87–90, 104, 111–112, 140–142
Electoral college, 75, 79, 85–89, 94, 141–142
Ellsworth, Oliver, 45, 46, 54, 68, 85, 97
Emancipation Proclamation, 97, 158, 159, 161
England, 33, 51, 76
Exclusion Bill, 14
Executive branch, 44, 49, 63, 64, 66, 68, 72, 75–81, 116, 125, 126, 146, 148–149, 150–152, 166. *See also* Presidency.
Expatriation Cases, 126

F

Fair Deal, 166
Farewell Address (Washington), 84, 90
Federal Communications Commission, 123–124
Federal courts, 52, 100, 116, 134, 138, 140
Federalism, 71, 73, 77, 82, 101, 138, 139, 142–143, 151, 155
Federalist, The, 58, 61, 78, 81, 115, 158
Federalists, 47, 67, 71, 78, 81, 84–90, 93, 159, 165
First Inaugural Address: of Jefferson, 90; of Lincoln, 97
Flag Salute Cases, 128, 129
Foreign affairs, 80–81, 152–157
Four Freedoms, 152
Frankfurter, Felix, 125, 126, 128, 129, 134, 137, 161
Franklin, Benjamin, 10, 31, 34, 38, 39, 43, 47, 57, 59, 70, 71, 74–75, 76, 85
Freedoms: of association, 133, 139; to broadcast, 123; of contract, 101, 102, 160; economic, 117; of enterprise, 101; from fear, 152; of petition, 51; of press, 51–52, 121–123, 133, 134; of religion, 20, 51, 56, 152; of speech, 51–52, 121, 122, 123, 133, 134, 152; of trade, 101; from want, 152. *See also* Liberty, Rights.

G

George III, 14–15, 23, 24, 28, 33, 67
Girouard v. United States, 159
Goldberg, Arthur J., 126, 130, 137–138, 161
Government: federal, 35–36, 44, 49, 138, 157; national, 35, 36, 44, 49, 63, 69; national-federal, 69; performance of, 33–38, 42; processes of, 26–33, 42; purpose of, 19–26, 41; representative, 115–116
Grand Committees, 45, 47, 70, 78, 80, 83

H

Hamilton, Alexander, 45, 47, 58, 66, 72, 73, 74, 78, 88, 158, 159, 166
Harlan, John M., 101, 118, 130, 134, 137, 160, 166
Hobbes, Thomas, 20–21
Holmes, Oliver Wendell, Jr., 101, 103, 122, 127
Homestead Act, 105
House Committee on Un-American Activities, 136
House of Representatives, 45, 68, 70, 72, 73, 75, 79, 82, 84, 85, 88, 89, 90, 94, 104, 147, 148, 156
Hughes, Charles E., 103, 132, 150, 159, 164, 166, 167

I

International Organizations, 153, 155

J

Jackson, Andrew, 90–93, 150, 166
Jackson, Robert H., 99, 125, 126, 128, 129, 134, 162, 164, 167
Jacksonian period, 93–94, 96, 139, 141, 159, 160, 166
Japan, 124, 125, 156
Jay, John, 31, 58
Jefferson, Thomas, 9, 11–13, 15, 25, 26, 29, 30, 32, 33, 51, 55, 58, 59, 78, 88–93, 127, 150, 159, 166
Johnson, William Samuel, 45, 47, 68
Joint committees, congressional, 149
Judiciary, 44, 49, 63, 64, 66, 68, 72, 75–81, 100, 102, 103, 116, 149, 150. *See also* Supreme Court.

K

Kansas-Nebraska Bill, 105
Kennedy, John F., 157

L

Labor, 101, 102, 108, 163
Laissez-faire, 103, 127
Law: civil, 21; common, 22; constitutional, 128; divine, 1–4; due process of, 22, 25, 26, 51, 52, 98, 100–103, 121, 122, 124, 126, 127, 133, 135–138, 160, 163, 164; eternal, 2, 5; equal protection under, 98, 100, 118, 131, 140, 163; Hebraic, 22; man-made, 2, 21, 120; natural, 1–5

League of Nations Covenant, 36
Legislative Reorganization Act of 1946, 147
Legislature, 44, 49, 50, 68, 72, 76, 77, 79–81, 116, 125, 147–149, 166. *See also* Congress, Senate.
Liberty, 22–24, 25, 52, 56. *See also* Freedom, Rights.
Lincoln, Abraham, 54–55, 65, 95, 97, 98, 150, 158
Locke, John, 4–9, 21, 26

M

MacArthur, Douglas, 125
McCarran Act (Internal Security Act of 1950), 122, 135, 138
McCarthy, Joseph R., 149
Madison, James, 32, 35, 42, 43, 47, 49, 57, 58, 61, 72, 75, 77, 78, 81–82, 83, 98, 115, 142
Marbury v. Madison, 166
Marshall, John, 150, 166
Martin, Luther, 44, 66–67, 70
Marxism, 73
Mason, George, 27, 28, 35, 43, 50
Massachusetts Constitution, 32
Massachusetts Declaration of Rights, 127
Mayflower Compact, 6
Mercantilism, 24, 101
Migratory Wildfowl Treaty, 155
Mill, John Stuart, 101, 120, 160
Miller, Samuel F., 125, 150, 166
Milton, John, 3, 7–9
Minimum wage laws, 102–103
Missouri Compromise, 96
Morris, Gouverneur, 35, 43, 47, 72, 73. 74, 85
Morris, Robert, 39, 43

N

National Association for the Advancement of Colored People, 137
National Labor Relations Act, 163
Nationalists, 35, 36, 47, 63–68, 70–73, 75–78, 81, 82, 84, 98
Naturalization Act, 159
Nature, state of, 5, 20–22, 26
Negro, the, 98, 100, 103–104, 105, 106, 117–118, 119, 146, 155, 161–163, 167. *See also* Civil rights, Slavery.
New Deal, 103, 109, 110, 111, 114, 127, 160, 166
New Jersey Plan, 44, 45, 67–68, 70, 76
New York Bakeries Case, 101–102
Notes on Virginia, 30, 32
Nuclear power, 145–146, 152
Nuremburg trials, 156

O

On Liberty, 120, 160

P

Panics: of 1873, 105, 106; of 1893, 106; of 1929, 106
Parties, political, 59–62, 67, 79, 84, 87–96, 104, 133, 156
Partisanship, 84, 95, 139, 149
Paterson, William, 44, 67
Pennsylvania Declaration of Rights, 31
Philadelphia Convention. *See* Convention of 1787.
Pinckney, Charles, 56, 88
Pinckney, Thomas, 88
Pluralism, 81–86, 139, 142
Politburo, 133–134, 167
Pope, Alexander, 21–22, 26
Populism, 105, 106
Preamble to the Constitution, 48, 56, 57, 101, 127
Presidency, 78–79, 80–81, 85–86, 91, 92, 94, 95–96, 106, 107, 116, 124, 125, 136, 139, 146, 148, 149–150, 152, 156, 157. *See also* Executive branch.
Progressivism, 106, 111
Puritanism, 3, 6–9, 11, 22, 23

R

Randolph, Edmund, 43–44, 46, 49
Reconstruction, 65, 105, 166
Republican form of government, 115–117, 119, 122, 131, 132, 166
Republican party, 88–92, 104–107, 109–113, 139, 141, 159, 166
Revolution, American, 9, 15, 40, 154
Revolution of 1688, 4–7, 9, 15
Rights: of assembly, 51, 163; to bear arms, 27; of citizenship, 126; civil, 22, 100, 117, 120, 161, 162; of communication, 119–124, 135, 139; to counsel, 160; to day in court, 101, 160; human, 120, 154; to liberty, 19, 22, 26; to life, 19–22, 26; to migrate, 99; of petition, 27–28; procedural, 51, 52, 100; of property, 19, 25; to pursuit of happiness, 19, 22, 25–26; to representative government, 28–29; of revolution, 33, 59, 60, 62, 116, 122, 132, 133, 135; of secession, 96; substantive, 51, 52; of suffrage, 29, 56, 63, 104, 116, 117, 140–

141, 162, 163; to trial by jury, 101, 126. *See also* Freedoms, Liberty.
Roosevelt, Franklin D., 95, 103, 109, 110, 145, 150
Roosevelt, Theodore, 102, 106, 150
Rousseau, Jean Jacques, 20–21
Rutledge, John, 45–46, 56, 57, 91

S

School Desegregation Cases, 118, 119, 165
Sectionalism, 104–106, 110–111
Sedition Acts: of 1798, 120, 122; of 1917, 122
Senate, 45, 69–71, 73–75, 79, 80, 85, 96, 147, 155, 156
Seniority system, 95, 107, 147, 148
Separate but equal doctrine, 100, 118, 165
Separation of church and state, 51, 127, 129–130
Separation of powers, 29–31, 76, 79, 80, 81, 136, 138
Shays' Rebellion, 41, 59
Sherman, Roger, 10–11, 44, 45, 67, 70, 76, 78, 115, 116
Slavery, 12, 23, 53–55, 82–83, 96, 97, 117
Smith Act, 122, 133–135, 138
Smith, Adam, 24, 101
Smith, Alfred E., 106, 111
Social compact, 4, 5–6, 8–9, 15, 16, 20, 21, 24, 38, 130
Social Security Act, 114
Social Security Cases, 160, 167
Sovereignty, 16, 21, 29, 32, 41, 48–53, 55, 64–70, 72, 76, 99, 117–119, 124, 127, 132, 138–139, 151–155, 157, 165, 167
States: courts in, 52, 100, 137, 138; governments of, 119, 139; governors of, 66; legislatures of, 65–66, 77, 88, 98, 101, 102, 129, 131, 139, 140, 150, 161
States' rights, 87
Statute of Religious Freedom, 127
Steel Plants Seizure Case, 125, 150
Stone, Harlan F., 103, 124, 127, 128, 164, 166
Subversive Activities Control Board, 122, 135
Supreme Court of U.S., 67, 79, 80, 85, 87, 98–103, 106, 109, 110, 114, 115, 118, 119, 121–138, 140–142, 150–152, 157–167. *See also* Judiciary.

T

Taney, Roger B., 150, 160, 166
Taxation, 82, 83, 103, 108, 110
Tennessee Reapportionment Case, 131
Texas v. White, 97
Tories, 14, 15–16, 20, 23, 61
Truman, Harry S., 125, 150

U

Unionists, 69, 70, 78, 84
United Nations, 36, 152–157
United States v. Macintosh, 1958–1959, 167

V

Veto power, 77–81, 103
Vice-Presidency, 79, 88, 89
Vinson, Frederick M., 125, 129, 134, 166
Virginia Constitution, 29
Virginia Declaration of Rights, 27–30, 50
Virginia Plan, 41–49, 53, 55–56, 58, 62, 63, 65, 67–73, 75–77, 82, 97
Virginia Statute of Religious Freedom, 51, 152

W

Warren, Earl, 119, 136, 165, 167
Washington, George, 11, 34, 35, 39–41, 43, 45, 47–50, 58, 59, 61, 67, 71, 79, 80, 83–85, 87, 88, 90, 150
Webster, Daniel, 90–92, 94, 104
Welfare state, 109–112, 114, 127, 148, 149, 160, 161, 166–167
Whigs, 6, 14–16, 19–38, 61–62, 90, 92–94, 104–106, 117, 133
Wilson, James, 32, 43, 46, 57, 75, 77, 98
Wilson, Woodrow, 95, 106, 156
World War II, 110, 119, 124, 125

1 2 3 4 5 6 7 8 9 10 11 12 13 14 15 16 17 18 19 20 21 22 23 24 25 SH 74 73 72 71 70 69 68 67 66 65 64